Advances in Japanese Business and Economics 5

For further volumes:
http://www.springer.com/series/11682

Advances in Japanese Business and Economics

Advances in Japanese Business and Economics showcases the research of Japanese scholars. Published in English, the series highlights for a global readership the unique perspectives of Japan's most distinguished and emerging scholars of business and economics. It covers research of either theoretical or empirical nature, in both authored and edited volumes, regardless of the sub-discipline or geographical coverage, including, but not limited to, such topics as macroeconomics, microeconomics, industrial relations, innovation, regional development, entrepreneurship, international trade, globalization, financial markets, technology management, and business strategy. At the same time, as a series of volumes written by Japanese scholars, it includes research on the issues of the Japanese economy, industry, management practice and policy, such as the economic policies and business innovations before and after the Japanese "bubble" burst in the 1990s.

Overseen by a panel of renowned scholars led by Editor-in-Chief Professor Ryuzo Sato, the series endeavors to overcome a historical deficit in the dissemination of Japanese economic theory, research methodology, and analysis. The volumes in the series contribute not only to a deeper understanding of Japanese business and economics but to revealing underlying universal principles.

Takashi Negishi

Elements of Neo-Walrasian Economics

A Survey

Springer

Takashi Negishi
Member
The Japan Academy
Japan

Professor Emeritus
The University of Tokyo
Japan

ISSN 2197-8859 ISSN 2197-8867 (electronic)
ISBN 978-4-431-54534-7 ISBN 978-4-431-54535-4 (eBook)
DOI 10.1007/978-4-431-54535-4
Springer Tokyo Heidelberg New York Dordrecht London

Printed on acid-free paper

Springer is part of Springer Science+Business Media (www.springer.com)

To my dear Aiko, for our golden wedding anniversary.

Preface

This book aims to explain to readers the basic idea of general equilibrium theory, which forms the core of current mainstream economics called the neoclassical school. Understanding this theory is absolutely necessary both for further study and for criticism of contemporary economic theories. I have tried, therefore, not only to explain traditional theories faithfully, but also to make clear the many problems that are still unsolved.

The book is based on many graduate or undergraduate lectures on microeconomics or price theory that I gave at The University of Tokyo. As a textbook or reference book for students who first study microeconomics, I recommend using Chap. 1, Chap. 2 (except Sect. 9), Chap. 3 (from Sect. 1 to Sect. 3, Sect. 6, Sect. 11), Chap. 4 (from Sect. 1 to Sect. 4), Chap. 5 (from Sect. 1 to Sect. 5, Sect. 8), Chap. 6 (except Sects. 6 and 7), Chap. 7 (from Sect. 1 to Sect. 5), Chap. 8 (from Sect. 1 to Sect. 6), and Chap. 9 (Sects. 1, 4, and 7). For more advanced readers, I suggest reading the remaining sections of each chapter and the literature recommended in the last part of the book. Problems are included at the end of each chapter to confirm that the content of the chapter has been understood and to suggest more advanced studies to readers. Incidentally, I have tried to avoid the use of advanced mathematics. Only an elementary knowledge of differential calculus and linear algebra is required to understand this book.

I thank Springer for taking what existed only as a typewritten English manuscript, converting it to LaTeX, and making it available both as an e-Book and printed book.

Tokyo, Japan
June 2013

Takashi Negishi

Preface

[illegible]

Contents

Chapter 1
Introduction

1.1 Economic Theory

Following chapters are intended to explain the basic structure, rather than recent contributions, of what has been called microeconomic theory of the neo-classical economics. Originally it is the economics of Marshall that was called the neo-classical economics by Thorstein Veblen who was critical of classical and neo-classical economic theories. The neo-classical theory that has been predominant in the post-war period is, however, to be called as neo-Walrasian theory. In other words, it is the traditional general equilibrium theory, pioneered by Walras and Pareto, and revived by such modern theorists as Hicks, Samuelson, Arrow, Debreu and Allais. What should be also added to this Walrasian tradition is that of Edgeworth who is now regarded, with Walras, as one of the two founding fathers of the equilibrium theory of modern mathematical economics. Microeconomics tries to explain the behavior of an economy through interactions among individual firms and individual consumers while macroeconomics deals with an aggregated economy as such (see Sect. 10.1). The former is also called as the price theory, since prices play important roles for interactions among firms and consumers.

Chapters 2–5 deal with the modern version of Walrasian general equilibrium theory and explain how goods are allocated and incomes are distributed among consumers and firms through the price mechanism of competitive markets. On the other hand, Chaps. 7–9 are devoted to welfare economics, which designs optimal allocation of resources and optimal distribution of incomes, and in which the concept of optimality suggested by Pareto plays an essential role. Edgeworth's view of competitive markets is introduced in Chap. 6 and it is shown how nicely it can be used to supplement Walrasian equilibrium theory. Finally, Chap. 10 considers the relation between microeconomics and macroeconomics, and discusses the so-called non-Walrasian general disequilibrium theory, which is, however, quite Walrasian in some sense.

Before the discussions of the details of the neo-classical micro-economic theory, it may be useful to consider what is the economic theory in general, and what

T. Negishi, *Elements of Neo-Walrasian Economics*, Advances in Japanese Business and Economics 5, DOI 10.1007/978-4-431-54535-4_1, © Springer Japan 2014

is the neo-classical microeconomics in particular. Perhaps what should first be emphasized is the hypothetico-deductive character of scientific theories. Universal theories cannot be reached by inductive inference from the observation of facts. This is because of the famous problem of induction that induction from particular instances to a universal theory requires an illogical leap in thought at some stage in the argument. No amount of observations of white swans can justify the statement that all swans are white. Scientific theories are not derived by inductive generalization from individual instance. They are merely based on hypotheses from which statements about facts are deduced by the aid of the rules of deductive logic. As Popper emphasized, they cannot be verified but can be falsified by empirical observations, since the observation of a single black swan is enough to refute the statement that all swans are white.

Not all the scientific hypotheses are, however, always falsifiable. From his study of Copernican revolution in astronomy, Kuhn insisted that an accepted theoretical framework called paradigm can be replaced by another only at the scientific revolutions. In other words, hypotheses basic and essential to a paradigm cannot always be falsified merely by observations inconsistent with the statements derived from such hypotheses. Lakatos argued further that the history of science has been and should be a history of competing research programs (paradigms). All the scientific research programs may be characterized as having an immutable hard core that is empirically not refutable and that is surrounded by a changeable protective belt of empirically refutable auxiliary hypotheses that has to bear the brunt of tests. Hypotheses which belong to hard core are, therefore, never empirically falsifiable. Since there have been many different schools in the history of economics, it is interesting to apply Lakatos's model of science to the case of economic science. Neo-classical economics is, then, certainly one of the major research programs in economics.

What is the hard core of the neo-classical economics as a research program? It is really not an easy question to answer and perhaps it is best to leave it to the readers of the following chapters. Instead, however, it is possible, at this stage, to point out two fundamental characteristics of the neo-classical economics as a school in economics. Firstly, the neo-classical economics is a collection of universal theories which are logically deduced from a small number of common basic premises such as the assumption of an economic man. Generally, these abstract theories are regarded as to be applicable in any age and in any country. Secondly, in neo-classical economics there is a fundamental belief in the function of competitive markets, which can be seen in its heavy uses of and reliance in the law of supply and demand, and the equilibrium analysis of markets.

1.2 Classical Economics

As a matter of fact, neo-classical economics has succeeded, in spite of the marginal revolution, these two characteristics from the classical economics. The purpose of the present and following sections is not to give a full description of the history of economics, but to give proper historical perspectives on neo-classical economics and on some names of neo-classical economists, which will appear very often in the following chapters. We can start, therefore, with the classical economics and shall discuss it only in its relation to neo-classical economics, though the name of Quesnay (1694–1774), at least, has to be mentioned. His *Tableau économique* (1758) is the first numerical model of an economy, i.e., a theoretical system based on simplifying assumptions to explain the behavior of an economy.

The classical economics was founded by Adam Smith (1723–1790) who wrote *The Wealth of Nations* (1776). He had wide knowledge of Newton's astronomy and mechanics, as was seen in one of his early writings, *The History of Astronomy*. Indeed, Smith drew an analogy between natural philosophy or natural science and moral philosophy or social science and argued that, after the former showed an example of systematic explanations of different observations based on a few common principles, something of the same kind should be done in the latter. He is also well known by his insistence on *laissez-faire* and criticism of government regulations. The pursuit of private interests can, through the guidance of the invisible hands of market mechanism based on the social division of labor, promote public benefits.

The economics of Adam Smith was followed by the complete domination of Ricardo's economics for a period of 100 years. Ricardo (1772–1823) published *On the Principles of Political Economy and Taxation* in 1817 and investigated the theory of the distribution of the product in conditions of equilibrium by the use of abstract economic models. He supported Say (1767–1832)'s law that supply creates demand and there is no possibility of glut. Although Malthus (1766–1834) who was more concerned with what determines the volume of output day by day in the real world argued against Ricardo in this respect, the former could not persuade the latter in the famous Ricardo–Malthus controversy. Say's law is, of course, an expression of the belief in the smooth functions of competitive markets. Classical economic theories were finally summarized and synthesized in his *Principles of Political Economy* (1848) by John Stuart Mill (1806–1873). According to Mill, the most fundamental law of the classical economics is the law of supply and demand. We have to fall back on this antecedent law, if the law of cost of production is not applicable, let alone the law of labor value, as in the case of international trade.

Senior (1790–1864) is one of the classical economists who are interested in the methodology of economics. In his *An Outline of the Science of Political Economy* (1836), it was argued that economics is not a fact-gathering expedition but a logical exercise in reasoning from a few postulates. Basic postulates of the classical economics are, according to Senior, (1) the assumption of an economic man who tries to obtain additional wealth with as little sacrifice as possible, (2) the Malthusian principle of population that the population is limited only by a fear of a deficiency of the means of subsistence, (3) the productivity of capital in the sense that the labor productivity can be increased by capital accumulation, which is made possible by abstinence of consumption, and (4) diminishing returns in agriculture. The first postulate is, of course, identical to the neo-classical axiom of the rationality and the fourth is extended into the convexity assumption on the feasible sets in the neo-classical theory of production (see Sect. 2.3).

1.3 Marginal Revolution and After

As the precursors of the marginal revolution against classical economics, we may name von Thünen (1783–1850), who is the founder of the location theory and pioneered the use of the concept of marginal productivity, Cournot (1801–1877), who developed theories of monopoly and oligopoly and clarified the implication of perfect competition (see Sects. 6.2 and 6.3), Dupuit (1804–1866), the pioneer of the consumers' surplus analysis (see Sect. 7.2), and Gossen (1810–1858), who is known for laws of marginal utility. Those who developed the marginalist theory of economics systematically are, however, W.S. Jevons (1835–1882), the author of *The Theory of Political Economy* (1871), Carl Menger (1840–1921), who wrote *Grundsätze der Volkswirthschaftslehre* (1871), and Leon Walras (1834–1910), the author of *Élements d'économie politique pure* (1874–1877). These economists, independently—at Manchester in England, Vienna in Austria and Lausanne in Switzerland—and almost at the same time, developed similar theories which are different from the classical one, on the basis of such marginal relations as marginal utility and marginal productivity.

For Walras, however, what is more important is not to insist on replacing the theory of marginal utility for the classical cost theory of value. While classical economics aimed to establish the law of causal relations among economic variables, Walras tried to develop the general equilibrium theory which emphasizes the mutual interdependency of economic variables. In Lausanne, Walras was succeeded by V. Pareto (1848–1923), who is well known by the concept of Pareto optimality in welfare economics. This Walrasian tradition is wholly succeeded by the current mainstream economics, i.e., the neo-classical economics. The general equilibrium theory assumes what Popper considers the true aim of the social sciences, since it is the very opposite of what he calls the conspiracy theory of society. Whatever happens in society is not the result of direct conspiracy of some powerful individuals and groups. The main task of social sciences is to try to analyse the unintended social repercussions of intentional human actions.

Jevons had a view of competitive markets different from that of Cournot and Walras. It was succeeded by F.Y. Edgeworth (1845–1926) in his *Mathematical Psychics* (1881), in which he explained how the arbitrage behavior of rational individuals can generate the unique market price for each commodity, i.e., the law of indifference, which Cournot and Walras simply presupposed. Edgeworth also pioneered, along with Cournot, the study of an important problem of modern mathematical economics, the problem of a large economy in which the number of individual participants is infinitely large (see Sect. 6.5).

The name of A. Marshall (1842–1924) should also be mentioned in connection with the marginal revolution, though his book, *Principles of Economics* (1890), was published slightly later than those of Jevons, Menger and Walras. Marshall did not deny the significance of classical economics, but tried to generalize Ricardo's theory of value and distribution as expounded by J.S. Mill. Marshall's vision of the time structure of demand and supply equilibria, i.e., temporary, short-run and long-run equilibria, was introduced into the general equilibrium theory by *Value and Capital* (1939) of J.R. Hicks. A.C. Pigou (1877–1959), who wrote *The Economics of Welfare* (1920), was Marshall's successor at Cambridge. The greatest topic in the Cambridge school after Marshall was, however, the appearance of a book of its self-criticism, J.M. Keynes (1883–1946)'s *The General Theory of Employment, Interest and Money* (1936). Keynes denied Say's law and the possibility of the automatic adjustments in markets, particularly in the labor market, and insisted the importance of the problem of the deficiency of effective demand. He admitted that Malthus was his predecessor in this respect. Although Keynesian revolution was done in terms of macroeconomics, there are several recent attempts to give microeconomic foundations to Keynesian economics (see Chap. 10). These are non-Walrasian in the sense of disequilibrium analysis. They are, however, still in the tradition of Walras, since the mutual interdependency among economic variables is emphasized in their general disequilibrium analysis.

1.4 Anti-Orthodox Economics (1)

If the classical and neo-classical economics can be called the orthodox economics, there have been many schools of economics which are to be called anti-orthodox. What is neo-classical economics can be seen also from the studies of what these schools distinguish themselves from the classical and neo-classical economics.

While the classical economics was developed mainly in England, an advanced capitalist country, the historical school of economics was formed in Germany, a less developed capitalist country in the second half of the nineteenth century. In contrast to general and universal theories established by the abstract and deductive method of the classical school, the historical school emphasized the importance of the concrete and inductive method and of the descriptive work on historical details. Classical economics was criticized on the grounds that the variety and diversity of economic institutions in different societies and centuries makes it impossible to explain all the variety of economic action by the single universal theory of the market economy. In the Methodenstreit (battle of methods) against the historical school, however, Carl Menger admitted the importance of institutions for economic actions and developed the organic theory of institutions which insists that they are the unintended social results of efforts in pursuit of rational individual interests. In other words, institutions can also be explained by the universal theory of rational behavior of individuals.

Max Weber (1864–1920), who was trained in the historical school, tried to bring the Methodenstreit to an end and agreed that all historical explanations require causal schemes which are of a general nature. He recognized that there is a need for abstract economic theory, but saw no reason why abstract schemes should have to be confined to schemes of rational economic conduct. He devised, therefore, the famous notion of the Idealtypus, an abstract model of the reality, which is his chief instrument of causal analysis in society to go beyond the rational schemes of economics and to grasp even the meaning of irrational actions. Weber is also known by his insistence of freedom from evaluation (Wertfreiheit) in the controversy on whether scientific value judgements (Werturteil) about social events and practical proposals are admissible, or even possible. This is succeeded by neoclassical welfare economics in its use of Pareto optimality and the distinction between resource allocation and income distribution (see Chaps. 7 and 9).

Institutionalism is the American version of the historical school. Perhaps the most famous of the representative scholars is Thorstein Veblen (1857–1929). Being influenced by the evolutionism of Darwin and Spencer, Veblen insisted that economics should be an evolutionary science which examines the emergence and the modification through time of economic institutions. He emphasized that the businessmen's goal of making money is in conflict with the industrial pursuits of engineers, which aim at the efficient production of commodities. His arguments provided a number of suggestive insights into the problems of market failures, pollution and unemployment (see Chaps. 8 and 10), though he went too far with his emotional bias against business. Also, his concept of conspicuous consumption can be used to show the possibility of an upward sloping demand curve, which the neoclassical theory of consumer behavior cannot do, unless the income effect is strong and works against the substitution effect (see Chap. 3). The tradition of institutional economics is succeeded by such contemporary economists critical of modern industrial economy and neo-classical economics as Galbraith and Myrdal.

Marx (1818–1883) was influenced by the three great intellectual achievements in the nineteenth century, classical German philosophy, English classical economics and French socialism. Though the classical economics was a historical in the sense that it aimed to find a universal law of capitalist economy which continues to exists indefinitely, Marx emphasized that the capitalist mode of production is historical and transitional, from the point of view of the materialist interpretation of history. According to Uno (1897–1977), however, Marx's *Das Kapital* (1867, 1885, 1894) should be regarded as a work which is concerned with principles of economics and to deal with the economic laws of motion of an autonomous, pure capitalist society, an abstract model of an economy, to which the mid-century British economy was approaching. In other words, principles of economics should not be confused with the theory of capitalist development, which aims to discuss the origin, development and death of the capitalism as well as its replacement by the socialism. Although the economics of *Das Kapital* was not mathematical, it may be interesting to see that recent mathematical models of Marxian economics are largely applications of the linear economic models of neo-classical economics, developed in the theory of general equilibrium, input–output analysis and linear-programming (see Chap. 5).

1.5 Anti-Orthodox Economics (2)

As we saw, Carl Menger defended the classical and neo-classical tradition in the Mothodenstreit against German historical school. It is also true that some of the important contributions made by the historical Austrian school, which was formed by those who followed Menger, were absorbed and developed in the general equilibrium theory of neo-classical economics. The economists of neo-Austrian school are, however, very critical of the equilibrium theory of neo-classical economics. The founding father of neo-Austrian school is Mises (1881–1973) who succeeded the subjectivist aspect of Menger. Both Mises and Hayek were against the neo-classical general equilibrium model of Lange in the so-called socialist calculation debate. They pointed out, like Lange, the importance of the role of markets, but they also emphasized that dynamic rivalry among entrepreneurs is essential for the function of markets. Neo-Austrians are critical of the static theory of market equilibrium in neo-classical economics, and argued for the importance of dynamic market process in which subjectively rational individuals learn from fragmented information.

The similarity between classical economics and neo-classical economics was pointed out in the previous sections. The economists of neo-Ricardian and post-Keynesian schools are, however, emphasizing the essential difference between the classical plutology (science of Wealth) and the neo-classical catallactics (science of exchange). They insist on the synthesis of Keynesian short-run theory and classical long-run theory. The essence of the classical economics is regarded, not the law of supply and demand, but the cost theory of value or labor theory of value, which insists that prices are determined exclusively by the cost of production and independent of demand. This tradition of the classical value theory was revived by P. Sraffa (1898–1983) in his *Production of commodities by Means of Commodities* (1960). It may be interesting, however, to see that this Ricardo–Sraffa theory has the mathematical structure which is very similar with that of linear economic models of neo-classical economics.

Problems

1.1. What is the relation between schools in economics and research programmes or paradigms?

1.2. Is it possible to consider the neo-classical synthesis between neo-classical and Keynesian economics, which was once attempted by Samuelson in his *Economics*?

Literature

See M. Blaug, *The Methodology of Economics* (1980) for the technical literature on philosophy of science, history of science and methodology of economics. For neo-classical economics, see T. Aspromourgos, "On the Origins of the Term 'Neo-classical'", *Cambridge Journal of Economics* (1986), A. Leijonhufvud, "Schools, 'revolutions' and research programmes in economic theory," S.J. Latsis (ed.), *Method and Appraisal in Economics* (1976), and R.D.C. Black, A.W. Coats and C.D.W. Goodwin (eds.), *The Marginal Revolution in Economics* (1973).
For the details of the history of economic theory, see M. Blaug, *Economic Theory in Retrospect* (1985), R.B. Ekelund and R.F. Hébert, *A History of Economic Theory and Method* (1983), and T. Negishi, *History of Economic Theory* (1989).

Chapter 2
Firms and Production

2.1 The Theory of the Firm

In a modern society, indispensable roles are played by many different firms. Firms offers a large part of the goods and services which are consumed in the society. The majority of the people live on incomes they receive from firms. Those who run firms and those who are employed by them spend most of their days in offices and factories of the firms and try hard to make their career in the firms. Consumers' taste and industrial technology are much influenced by firms' activities in advertising, marketing, researches and developments. The study on firms should, therefore, be an inter-disciplinary task among economics, sociology, psychology, business administration, engineering and system analysis. Except for the case of a small private firm, a firm is and organization composed by many decision-makers, with partly common, but partly conflicting interests, controlling different means and basing their decisions on partly different information. Even the economic theory of firms, therefore, should be in general based, not on a simple optimization theory, but on the theory of games or the theory of teams.

Fortunately, however, the theory of the firm is expected to play a quite limited role in the neo-classical theory of microeconomics. It is merely an auxiliary device to explain the form of supply functions (curves) of output (the consumables and the intermediate goods) and of demand functions (curves) of input (the service of factors of production and the intermediate goods). For such a limited purpose, the most simple theory of a profit maximizing firm will do. It is true that such a firm is merely a caricature stripped of many important aspects of firms of the real economy. It is also true, however, that such a simple theory can be a starting point of a more general theory of the firm. Whether it is a good starting point or not depends on how approximately it can explain the behavior of firms in the real economy.

The profit to be maximized by a firm is defined as the difference between the revenue it receives from the sale of its outputs and the costs it incurs from the purchase of its inputs. In this chapter, let us assume that our firm is a competitive firm which takes prices prevailing in the market as given, irrespective of the level of

T. Negishi, *Elements of Neo-Walrasian Economics*, Advances in Japanese Business and Economics 5, DOI 10.1007/978-4-431-54535-4_2, © Springer Japan 2014

its outputs and inputs. The rationale for such price-taking behavior will be discussed in Chaps. 4 and 5 in the below. The profit of the firm is, then, simply a linear function of its outputs and inputs. The maximization of the profit with respect to outputs and inputs is, however, subject to technological relations among outputs and inputs. Unless we are in the land of Cockaigne, for example, outputs cannot be increased indefinitely from the given inputs. Generally, there exist complex substitutability and complementarity among outputs and inputs. The problem of the firm is, therefore, that of a constrained maximization of the profit, being subject to the so-called production function which summarizes technological restrictions on the production, i.e., the transformation of inputs into outputs.

2.2 Production Functions

An example of such production functions which have been often used in theoretical as well as empirical studies is the so-called Cobb–Douglas production function.

$$Y = AL^a K^b \tag{2.1}$$

where A, a and b are positive constants and Y, L and K denote, respectively, the output, the input of labor service, and the input of capital service. Since (2.1) can be rewritten in the log-linear form

$$\log Y = \log A + a \log L + b \log K, \tag{2.2}$$

parameters of production function A, a and b can be easily estimated empirically from data of Y, L and K. If $a + b = 1$, the constant returns to scale prevails, while $a + b < (>)\ 1$ implies the existence of the diminishing (increasing) returns.

More generally, consider an economy of m goods which include the consumables, the intermediate goods and the service of factors of production. Let y_j denote the output of the j-th good if it is positive, and the input of the j-th good if it is negative ($j = 1, \ldots, m$). The production function of a firm can, in general, be written as

$$f(y_1, \ldots, y_j, \ldots, y_m) = 0 \tag{2.3}$$

in the form of implicit function. If the j-th good is neither output nor input of the firm, consider simply that $y_j = 0$. In the case of Cobb–Douglas production function (2.1), it can be written in the form (2.3) as

$$Y - A(-L)^a(-K)^b(-1)^{a+b} = 0, \tag{2.4}$$

since Y denote the level of output while L and K denote the absolute value of the level of inputs.

Fig. 2.1

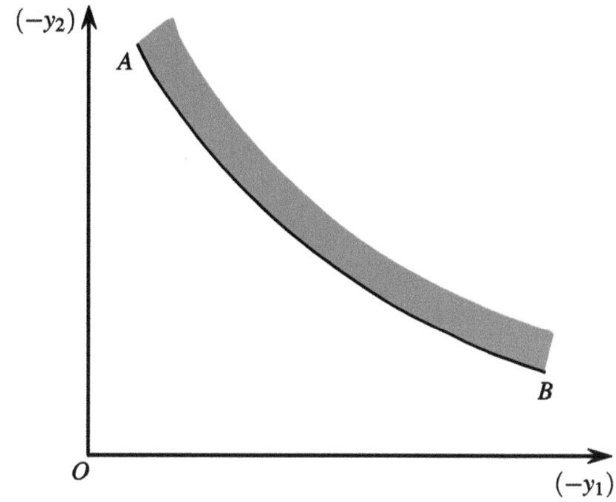

Let p_j denote the price of the j-th good ($j = 1, \ldots, m$), which prevails in the market and is taken by the firm as unchanged. The profit of the firm is, then, a simple linear function

$$\pi = \sum_j p_j y_j \tag{2.5}$$

since inputs are denoted by negative y_j's. The firm's problem is to maximize (2.5) subject to (2.3). While the profit (2.5) to be maximized is a simple linear form, the constraint (2.3) is generally non-linear. The nature of the maximization problem depends, therefore, on the form of production function (2.3).

The form of production function generally assumed is usually shown by curves which shows the relation between inputs of two goods, outputs of two goods, and an input of a good and an output of a good. The curve *AB* in Fig. 2.1 is the so-called isoquant which shows the relation between required inputs of the first two goods $(-y_1)$ and $(-y_2)$, when inputs and outputs of all the other goods are given. Usually, it is drawn as convex to the origin. Similarly, the curve *CD* in Fig. 2.2 shows the possible combination of output of the j-th good y_j and that of the k-th good y_k, when inputs and outputs of other goods are given, and is drawn, as usual, concave to the origin. Finally, Fig. 2.3 gives a curve *EF* which shows the possible relation between the input of the j-th good $(-y_j)$ and the output of the k-th good y_k, when inputs and outputs of other goods are given. This curve is usually drawn so that the productivity of the input in terms of the output diminishes as the scale production expands. As a matter of fact the usually assumed forms of these three curves represent the same single assumption made on the production function (2.3).

Fig. 2.2

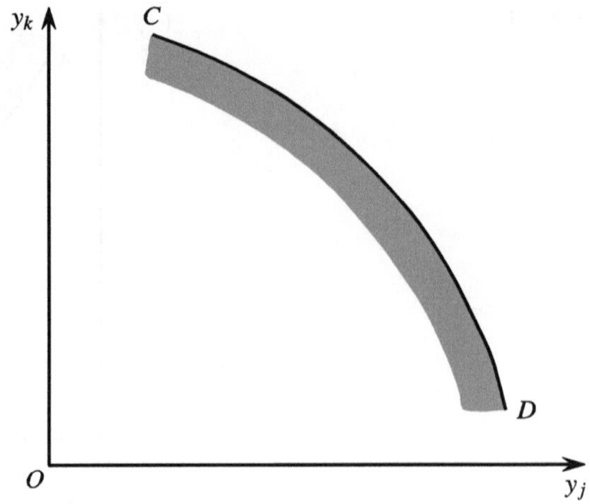

Fig. 2.3

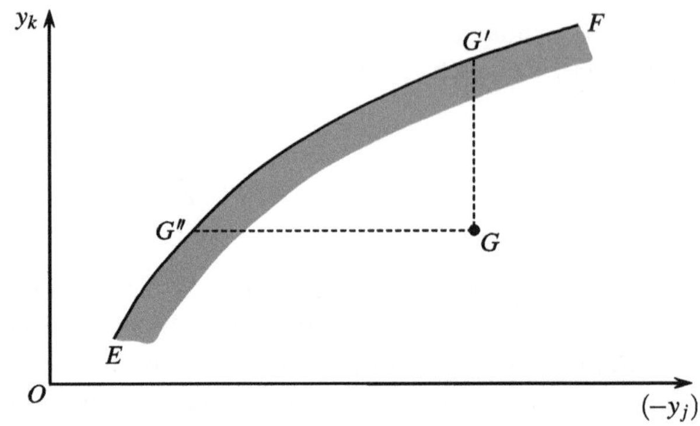

2.3 Feasible Set

To see this, consider the shaded areas in Figs. 2.1–2.3, bounded, respectively, by curves *AB*, *CD* and *EF*. Any point in these areas represents the technologically possible combination, though not necessarily efficient combination, of inputs and outputs, if we assume the free disposal of inputs and outputs. For example, consider the point G in Fig. 2.3. We can reach to this point from the point G' on the curve *EF* by throwing away the output $G'G$. It can also be reached from the point G'' on the curve *EF* by an increase in input $G''G$, which is to be left unused. This point is clearly technologically possible, though not efficient. Points on the curve *EF* are, on the other hand, not only technologically possible, but also efficient. Similarly, curves *AB* and *CD* in Figs. 2.1 and 2.2 represent technologically efficient combinations while points inside of the shaded areas represent possible but inefficient combinations of inputs and outputs.

The shaded areas in Figs. 2.1–2.3 are called feasible sets of combinations of inputs and outputs. In terms of production functions, any point on the boundary

Fig. 2.4

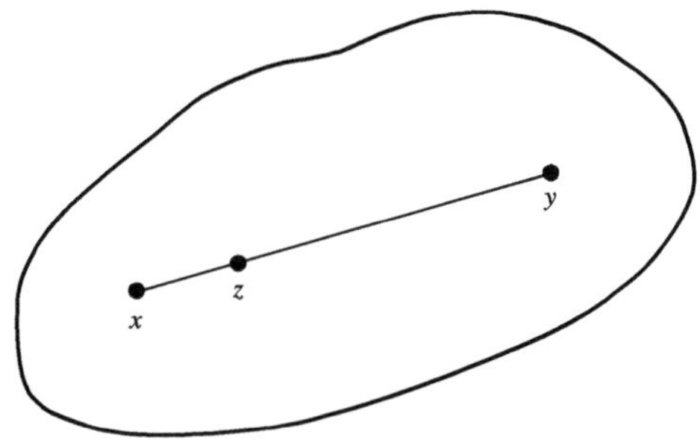

curves *AB*, *CD* and *EF* satisfies the equality form of production function like (2.3) while any point in the feasible sets satisfies the inequality form of production function

$$f(y_1, \ldots, y_j, \ldots, y_m) \leq 0. \tag{2.6}$$

For example, in the case of Cobb–Douglas production function, the inequality form is

$$Y - A(-L)^a(-K)^b(-1)^{a+b} \leq 0, \tag{2.7}$$

which is satisfied by any feasible, i.e., technologically possible, combination of Y, L and K.

The shaded areas in Figs. 2.1–2.3 share a common property. They are all convex sets. As is seen in Fig. 2.4, a set of points is convex if it also contains any point z on the line segment between x and y whenever it contains any points x and y. In other words, whenever it contains any points x and y, a convex set contains also their weighted average with arbitrary positive weights. Now we are ready to state the assumption on production functions, which is usually made in the neoclassical theory of microeconomics. The feasible sets of production functions are convex. In terms of production function, if any two input–output vectors, $y = (y_1, \ldots, y_j, \ldots, y_m)$ and $y' = (y'_1, \ldots, y'_j, \ldots, y'_m)$, satisfy the inequality form of the production function (2.6), then, any positive linear combination of them, i.e.,

$$\begin{aligned} y'' &= ty + (1-t)y' \\ &= (ty_1 + (1-t)y'_1, \ldots, ty_m + (1-t)y'_m) \end{aligned} \tag{2.8}$$

for any $0 < t < 1$, also satisfies the production function (2.6). This assumption that

$$\text{if} \quad f(y) \leq 0 \quad \text{and} \quad f(y') \leq 0, \quad \text{then} \quad f(y'') \leq 0 \tag{2.9}$$

is called the convexity assumption.

Fig. 2.5

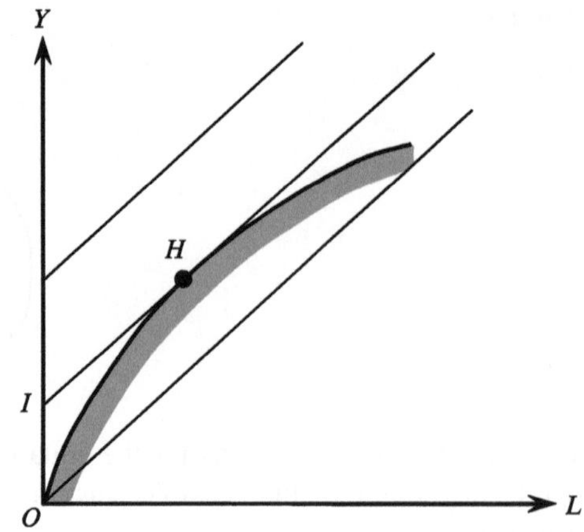

If this convexity assumption is made, the maximization of profit (2.5) under the condition (2.6) becomes a very simple problem, as is seen in Fig. 2.5. Consider a simple case where the firm produces a single product Y and the only variable input is labor L. Figure 2.5 is a reproduction of Fig. 2.3. The equi-profit lines are parallel lines with the slope $\frac{w}{p}$, where p and w denote, respectively, the price of the product and the rate of wage. The profit is maximized at H, where a profit line is tangent to the boundary *EF* of the feasible set and the profit in terms of the product is indicated by *OI*. At H, the marginal productivity of labor, $\frac{dY}{dL}$, is equal to the real wage, $\frac{w}{p}$, so that the so-called first postulate of the classical economics is established. Usually, the condition of the maximization of (2.5) under the constraint (2.6) is that the marginal rate of substitution between any two goods, i.e., the slope of the relevant boundary curves of feasible set, is equal to the price ratio of these two goods. This tangency condition is not generally true, however, when the convexity assumption is not imposed. Consider the difficulty of such a case, which, for example, can be seen in Fig. 2.6.

To assume the convexity so as to make the problem simple is one thing, however, and to justify such an assumption is quite another. The production function is a summary statement of the firm's structure of production. To justify the convexity assumption on production function, therefore, we have to scrutinize the details of the structure of production hidden behind the production function. In view of the fact that the technique of linear programming has been successfully applied to organize the production efficiently in many different firms, we may use the linear programming model of production for this purpose, since the success of linear programming in the production planning of many firms implies that its structure reflects the firms' structure of production fairly well.

Fig. 2.6

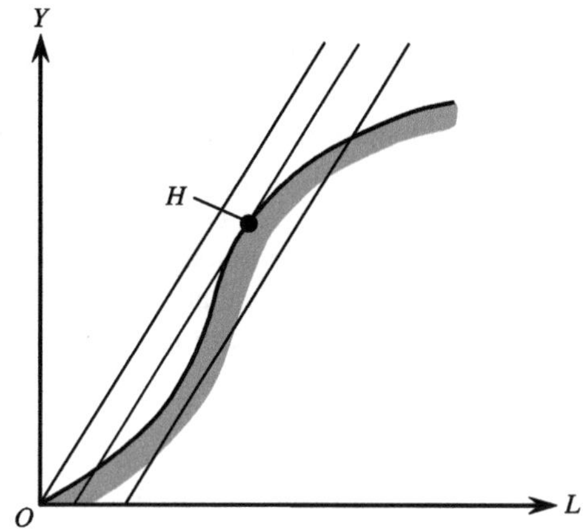

2.4 Linear Programming Model

Linear Programming is a mathematical technique to maximize a linear function subject to constraints of linear inequalities. While the profit (2.5) to be maximized is a linear function of inputs and outputs, the constraint of production function (2.6) is a non-linear inequality in our theory of a perfectly competitive firm. To apply linear programming, therefore, we have to decompose the production function into more basic linear production processes which transform inputs into outputs. Let us suppose that there exist n different production processes behind a single production function and denote by x_i (≥ 0) the activity level of the i-th process ($i = 1, \ldots, n$). If we denote by a_{ij} the amount of the j-th good produced (positive) or consumed (negative) by the unit activity level of the i-th process, i.e., when $x_i = 1$, two basic assumptions of linear programming model of production can be stated as follows.

Divisibility. The amount of the j-th good produced or consumed by the i-th process when its activity level is x_i is simply $a_{ij}x_i$ for any $x_i \geq 0$. In other words, the process can be continuously divided or extended and inputs and outputs are proportional to the activity level of the process.

Additivity. If the i-th process is operated at the level x_i and the i'-th process is operated at the level of x_i', simultaneously, their joint output or joint consumption of the j-th good is simply $a_{ij}x_i + a_{i'j}x_{i'}$ for any $x_i \geq 0$ and $x_{i'} \geq 0$. In other words, processes are independent and there is no external economies or diseconomies among processes.

Decomposition of a firm's production into different process is arbitrary. One may consider that different factories of a firm are independent production processes. Alternatively, a different technology of production may be considered as a different production process. If the firm produces several different products, the production of different goods may be considered as different processes. The point is that the production of a firm should be decomposed into production processes so that we can safely assume divisibility and additivity assumptions. Obviously whether these assumptions are satisfied depends on how we decompose the firm's production into processes. This is why the application of linear programming is sometimes called not the problem of theory but that of art.

Processes transform inputs into outputs. As for inputs, however, we have to distinguish two different types. The first one is that of variable inputs, which a competitive firm can purchase freely whatever amount it likes at a given market price. The second one is that of more or less fixed or limitational inputs, the total amount of which a firm can use are given, at least in the short-run, i.e., within a given period. Examples of variable type inputs are raw materials, energies and labor service of untrained or part-time workers. On the other hand, examples of the second type inputs are land of given characteristics in agriculture, capacity of fixed plants in manufactures, and labor service of managers and trained workers. A firm inherited a given amount of these fixed factors of production from the previous period and has to make a plan of its production in the current period within the fixed supply of these factors.

Suppose there are r different factors of the second type and let s_k (> 0) denote the amount of the fixed supply of the k-th such factor which the firm can use freely ($k = 1, \dots, r$). If the i-th process consumes A_{ik} (≥ 0) of the k-th such factor as inputs at its unit activity level, the total consumption of n processes $\sum_i A_{ik} x_i$, from the assumption of divisibility and additivity, when the i-th process is operated at the level of x_i ($i = 1, \dots, n$). The condition for the feasibility of activity vectors of processes, $x = (x_1, \dots, x_n)$, is then

$$\sum_i A_{ik} x_i \leq s_k \quad (k = 1, \dots, r). \tag{2.10}$$

If we denote by positive a_{ij} the output of the j-th marketable good by the i-th process, and by the negative a_{ij} the first type input of the j-th marketable good by the i-th process, when $x_i = 1$, then, the total output (positive) or input (negative) of the firm is $y_j = \sum_i a_{ij} x_i$, when the i-th process is operated at the level of x_i. In view of (2.5), the profit is

$$\pi = \sum_j p_j \sum_i a_{ij} x_i. \tag{2.11}$$

The firm now maximizes a linear function (2.11) with respect to activity vector $x = (x_1, \dots, x_n)$ subject to constraints of linear inequalities (2.10), which is a linear programming problem.

2.5 Convexity of Feasible Set

Let us denote by A the $n \times r$ matrix of A_{ik} $(i = 1, \ldots, n,\ k = 1, \ldots, r)$, the feasibility condition (2.10) of activity vector x is rewritten as

$$Ax \leq s \tag{2.12}$$

where $s = (s_1, \ldots, s_r)$ is the given availability vector of the second type inputs. The convexity of the feasible set of activity vectors x of processes is easily seen by the fact that for any x and x'

$$\text{if} \quad Ax \leq s \quad \text{and} \quad Ax' \leq s, \quad \text{then} \quad Ax'' \leq s, \tag{2.13}$$

where $x'' = tx + (1 - t)x'$ for any t such that $0 < t < 1$.

If we denote by a the $n \times m$ matrix of a_{ij} $(i = 1, \ldots, n,\ j = 1, \ldots, m)$, the input–output vector y of the firm corresponding to the activity vector x of processes can be expressed as

$$y = ax. \tag{2.14}$$

If input–output vectors y and y' of a firm correspond, respectively to activity vectors x and x' of processes, then, $y'' = ty + (1 - t)y'$ corresponds exactly to $x'' = tx + (1 - t)x'$ for any t such that $0 < t < 1$. Suppose any feasible x and x' which satisfy (2.12). The corresponding y and y' satisfy, respectively, $f(y) \leq 0$ and $f(y') \leq 0$. In view of (2.13), then, y'' satisfies $f(y'') \leq 0$. The convexity assumption (2.9) is, therefore, justified.

If linear programming model can be applied to the production of a firm, the feasible set of the firm's input–output vectors of marketable goods can be shown convex. What makes the convexity assumption justifiable is the existence of fixed factors, of which only a given amount can be used in the short-run.

2.6 Marginal Cost

To see the implications of the convexity of the feasible set, let us consider a simplified case of a single product firm. Since the profit is the difference between the revenue from the sale of the single product and the cost of variable, i.e., marketable inputs which are used to produce the product, and prices are taken as given by the firm, the maximization of the profit requires first the minimization of the cost for any given level of output of product Y. The minimum cost C of the firm is then considered a function of Y. Obviously, it is an increasing function. In Fig. 2.7, cost curves are drawn as upward sloping. The problem is whether the curve *OA* or *OB* is the minimum variable cost curve, which is derived from our linear programming

Fig. 2.7

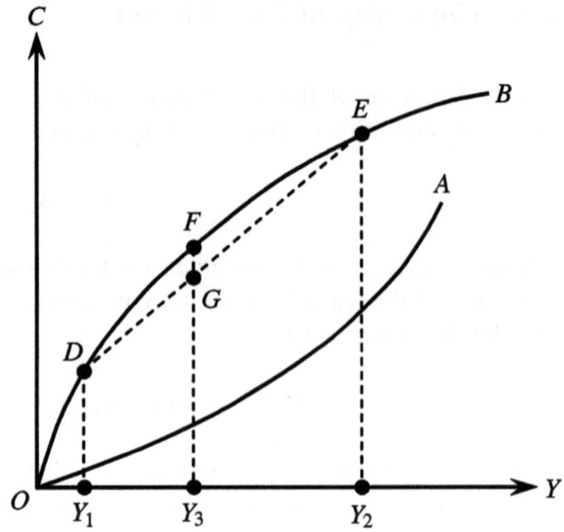

model of production. In other words, whether its slope, i.e., the marginal cost $\frac{dC}{dY}$, is increasing or diminishing with respect to the level of output Y.

Suppose the curve OB is the case. The minimum variable costs necessary for the outputs Y_1, Y_2 and $Y_3 = tY_1 + (1-t)Y_2$, for $0 < t < 1$, are indicated, respectively, as Y_1D, Y_2E and Y_3F. If Y_1 and Y_2 correspond, respectively, to activity vectors x and x' of processes,

$$Y_1D = -\sum_i x_i \sum_j a_{ij} p_j, \tag{2.15}$$

$$Y_2E = -\sum_i x_i' \sum_j a_{ij} p_j \tag{2.16}$$

where p_j and a_{ij} (< 0) denote, respectively, the price of the j-th marketable input and the amount of the same input necessary for the unit level of activity of the i-th process. Since the feasible set of the activity vectors is convex, Y_3 can be produced from the activity $x'' = tx + (1-t)x'$ of processes, with the cost $Y_3G = tY_1D + (1-t)Y_2E$, i.e.,

$$Y_3G = -\sum_i x_i'' \sum_j a_{ij} p_j \tag{2.17}$$

which is smaller than the minimum cost Y_3F, as is seen in Fig. 2.7. This contradiction implies that our supposition was wrong and that the minimum cost curve is not like the curve OB.

The marginal cost cannot be diminishing. It should be increasing, or at least constant. The constant marginal cost, however, cannot be maintained for a wide

Fig. 2.8

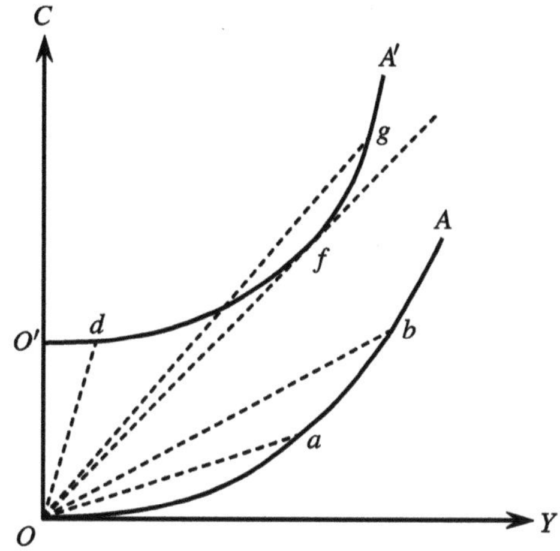

range of output, which can be seen by the consideration of the following simple example. Suppose a firm has two processes to produce a single product from the input of labor service purchasable at the given wage rate. Each process requires the input of a fixed factor, say, the service of machine specific to each process. For a low level of output, the firm uses the process which requires smaller labor input for a unit of output and the marginal cost is constant at the constant labor cost of this process. If the output is increased up to the point where the fixed factor specific to this lower cost process is fully used up, a further increase in output has to be supplied by the use of the process which requires larger labor input for a unit of output. The marginal cost is increased to the level of labor cost of this higher cost process.

The minimum variable cost curve is, therefore, roughly like the curve *OA* in Figs. 2.7 and 2.8, though it may be partly linear. If the number of processes and that of fixed type factors of production are very large, the minimum cost curve can be approximated by the curve *OA* fairly well. If the marginal cost is increasing in this way, the marginal cost curve, which is also upward sloping, is the supply curve of a single product firm, since its profit to be maximized is $pY - C(Y)$, where p is the given price of product, Y is the level of output and $C(Y)$ is the minimum cost function, and the condition for the maximization is $p = \frac{dC}{dY}$, from which the supply Y can be read as a function of P.

2.7 Average Cost

While the slope of the minimum cost curve *OA* in Figs. 2.7 and 2.8 gives the marginal cost, the average cost $\frac{C(Y)}{Y}$ can be given by the slope of lines (like *Oa*, *Ob* in Fig. 2.8) between points on the curve and the origin. In the case of the curve *OA*,

Fig. 2.9

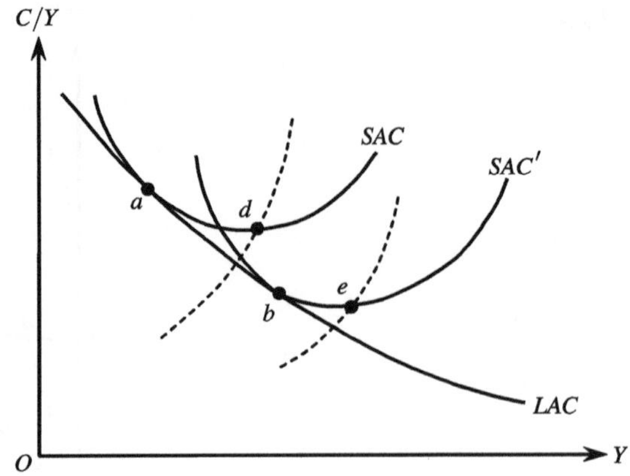

the average cost is increasing with respect to the level of output, as is seen in Fig. 2.8. According to the empirical studies of average cost, however, it often diminishes first and then increases as the level of output is increased. In other words, the average cost curve is neither simply downward sloping nor simply upward sloping. It is, as it were, a U shaped curve. If there exists the so-called fixed cost which does not vary with the level of output, the U shape of the average cost curve can be easily explained as is seen in Fig. 2.8. Suppose OO' is the fixed cost so that the variable cost curve starts, not from the origin O as the curve OA but from the displaced origin O' as the curve $O'A'$, to show the total cost C as a function of output Y. The average cost $\frac{C}{Y}$ diminishes first and then increases as the changes of the slope of lines *Od*, *Of* and *Og* indicate.

The fixed cost does exist in our linear programming model of production since inputs of fixed factors of production are necessary in addition to variable, marketable inputs to produce the outputs. For example, the salary and wages of those employees who are employed by the long-term contacts are fixed cost to the firm since they do not vary with the current level of output. Similarly, interest cost of bonds issued to finance the purchase of capital assets like plants machines, etc. is also a fixed cost to the firm, which should be paid irrespective of the current level of output. The U shaped average cost curve can thus be explained by the fixed cost related to the fixed limitational inputs and by the rising marginal cost curve, derived from the convexity of feasible set of activity vectors of processes, in our linear programming model.

In the long-run, a firm can change some, at least, of the amount of the fixed supply of the fixed limitational factors (s_k's in Sect. 2.4). If they are increased, the fixed cost OO' in Fig. 2.8, is also increased, but the marginal cost, i.e., the slope of the curve $O'A'$ rises more slowly. In Fig. 2.9, the U shaped short run average cost *SAC* curve is shifted to the right as the firm's stock of fixed factors is increased. *SAC* is shifted to *SAC*′ when some of s_k's are increased. It is natural that *SAC*′ gives lower

$\frac{C}{Y}$ for larger output, but higher $\frac{C}{Y}$ for smaller output. The long-run average cost *LAC* curve is the envelope of such shifted *SAC* curves and indicates the minimum average cost to produce each level of output when s_k's are changeable. If the input coefficients for marketable inputs of processes (negative a_{ij}'s) are unchanged, and not all s_k's are changeable, *LAC* curve should be eventually upward sloping. If all the s_k's are changeable, however, *LAC* curve is horizontal, since the constant returns to scale prevails when all the s_k's are changed proportionally. Finally, *LAC* curve can always be downward sloping as in Fig. 2.9, if $-a_{ij}$'s decrease as s_k's are increased. Machines with larger capacities may be more efficient in the sense that they require smaller variable inputs for a unit of output.

It is to be noted that generally *LAC* curve is tangent to *SAC* curves at the points like a and b which are different from the points of the minimum *SAC* like d and e where marginal cost curves (dotted curves in Fig. 2.9) intersect with *SAC* curves, unless *LAC* curve is horizontal. In other words, generally it is not the locus of the points of minimum short-run average cost. It is, however, not entirely wrong to consider the locus of such points as the long-run average cost curve, as will be seen in next section. What is wrong is to confuse two curves which are relevant, respectively, in two different situations.

2.8 Marshallian Externality

In this section, let us digress on Marshallian external economies and diseconomies. The cost of a single firm is considered as a function not only of the level of its own output, but also of the level of the aggregate output of the industry. When an industry expands, for example, the efficiency of public facilities like roads, sea and air ports, and railways, is likely to be increased, so that the cost of a single firm in the industry is reduced (external economy). Alternatively, an industrial expansion may increase congestion in the use of such facilities and the cost of individual firms may be increased (external diseconomy). In these cases, the cost curve of a firm cannot be drawn unless the level of the aggregate output of the industry is specified. Marshallian device for this problem is the representative firm which is a small replica of an industry with free entry.

Now the long-run average cost (*LAC*) curve is not the envelope but the locus of the minimum point of the short-run average cost (*SAC*) curves. In Fig. 2.10, we measure horizontally the volume of the industrial output or the corresponding output of the representative firm, and vertically, prices and costs. Curves *SAC* are short-run average cost curves of the representative firm, and curves *SMC* are short-run marginal cost curves of the representative firm, which is, however, also the short-run supply curve of the industry. Curves D_1, D_2, etc. are demand curves for the industry. Finally, the curves *LAC* is the long-run average cost curve of the representative firm, which is also the long-run supply curve of the industry.

Fig. 2.10

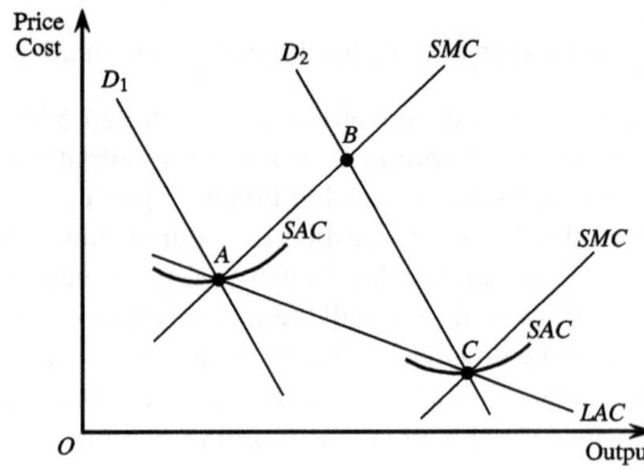

Suppose the demand curve is D_1, which intersects with *LAC* at the point A. The point A signifies the long-run equilibrium of the industry. The short-run average cost of the representative firm, which corresponds to the industrial output given by the abscissa of the point A, reaches the minimum at the point A, so that the point A is also on the curve *SMC*. Since the normal profit is considered to be included in the cost, the representative firm is earning the normal profit at the point A, and the volume of the industrial output remains unchanged. If the demand curve is shifted to D_2, the equilibrium is shifted first to the point B, at which D_2 intersects with the short-run supply curve *SMC*. Gradually, however, the cost curves of the representative firm are shifted downward by the external economies caused by the expansion of the industrial output due to the entry of new firms and the expansion of individual firms caused by the profit higher than the normal one at the point B. The long-run equilibrium is again established at the point C. Similar consideration can also be made in the case of external diseconomies.

The long-run average cost curve of the representative firm when Marshallian externality exists is thus the locus of the minimum point of the short-run average cost curves, like point A, C, etc., and should not be confused with the long-run average cost curve of a single competitive firm, which is, as was seen in Sect. 2.7, the envelope of the short-run average cost curves. The former curve is the locus of the industrial equilibria while the latter has nothing to do with the equilibrium of the industry.

2.9 Profit Function

Let us return to the consideration of the general case of a multiple product firm. In the short-run, the available quantities of some fixed factors of production are limited, and the feasible set of the firm's production function (2.6) is a convex set, where y_j denotes output of the j-th good, if it is positive, or input as a variable factors of production of the j-th good, if it is negative. Being subject to this condition, the firm maximizes the profit (2.5) where the firm takes the price of the j-th good, p_j, as given in the market, $j = 1, \ldots, m$. Since the maximized profit changes as the given prices are changed, it can be considered as a function of prices,

$$\pi(p) \tag{2.18}$$

where $p = (p_1, \ldots, p_m)$ is the vector of given prices.

We can show that this profit function is a convex function of prices. A convex function of a single variable is shown in Fig. 2.11. It has the positive second order derivative and the minimum point where the first order derivative is zero. More generally, the convex function is defined as follows. A function $f(x)$ of $x = (x_1, \ldots, x_m)$ is convex if and only if

$$tf(x) + (1-t)f(x') \geq f(tx + (1-t)x') \tag{2.19}$$

for any x and x', where t is any positive constant less than one. If $f(x)$ is not linear, and differentiable, furthermore, strict inequality has to hold.

To show that the profit function (2.18) is a convex function of p, consider any price vectors p and p' and their positive linear combination $p'' = tp + (1-t)p'$ for any $0 \leq t \leq 1$. Let y, y' and y'' be, respectively, the profit maximizing input–output vectors corresponding to p, p' and p'', i.e., $\pi(p) = py = \sum_j p_j y_j$, $\pi(p') = p'y' = \sum_j p'_j y'_j, \pi(p'') = p''y'' = \sum_j p''_j y''_j$. Then,

$$\pi(p'') = t\sum_j p_j y''_j + (1-t)\sum_j p'_j y''_j. \tag{2.20}$$

Since y and y' are profit maximizing input–output vectors corresponding, respectively, to p and p',

$$\sum_j p_j y''_j \leq \sum_j p_j y_j = \pi(p) \tag{2.21}$$

and

$$\sum_j p'_j y''_j \leq \sum_j p'_j y'_j = \pi(p'). \tag{2.22}$$

In view of (2.20), (2.21) and (2.22), therefore,

$$t\pi(p) + (1-t)\pi(p') \geq \pi(p'') = \pi(tp + (1-t)p') \tag{2.23}$$

Fig. 2.11

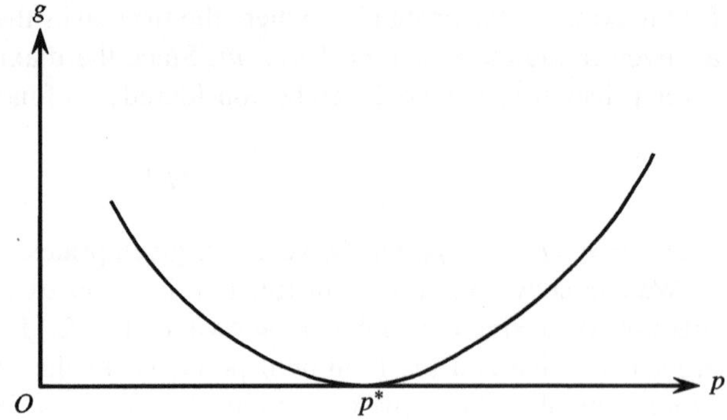

and the profit function is a convex function. If y and y' maximize profit uniquely at p and p' respectively, the strict inequality holds in (2.23).

An important implication of the convexity of the profit function is that the profit maximizing output or input y_j is derived from the profit function by the differentiation with respect to price p_j. To see this, let $y^* = (y_1^*, \ldots, y_m^*)$ be the profit maximizing input–output vector when the given price vector is $p^* = (p_1^*, \ldots, p_m^*)$. Consider the following function g.

$$g(p) = \pi(p) - \sum_j p_j y_j^*. \tag{2.24}$$

Since the maximum profit is $\pi(p)$ when the price vector is p and y^* maximizes the profit when the price vector is p^*, obviously $g(p) \geq 0$ and $g(p^*) = 0$. As is seen in Fig. 2.11, g reaches the minimum at $p = p^*$. Since $g(p)$ is a convex function, the condition for the maximization is

$$\frac{\partial g(p^*)}{\partial p_j} = \frac{\partial \pi(p^*)}{\partial p_j} - y_j^* = 0 \quad (j = 1, \ldots, m) \tag{2.25}$$

if π is assumed to be differentiable. Since this is true for any p^*, we have the so-called Hotelling's lemma

$$y_j(p) = \frac{\partial \pi(p)}{\partial p_j}. \tag{2.26}$$

2.10 Supply and Demand Function

The profit maximizing output or input function $y_j(p)$ is the firm's supply function of the j-th product or demand function of the j-th variable factor of production. The supply (demand) of the j-th good is an increasing (a diminishing) function of the price of the j-th good. This can be easily seen by comparison of two situations, respectively, with price vector p and price vector p'. If the profit maximizing vectors are, respectively, y and y', we have

$$\sum_j p_j y_j \geq \sum_j p_j y'_j \tag{2.27}$$

and

$$\sum_j p'_j y'_j \geq \sum_j p'_j y_j. \tag{2.28}$$

By subtracting (2.28) from (2.27), then, we have

$$\sum_j (p_j - p'_j)(y_j - y'_j) \geq 0. \tag{2.29}$$

If the difference between p and p' is only for the price of the j-th good,

$$(p_j - p'_j)(y_j - y'_j) \geq 0. \tag{2.30}$$

Since strict inequalities hold in (2.27), (2.28) and therefore in (2.29) and (2.30), if y and y' are unique profit maximizing vectors respectively at p and p', (2.30) implies that the supply of the j-th good ($y_j > 0$) is increasing and the demand for the j-th good ($y_j < 0$) is diminishing with respect to its price p_j. Firm's supply curves are upward sloping and demand curves are downward sloping.

Since the profit maximizing input–output vectors are derived from the convex profit function as we saw in the previous section (see (2.26)), this property of firm's supply and demand functions corresponds to the positive second order derivative of a convex function π with respect to p_j, i.e.,

$$\frac{\partial^2 \pi}{\partial p_j^2} = \frac{\partial y_j}{\partial p_j} > 0. \tag{2.31}$$

The use of the profit function also leads us to the symmetry of the cross price effects,

$$\frac{\partial y_j}{\partial p_k} = \frac{\partial^2 \pi}{\partial p_k \partial p_j} = \frac{\partial y_k}{\partial p_j}. \tag{2.32}$$

We can, therefore, define the substitutability and complementarity among inputs to produce a given output consistently by the cross price effects, i.e., two inputs are substitute if $\frac{\partial y_j}{\partial p_k} = \frac{\partial y_k}{\partial p_j}$ is negative and complementary if it is positive (since y_j and y_k are negative).

Problems

2.1. Draw curves *AB* and *EF* in Figs. 2.1 and 2.3 for the case of the Cobb–Douglas production function

$$Y = AL^a K^{(1-a)}$$

where Y, L and K denote, respectively, the output, the input of labor, and the input of capital, and A and a are constants such that $A > 0$, and $0 < a < 1$.

2.2. Derive the condition for the maximization of the profit $pY - wL - rK$, where p, w and r denote, respectively, the price of the product, the rate of wage, and the rental price of the capital, taken by firm as constants, being subject to the Cobb–Douglas production function given in Problem 2.1. Show the economic implication of the constant a.

2.3. Consider the so-called *CES* production function

$$Y^{(-b)} = aK^{(-b)} + (1-a)L^{(-b)} \quad (0 < a < 1,\ b > -1)$$

and show that the returns to scale are constant, and that the function approaches the Cobb–Douglas function as b approaches zero (use L'Hospital's rule). Draw curves *AB* and *EF* in Figs. 2.1 and 2.2.

2.4. The absolute value of the slope of the isoquant (curve *AB* in Fig. 2.1) is called the marginal rate of substitution between two inputs. In the case of Cobb–Douglas function and *CES* functions given in Problems 2.1 and 2.3, it is $R(K, L) = -\dfrac{dK}{dL}$, given Y. The elasticity of substitution between two inputs is defined as the elasticity (i.e., the ratio of relative changes) of the ratio of two inputs with respect to the marginal rate of substitution between them, as we move along an isoquant. In our case,

$$s = \frac{d \log(K/L)}{d \log R} = \frac{\dfrac{d(K/L)}{(K/L)}}{\dfrac{dR}{R}}.$$

Calculate s both for Cobb–Douglas and *CES* functions (Express R as a function of K/L). Why is the latter called *CES*?

2.5. Consider the problem of the maximization of the profit (2.11) subject to the conditions (2.10) in Sect. 2.4, by using the method of Lagrangian multipliers. Show the significance of multipliers as implicit or shadow prices of the fixed or limitational factors of production. Demonstrate that the maximized profit is exhaustively distributed to the fixed factors. Discuss the firm's policy to increase the stock (s_k's) of such factors in the long-run, when they can be bought at certain prices in the market.

2.6. Let us define that a set is strictly convex if it contains any point z on the line segment between x and y as an inner point (a point of a set, which does not belong to the boundary of the set), whenever it contains any two points x and y. Demonstrate that the profit maximizing input–output vector is unique, if the feasible set is strictly convex.

2.7. Discuss the difficulty of non-convexity case given in Fig. 2.6 (Compare profits at points H and O).

2.8. In Fig. 2.7, show that the minimum cost function is a convex function of the level of output.

2.9. A function h is defined as a concave function, if $h = -f$ and f is a convex function as defined in Sect. 2.9 (see (2.19)). State the condition of a concave function h directly in terms of h.

2.10. Show that the minimum cost function is a concave function of prices of inputs. Demonstrate the so-called Shephard's lemma that the cost-minimizing input of the j-th variable input to produce the given output is derived from the minimum cost function by the differentiation with respect to its price.

Literature

For further studies in general, see J.R. Hicks, *Value and Capital* (1946), pp. 319–323, E. Malinvaud, *Lectures on Microeconomic Theory* (1972), pp. 43–70, and H.R. Varian, *Microeconomic Analysis* (1978), pp. 1–51.
For *CES* production function, see R.G.D. Allen, *Macro-Economic Theory* (1967), pp. 48–49, 35–52. See also M.C. Kemp, *The Pure Theory of International Trade* (1964), p. 57.
Linear programming model of production in the firm was developed in R. Dorfman, P.A. Samuelson and R.M. Solow, *Linear Programming and Economic Analysis* (1958), pp. 130–185.
Marshallian long-run average cost curve is explained beautifully by R. Frisch, "Alfred Marshall's Theory of Value," *Quarterly Journal of Economics* (1950). See also J. Viner, "Cost Curves and Supply Curves," A.E.A. *Readings in Price Theory* (1952).
Some examples of recent attempts to go beyond the neo-classical theory of the firm are, M. Aoki, *The Co-operative Game Theory of the Firm* (1984), O.E. Williamson, *Corporate Control and Business Behaviour* (1970), and ibid., *Markets and Hierarchies* (1975).

Chapter 3
Households and Consumption

3.1 The Theory of the Consumer

Consumption of goods in households is the main purpose and the final result of a large part of economic activity. To demand for the consumables, however, households have to supply the service of factors of production to earn their incomes in the modern market economy. The role of the theory of the household is, therefore, to explain not only its demand for goods (the consumables) but also its supply of goods (the service of factors of production). But, fortunately, the households' supply of the factors of production can be easily explained by an extension of the theory of their demand for goods. This is the reason why we can start with the theory of the behavior of a consumer who spends the given income to demand for the consumers' goods. While the theory of the firm is developed as the theory of the constrained maximization, i.e., the maximization of profit subject to the production function, the theory of the consumers' behavior also considers the constrained maximization, i.e., the maximization of utility subject to the budget constraint.

The budget constraint implies that the expenditure on the consumers' goods should not exceed the given income. Since individual consumer's influence on the market price is safely considered to be negligible, we can assume that the consumer takes the market prices as given. The budget constraint is, then, a simple linear inequality in terms of quantities of consumers' goods. Unlike the production function in the case of the theory of the firm, there is no problem to be discussed for the constraint in the case of the theory of the consumer. As for the maximand, however, the latter theory has a difficult problem while the maximand of the competitive firm is, as we saw, a simple linear function. The profit is an objective, perfectly measurable quantity, while the utility is a subjective concept and its measurability is not necessarily assured. As we started with the consideration of the production function in Chap. 2, therefore, firstly we have to scrutinize the concept of the utility in this chapter.

T. Negishi, *Elements of Neo-Walrasian Economics*, Advances in Japanese Business and Economics 5, DOI 10.1007/978-4-431-54535-4_3, © Springer Japan 2014

3.2 Utility Function

Consider the economy of m goods. If we denote the quantity of the j-th good to be consumed by a consumer by x_j $(j = 1, \ldots, m)$, the budget constraint is

$$\sum_j p_j x_j \leq Y, \tag{3.1}$$

where Y and p_j denote, respectively, the given income and the market price of the j-th good, which the consumer takes as given. Being subject to the budget constraint (3.1), the consumer chooses a consumption vector $x = (x_1, \ldots, x_m)$ so that the utility

$$U(x) = U(x_1, \ldots, x_m) \tag{3.2}$$

is maximized. If it can be expressed as a function of the quantity of goods to be consumed, however, the utility should first be able to be measured as a quantity. How measurable is such a subjective concept as the utility? Can it be measured uniquely?

Different things can be measured in different degrees. Consider first the case of the length of a physical object, say, a stick, which seems to be measurable in the most definite way. Even in this case, however, we cannot measure it uniquely. According to one measure, it is 1 m. But it is 39.37 in., according to another measure. The length of x meters is also expressed as that of $y = 39.37x$ in. Different measures are related in such a way that we can convert one measure into another by multiplying a constant like 39.37. Since the unit of measurement is arbitrary, the length of a thing can only be measured uniquely up to a positive scalar multiplication.

Next consider the case of temperature. Centigrade scale divides the interval between the freezing point and the boiling point of water into 100°, 0° representing the freezing point and 100° the boiling point. According to Fahrenheit scale, however, the boiling point of water is at 212° and the freezing point at 32° above the zero of the scale, the zero point approximating the temperature produced by mixing equal quantity by weight of snow and salt. Two scales are related by the linear equality that $\text{Fahrenheit} = \frac{9}{5}\text{Centigrade} + 32$. In other words, the measurement of the temperature is unique only up to the increasing linear transformation. Unlike the case of the measurement of the length, not only the unit but also the zero point are different between two scales of the temperature.

The final case is the measure of the hardness in the sense that the diamond is the hardest substance so that it is used to cut the glass which is less hard. In this case, any quantitative measure will do, provided that it ranks the hardness of things in the identical order. In other words, if x denotes the degree of hardness according to a measure, any other measure which denotes the degree of hardness as $y = f(x)$

is permissible, provided that f is an increasing function of x, i.e., $\frac{df}{dx} > 0$. While measures in the first two cases are called cardinal, measures in this case are called ordinal, since only the rank or order does matter.

If one considers that the utility is at least as measurable as the temperature, the utility is cardinal and the utility function is unique up to the increasing linear transformation. If a function U given in (3.2) is a utility function of a consumer, any other function V such that

$$V(x) = aU(x) + b, \tag{3.3}$$

where a (> 0) and b are constants, is also a utility function of the same consumer. If U is a strictly concave (convex) function, i.e.,

$$U(tx + (1-t)x') > (<)\, tU(x) + (1-t)U(x') \tag{3.4}$$

for any x and x', where t is any positive number less than one, then V is also a concave (convex) function. Therefore, the utility is cardinal in the situation where the diminishing (increasing) marginal utility does make sense, since concave (convex) utility function implies that the marginal utility $\frac{\partial U}{\partial x_j}$ is diminishing (increasing), i.e., $\frac{\partial^2 U}{\partial x_j^2} < 0$ (> 0).

Although we have to use the cardinal utility in a specific situation (see Sect. 3.11), generally we can develop the theory of the consumer without imposing the cardinality on utility function. In other words, if $U(x)$ is a utility function of a consumer, then, any other function V such that

$$V(x) = f[U(x)] \tag{3.5}$$

is also a utility function of the same consumer, provided that f is an increasing function. If the utility is ordinal, the concavity (convexity) of the utility function does not make sense. Even if U happens to be a concave (convex) function, V may not be so, since f is an arbitrary function, provided it is increasing. Instead of the concavity, it is usually assumed in the theory of the ordinal utility that the utility function is a strictly quasi-concave function, which means that for any x and x' such that $U(x) = U(x')$,

$$U(tx + (1-t)x') > U(x) = U(x') \tag{3.6}$$

where t is any positive number less than one. This property remains unchanged if U is transformed into V by f.

3.3 Indifference Map

To see the implication of the quasi-concavity of the utility function, let us first consider the case of two goods. If $U(x_1, x_2)$ is an ordinal utility function of a consumer, any other function V such that

$$V(x_1, x_2) = f[U(x_1, x_2)] \tag{3.7}$$

is also the utility function of the same consumer, provided f is an increasing function. Although the behavior of the consumer is studied by the maximization of a particular utility function U subject to the budget constraint

$$p_1x_1 + p_2x_2 \leq Y, \tag{3.8}$$

we should be careful to assure that it is entirely unaffected by the change in the utility function from U to V.

A way to do this is to get rid of function f in (3.7) by considering

$$V(x_1, x_2) = f[U(x_1, x_2)] = \overline{V} \tag{3.9}$$

for any given $\overline{V}$ and differentiating (3.9) to obtain

$$V_1dx_1 + V_2dx_2 = \frac{df}{dU}(U_1dx_1 + U_2dx_2) = 0 \tag{3.10}$$

where V_j and U_j are marginal utility of the j-th good, i.e., $\frac{\partial V}{\partial x_j}$ and $\frac{\partial V}{\partial x_j}$. Since $\dfrac{df}{dU} > 0$, we have from (3.10)

$$-\frac{dx_2}{dx_1} = \frac{V_1}{V_2} = \frac{U_1}{U_2} \tag{3.11}$$

which implies that for a unit increase in the quantity of the first good ($dx_1 = 1$) the decrease in the quantity of the second good ($-dx_2$) should be equal to $\dfrac{V_1}{V_2} = \dfrac{U_1}{U_2}$ so as to keep the level of the utility unchanged. This ratio of changes in the quantity of two goods is called the marginal rate of substitution. It is the inverse ratio of the marginal utility of two goods and unaffected by the transformation of utility function from U to V.

Figure 3.1 is the indifference map, the collection of indifference curves showing loci of indifferent consumption vectors $x = (x_1, x_2)$ which satisfy (3.9) for different levels of utility $\overline{V}$, $\overline{V}'$, $\overline{V}''$, etc. If the marginal utilities are positive, indifference curves are downward sloping since their slopes are given by (3.11) and the levels

Fig. 3.1

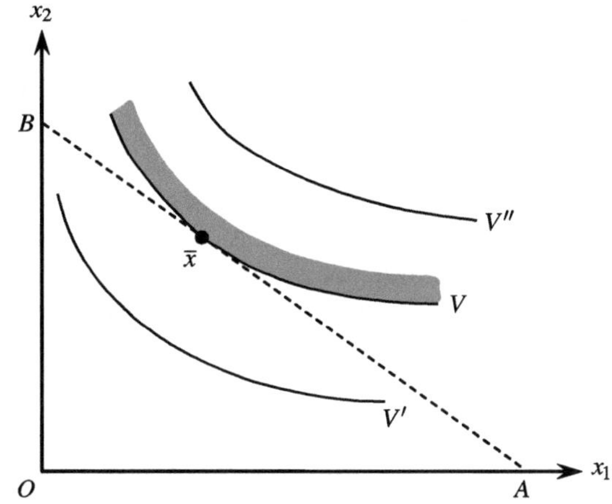

of utility are such that $\overline{V}' < \overline{V} < \overline{V}''$. In view of (3.11) which describes the shape of the indifference curve passing any point in Fig. 3.1, the indifference map is unaffected by the change of utility function from U to V. In other words, all the utility function V defined in (3.7) share the identical indifference map with U.

In Fig. 3.1, indifference curves are, as usual, drawn convex to the origin. This implies that the utility function is strictly quasi-concave as defined in (3.6). If, for example, x and x' are on the indifference curve V so that $U(x) = U(x')$, the point $x'' = tx + (1-t)x'$ lies inside of the shaded area bounded by the curve so that $U(x'')$ is higher than $U(x)$ and $U(x')$, for any $0 < t < 1$. Since the shaded area is the set of consumption vectors indifferent or preferred to a point on the boundary curve having the level of utility V, generally we can say that the utility function is strictly quasi-concave, if and only if the set of consumption vectors $[x \mid U(x) \geq V]$ for any V is a strictly convex set, i.e., such a set that it contains any point z on the line segment between x and y as an inner point (not a boundary point) whenever it contains any two points x and y.

In the two goods case, the maximization of utility U subject to the budget constraint (3.8) can be easily solved as is seen in Fig. 3.1. The dotted line AB signifies the equality form of the budget constraint (3.8). The utility is maximized at $\overline{x}$, where an indifference curve is tangent to the budget line and the marginal rate of substitution (the slope of the indifference curve) is equalized to the price ratio $\frac{p_1}{p_2}$ (the slope of the budget line), since OA is equal to $\frac{Y}{p_1}$ and OB is equal to $\frac{Y}{p_2}$ in Fig. 3.1. Similarly, the condition for the maximization of utility (3.2) being subject to the budget constraint (3.1) in the general m goods case is the equality of the marginal rate of substitution and the price ratio for any two goods, in addition to the equality form of (3.1), if the utility function is strictly quasi-concave. The solution for this constrained maximization problem gives the demand for goods $x_1, \ldots, x_m$ as functions of prices $p_1, \ldots, p_m$, when the income Y is given.

If the utility function is strictly quasi-concave, such a demand function is well behaved in the sense that it is a single valued and continuous, as is seen from Fig. 3.1. If indifference curves are not convex to the origin and the shaded area is not a convex set, demand changes substantially as a result of a slight changes in prices, which is a result generally not expected empirically. To justify the assumption of the strict quasi-concavity of utility function is, therefore, very important as a foundation of the theory of the consumer. As in the case of the convexity of the feasible set of the production function, which we discussed in Chap. 2, a way to demonstrate the quasi-concavity of utility function is to consider the details of maximization process hidden behind the summarized expression of the function.

3.4 Linear Programming Model of Consumption

Goods are consumed in many different consumption activities of the household, which create utility to the consumer. Suppose there are n consumption activities and denote by z_i the level of the i-th activity, $i = 1, \ldots, n$. Each consumption activity requires the two different kinds of inputs. Firstly, the i-th activity consumes a_{ij} units of the j-th marketable goods, $j = 1, \ldots, m$, when it is operated at the unit level, i.e., $z_i = 1$. In addition to this, secondly, it requires the use of A_{ik} units of the k-th fixed or limitational factors, which cannot be purchased at all, or in the short-run, at least, when the i-th activity is operated at the unit level. At the beginning of each period, the household has a stock of such fixed factors, i.e., s_k ($k = 1, \ldots, r$), of the k-th factor. For example, having parties at one's home requires the consumption of liquors and foods, which can be purchased at the given prices. In addition to this, however, it also requires one's own precious time. Furthermore, the level of such activity is subject to the capacity of rooms, gardens and kitchen, since the number of guests is limited by these factors which cannot be increased, at least, in the short-run.

Assuming the divisibility and additivity (see Sect. 2.3) of activities, we can show the feasibility condition of activity vector $z = (z_1, \ldots, z_n)$ by

$$\sum_i A_{ik} z_i \leq s_k \quad (k = 1, \ldots, r) \tag{3.12}$$

and see easily that the feasibility set of z, i.e., the set of z which satisfies (3.12) is a convex set. Similarly, the total consumption of the j-th marketable good is given by

$$x_j = \sum_i a_{ij} z_i \quad (j = 1, \ldots, m) \tag{3.13}$$

when the level of consumption activities are given as z. Finally, if we suppose that the utility a_{i0} is created by the unit level of the i-th activity, the total utility created by z is

$$U = \sum_i a_{i0} z_i. \tag{3.14}$$

The utility function $U = U(x)$ gives the result of the maximization of (3.14), with respect to z, subject to (3.12) and (3.13), when the consumption vector $x = (x_1, \ldots, x_m)$ is given. In view of (3.13) and (3.14), it can be shown from the convexity of the feasible set of z that the feasible set (possible, but not necessarily efficient combination) of $(U, x_1, \ldots, x_m)$ is convex and the utility function $U(x)$ is concave. This result depends, of course, on our choice of a particular measure of utility in (3.14) and is not invariable for the possible transformation of utility measure (3.5). But the convexity of the set $[x \mid U(x) \geq \overline{V}]$ for any $\overline{V}$ is also derived from the convexity of feasible z and is unaffected by the change of utility function in (3.5). In two goods case, where the quantity of goods other than the first two are assumed to be given, the shaded area in Fig. 3.1 is convex, though it is not strictly convex. In other words, an indifference curve has line segments, where marginal rate of substitution remains unchanged.

Such a line segment cannot, however, be very long and the marginal rate of substitution has to be changed for a substantial change in consumption vector. Starting from a point on an indifference curve in Fig. 3.1, for a reduction in the quantity of the second good x_2, the quantity of the first good x_1 has to be increased to keep the level of utility unchanged. Since an indifference curve is a locus of efficient consumption vectors for a given level of utility, such an increase in x_1 should be made by an increase in the level of a consumption activity in which the ratio of a_{i0} in (3.14) to a_{i1} in (3.13) is the largest, provided that the fixed factor specific for the activity is not fully employed. If the reduction in x_2 is continued, however, such a specific fixed factor necessary for the activity is eventually exhausted. For a further reduction in x_2, then, an activity with smaller $\dfrac{a_{i0}}{a_{i1}}$ has to be used to increase x_1. The ratio of necessary change in x_1 to the same change in x_2 has to be changed, so that the marginal rate of substitution changes. By increasing the number of activities and that of fixed factors, we can approach approximately to the case of smooth indifference curves with no line segment, i.e., the case of a strictly quasi-concave utility function.

3.5 Preference

If the utility function is ordinal, the information on the taste of a consumer contained in such a function (or a set of functions in (3.5)) can be described without the use of utility function, since only the order or rank of consumption vectors does matter. Let us denote as xRy if and only if $U(x) \geq U(y)$, where $x = (x_1, \ldots, x_m)$ and $y = (y_1, \ldots, y_m)$ are consumption vectors and U is an ordinal utility function. In other words, the consumer either prefers x to y or is indifferent between them. If x and y are indifferent, i.e., $U(x) = U(y)$, then xRy and yRx. If x is preferred to y,

Fig. 3.2

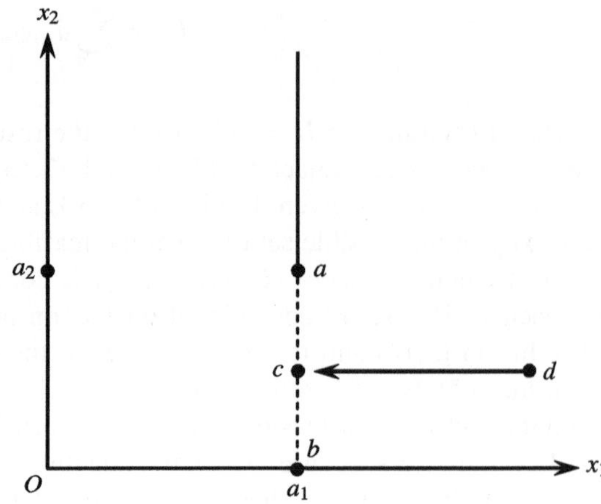

i.e., $U(x) > U(y)$ then xRy but not yRx. When utility function is well behaved, the following assumptions are satisfied by preference relation R.

Completeness	For all x and y, either xRy or yRx.
Reflexibility	For all x, xRx.
Transitivity	For all x, y and z, if xRy and yRz, then xRz.
Continuity	For all y, the set $[x \mid xRy]$ and the set $[x \mid yRx]$ are closed sets.
Strong Monotonicity	If $x = y$ but $x \neq y$, then xRy but not yRx.
Strong Convexity	For any y, the set $[x \mid xRy]$ is strictly convex.

Continuity, Strong Monotonicity and Strong Convexity correspond, respectively, to our assumptions on utility function that it is continuous function, that all goods have positive marginal utility and that it is a strictly quasi-concave function.

The implication of the assumption of Continuity can be seen by the consideration of an interesting example, i.e., lexicographical preference. In two goods case, suppose that xRy but not yRx if either (1) $x_1 > y_1$ or (2) $x_1 = y_1$ and $x_2 > y_2$. In Fig. 3.2, the quantity of the first good x_1 is measured horizontally, and that of the second good, x_2, vertically. Consider the point $a = (a_1, a_2)$. The set $[x \mid xRa]$ and the set $[x \mid aRx]$ are, respectively points on or to the right of the vertical line through the point $b = (a_1, 0)$ but not including the line segment ab and points to the left of the vertical line through the point b including the line segment ab. This preference relation, therefore, violates the assumption of Continuity, since the closed set is a set which contains all the points on the boundary. In this case, the preference cannot be shown by a continuous function. If utility function $U(x)$ is continuous, we must have $U(x^*) \geq U(y)$ for any sequence of consumption vectors x^i, which converges to x^* and $U(x^i) > U(y)$ for all i. In Fig. 3.2, however, a sequence of consumption vectors starting from the point d and converges to the point c does not have this

Fig. 3.3

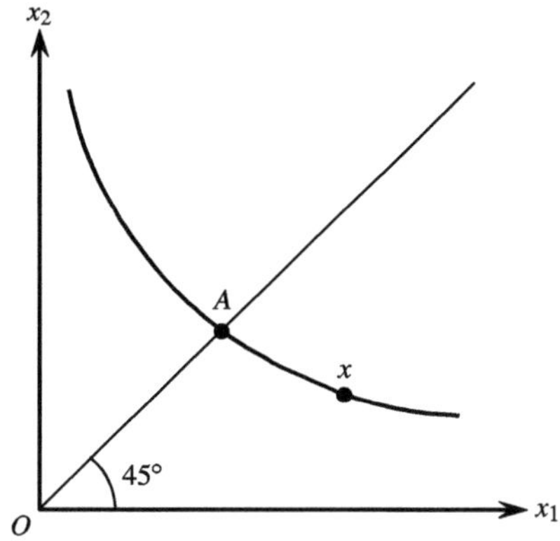

property, since $U(c) < U(a)$ even though $U(x^i) > U(a)$ for any consumption vector x^i in the sequence.

Even though the taste of a consumer can be fully described by the preference relation R, the utility function is also a very convenient device to work with in the theory of consumption. We can construct, fortunately, a corresponding utility function from the preference relation R, if the latter satisfied assumptions of Completeness, Reflexibility, Continuity and Strong Monotonicity. In two goods case shown in Fig. 3.3, $U(x)$ is measured by the length of *OA*, where *A* is the intersection of the indifference curve passing x and the 45° line. Generally, according to a utility function corresponding to R, $U(x)$, the utility of a consumption vector x is such a number that $xRU(x)e$ and $U(x)eRx$, where e is the vector consisting of all ones. Of course, any function $V(x)$ which satisfies (3.5) with U is also a utility function corresponding to R.

3.6 Substitution and Income Effects

The role of the theory of the consumer in the neo-classical microeconomics is to explain the consumers' demand for goods as functions of prices in general, and particularly, the demand for a good as a decreasing function of its own price (i.e., the downward sloping demand curve). To do this, it is convenient to divide the effect of price change on demand into two parts, the substitution effect and the income effect. This is seen for the two goods case in Fig. 3.4. Initially, the budget constraint is *AB*. The utility is maximized on the budget line *AB* at the point a where an indifference curve is tangent to the line *AB*. Suppose the price of the first good is raised, so that the budget line is rotated around A to *AC*. The new equilibrium point of the consumer is the point b, where an indifference curve is tangent to the line *AC*. We do not, however, consider that the equilibrium point a is shifted directly to the point b. It is first moved to c on the same indifference curve (the substitution effect) and then to the new equilibrium point b (the income effect).

Fig. 3.4

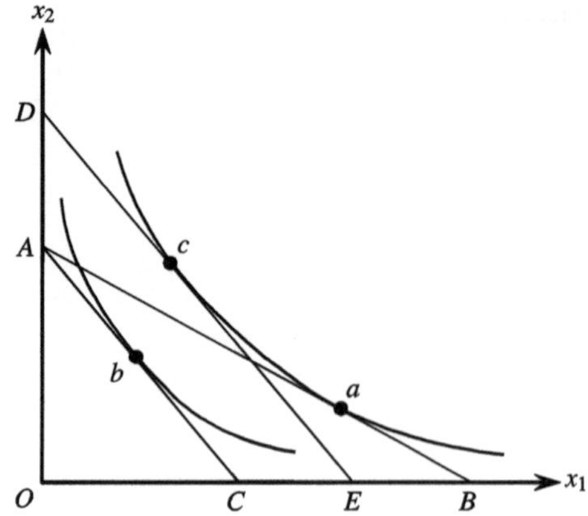

The point c is constructed as an equilibrium of the consumer, which is obtained if the consumer is compensated in income so that he can still enjoy the unchanged utility level after the rise in the price of the first good. The indifference curve which passes the point a is tangent, at the point c, to the line DE, which is parallel to the new budget line AC. In other words, the line AC is shifted to DE by the income compensation for the price change. Since the indifference curve is convex to the origin and tangent to budget lines AB and DE, respectively, at a and c, it is clear that the demand for the first good (x_1) is reduced by a rise in its price between a and c. In other words, the demand curve for it is downward sloping as far as the substitution effect is concerned. This is because the rational individual who maximizes utility subject to budget condition will substitute cheaper goods for more expensive ones so that the cost to achieve the given level of utility is kept to be minimized.

Besides this negative substitution effect, however, there is also the income effect which moves the equilibrium from c to b. This is because the real income (the level of utility) is reduced by the rise in the price of the first good, when the nominal income is kept unchanged. In the case of Fig. 3.4, the demand for the first good is decreased by the reduction of the real income, which is caused by a rise in its price. Income effect works, therefore, also to make the demand curve downward sloping in this case. This is, however, not always true, since the point b may be located to the right of the point c, so that the demand for the first good is increased (decreased) by a fall (rise) in the real income. In such a case of the inferior good, the total effect of price change on demand is indeterminate, since the income effect works against the substitution effect. If the former effect is stronger, the demand curve cannot be downward sloping (Giffen paradox).

The case of inferior good is by no means exceptional. Whether a good is inferior or not is not the problem of the good itself but the problem of the taste and income level of the consumer. When one's income is so low that to eat steak is unimaginable, the consumption of hamburgers is increased as income rises. If the income level is high enough so that both steak and hamburgers are consumed, however, a further rise in income reduces the consumption of hamburgers, since it is substituted by the consumption of steak. If we disaggregate the model of the consumer and increase the number of goods, therefore, the possibility of inferiority of a good to a consumer cannot be assumed away and the sign of income effect is generally indeterminate. If the number of goods is large and the share of a single good in the consumer's budget is small, however, the size of the income effect is rather small, since the real income is not reduced very much by a rise in the price of a single good.

On the other hand, the negative sign of the substitution effect is not changed even if the number of goods are increased. Consider the general m goods case. Let $x^1 = (x_1^1, \ldots, x_m^1)$ denote a consumption vector which corresponds to the point a in Fig. 3.4 and $x^2 = (x_1^2, \ldots, x_m^2)$ denote a consumption vector which corresponds to the point c in the same figure. In other words, x^1 is the original equilibrium of the consumer, and x^2 is a hypothetical one where the consumer is compensated in income against changes in prices. Let $p^1 = (p_1^1, \ldots, p_m^1)$ and $p^2 = (p_1^2, \ldots, p_m^2)$ be, respectively, the original price vector and the changed price vector. The sign of the substitution effect is the sign of $(x_j^1 - x_j^2)(p_j^1 - p_j^2)$, if the difference between p^1 and p^2 is only in the price of the j-th good.

To see the sign of the substitution effect in the general m goods case, it is convenient to use the weak axiom of revealed preference, an approach to the theory of the consumer based exclusively on observed or observable market data, in particular on value sums. It is defined that x^1 is revealed preferred to x^2 if and only if

$$p^1x^1 = \sum_j p_j^1 x_j^1 \geq \sum_j p_j^1 x_j^2 = p^1 x^2. \tag{3.15}$$

Then, the weak axiom states that if x^1 is revealed preferred to x^2, x^2 cannot be revealed preferred to x^1. In view of (3.15), this means that $p^1x^1 \geq p^1x^2$ implies $p^2x^2 < p^2x^1$. In other words, if x^1 is chosen at prices p^1 even if x^2 could have been purchased, then it is clear that x^1 is preferred to x^2 and it should be impossible at prices p^2 to purchase x^1 if x^2 is actually chosen at p^2. Since x^1 and x^2 are indifferent, neither is revealed preferred to the other so that $p^1x^1 < p^1x^2$ and $p^2x^2 < p^2x^1$. We have, therefore, $(p^1 - p^2)(x^1 - x^2) < 0$. If the difference between p^1 and p^2 is only in the price of the j-th good, then, $(p_j^1 - p_j^2)(x_j^1 - x_j^2) < 0$.

If the number of goods is large, the substitution effect is not only negative but also large, since there are many close substitutes to a good. Even if the income effect works against the substitution effect, then, it is likely that the substitution effect outweighs the income effect and the demand curve is downward sloping.

3.7 Indirect Utility Function

The equation which divides the effect of price change on demand into the substitution and income effects is called Slutsky equation, since it was originally worked out by E. Slutsky, a Russian mathematical economist. To derive this equation formally, we need some auxiliary devices, indirect utility function, the minimum expenditure function, the compensated demand function, and Roy's identity.

The indirect utility function is a summary statement of the maximization of utility subject to the budget constraint, i.e., the maximization of (3.2) subject to (3.1). Since the nominal income Y and prices $p = (p_1, \dots, p_m)$ are given, the solution of this problem $x = (x_1, \dots, x_m)$ is a function of p and Y, and therefore the resulted maximized utility is given by the indirect utility function $V(p, Y) = U[x(p, Y)]$.

By substituting (3.1) into (3.2), eliminating, say, x_1, and maximizing U with respect to $x_2, \dots, x_m$, or by using Lagrange's multiplier method, we obtain

$$\frac{\frac{\partial U}{\partial x_j}}{p_j} = \frac{\partial V}{\partial Y} \quad (j = 1, \dots, m) \tag{3.16}$$

as the conditions to be satisfied by the solution of the problem, $x(p, Y)$. If this is not clear, see Problem 3.7. Since (3.1) should also be satisfied by $x(p, Y)$, we obtain further

$$\sum_j p_j \frac{\partial x_j}{\partial p_i} = -x_i \quad (i = 1, \dots, n) \tag{3.17}$$

by differentiating (3.1) with respect to p_i. Finally, by differentiating the indirect utility function $V(p, Y) = U[x(p, Y)]$ with respect to p_i, we have

$$\frac{\partial V}{\partial p_i} = \sum_j \frac{\partial U}{\partial x_j} \frac{\partial x_j}{\partial p_i}. \tag{3.18}$$

In view of (3.16) and (3.17), however, this implies

$$\frac{\partial V}{\partial p_i} = \frac{\partial V}{\partial Y}(-x_i) \tag{3.19}$$

which is called Roy's identity.

While we tried to show that the direct utility function $U(x)$ is quasi-concave, it is easily shown that the indirect utility function $V(p, Y)$ is a quasi-convex function of p, i.e.,

$$V(tp + (1-t)p', Y) \leq V(p, Y) = V(p', Y) \tag{3.20}$$

Fig. 3.5

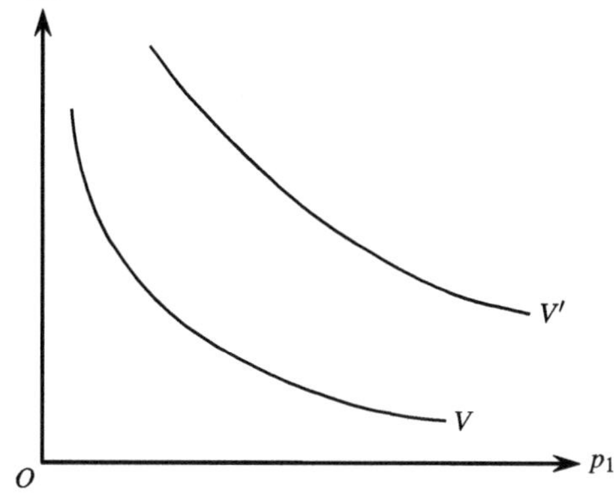

for any $0 < t < 1$. In Fig. 3.5, indifference curves are convex to the origin, and the level of utility is such that $V > V'$ since V is a decreasing function of p. To see this, first note that $x(tp + (1-t)p', Y)$, i.e., the solution of the maximization of the utility (3.2) subject to the budget constraint (3.1) for $p = tp + (1-t)p'$, satisfies either $px \leq Y$ or $p'x \leq Y$. Suppose not. Then, $x(tp + (1-t)p', Y)$ does not satisfy (3.1) for $p = tp + (1-t)p'$, since $px > Y$ and $p'x > Y$, which is clearly a contradiction. Now, therefore, either $V(p, Y)$ or $V(p', Y)$ is not smaller than $U[x(tp+(1-t)p', Y)] = V(tp+(1-t)p', Y)$, since V denotes the maximum value of u, subject to (3.1). If $V(p, Y) = V(p', Y)$, then, we have (3.20) established.

3.8 Minimum Expenditure Function

In the theory of the firm (Chap. 2), we consider the minimum cost function to produce the given output. Similarly, we can consider the minimum expenditure necessary to achieve to the given level of utility. This is a summary statement of the minimization of the expenditure

$$px = \sum_j p_j x_j \tag{3.21}$$

subject to the constraint

$$U(x) = U(x_1, \ldots, x_m) \geq V, \tag{3.22}$$

where V is the given level of the utility. The solution of the problem $x = (x_1, \ldots, x_m)$ and the resulted minimum expenditure e are considered as functions of $p = (p_1, \ldots, p_m)$ and V, i.e., $x(p, V)$ and $e(p, V)$. It is intuitively clear that $x(p, V)$ remains unchanged if all the prices are changed proportionally, i.e.,

Fig. 3.6

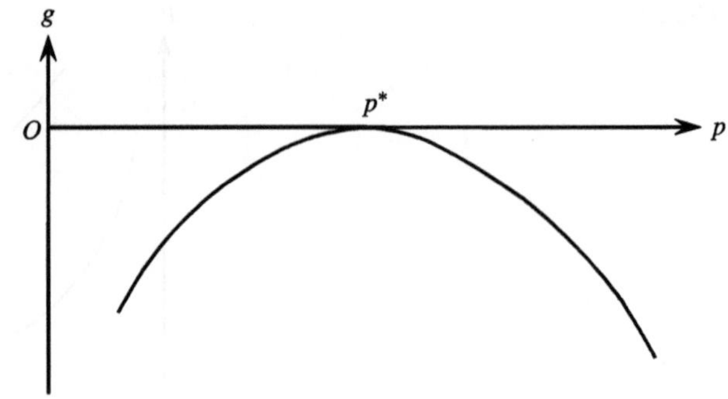

$x(kp, V) = x(p, V)$ for any $k > 0$. Suppose not. Then, $U[x(p, V)] \geq V$ and $px(p, V) < px(kp, V)$, since $U[x(kp, V)] \geq V$ by definition. Since $k > 0$, however, this leads to $kpx(p, V) < kpx(kp, V)$, which contradicts with the definition of $x(kp, V)$.

As in the case of the minimum cost function, the minimum expenditure function is a concave function of prices p, i.e.,

$$e(tp + (1-t)p', V) \geq te(p, V) + (1-t)e(p', V) \tag{3.23}$$

for any $0 < t < 1$. This is because $px(tp + (1-t)p', V) \geq e(p, V)$, $p'x(tp + (1-t)p', V) \geq e(p', V)$, and $e(tp + (1-t)p', V) = tpx(tp + (1-t)p', V) + (1-t)p'x(tp + (1-t)p', V)$. Now, suppose $x^* = (x_1^*, \ldots, x_m^*) = x(p, V)$ when $p = p^*$. Since the minimum expenditure function $e(p, V)$ is concave, we can have

$$\frac{\partial e(p, V)}{\partial p_j} - x_j^* = 0 \quad (j = 1, \ldots, m) \tag{3.24}$$

as the condition for the maximization of

$$g(p) = e(p, V) - \sum_j p_j x_j^*, \tag{3.25}$$

which occurs at $p = p^*$, where, of course, $g(p^*) = 0$, and $g(p) \leq 0$. See Fig. 3.6. In other words, the unchanged consumption pattern does not keep the expenditure minimum when prices are changed, but the changes in the minimized expenditure caused by an infinitesimal price change can be calculated by the unchanged pattern of consumption.

Combining the concepts of the indirect utility function and the minimum expenditure function, we can consider the problem of the minimization of the expenditure (3.21) subject to the condition (3.22) for $V = V(p^*, Y)$. Let us denote the solution (consumption vector) of this problem as $h[p, V(p^*, Y)]$ and call it the compensated demand function, since it corresponds to the point c in Fig. 3.4, the demand for goods when the consumer is compensated in income after prices changed from p^* to p. Compensated demand coincides with the original demand, $x(p, Y)$, i.e., the solution of the maximization of (3.2) subject to (3.1), if $p = p^*$. Suppose $y = h[p, V(p, Y)] \neq x(p, Y)$. Then, $py < px(p, Y)$ and $U(y) \geq U(x(p, Y))$. If $U(x)$ is an increasing function of x, there is y' in the neighborhood of y such that $py' < px(p, y) = Y$, and $U(y') > U(x(p, Y))$, which contradicts with the definition of $x(p, Y)$. Therefore, $x(p, Y) = h[p, V(p, Y)]$.

3.9 Slutsky Equation

Now we are ready to derive Slutsky equation. Differentiate the demand function $x(p, Y) = h[p, V(p, Y)]$ with respect to p_j at $p = p^*$. In view of the definition of the compensated demand function h, this gives us

$$\begin{aligned}\frac{\partial x(p, Y)}{\partial p_j} &= \frac{\partial h[p, V(p, Y)]}{\partial p_j} \\ &= \frac{\partial h[p, V(p^*, Y)]}{\partial p_j} + \frac{\partial h[p^*, V(p, Y)]}{\partial p_j}.\end{aligned} \tag{3.26}$$

The extreme left-hand side denotes the effect on demand of a change in the price of the j-th good while the extreme right-hand side divides it into the substitution effect (the first term) and the income effect (the second term). The substitution effect is the effect of price change with the compensation in income, which keeps the level of utility unchanged. The income effect is the effect of price change through the change in the level of real income, i.e., the level of utility.

The j-th part of (3.26) is

$$\frac{\partial x_j(p, Y)}{\partial p_j} = \frac{\partial h_j[p, V(p^*, Y)]}{\partial p_j} + \frac{\partial h_j[p^*, V(p, Y)]}{\partial p_j}. \tag{3.27}$$

From the definition of h as the solution of the expenditure minimization for $V = V(p^*, Y)$, definition of the minimum expenditure function $e(p, V)$ and (3.24), where x_j^* is $h_j[p, V(p^*, Y)]$ when $p = p^*$, the first term in the right-hand side can be written as

$$\frac{\partial h_j[p, V(p^*, Y)]}{\partial p_j} = \frac{\partial^2 e(p, V(p^*, Y))}{\partial p_j^2} \tag{3.28}$$

which is negative, since the minimum expenditure function is concave with respect to p. Therefore, the substitution effect is negative. The second term can be written as

$$\frac{\partial h_j[p^*, V(p, Y)]}{\partial p_j} = \frac{\partial x_j(p, Y)}{\partial Y}(-x_j(p, Y)) \tag{3.29}$$

Fig. 3.7

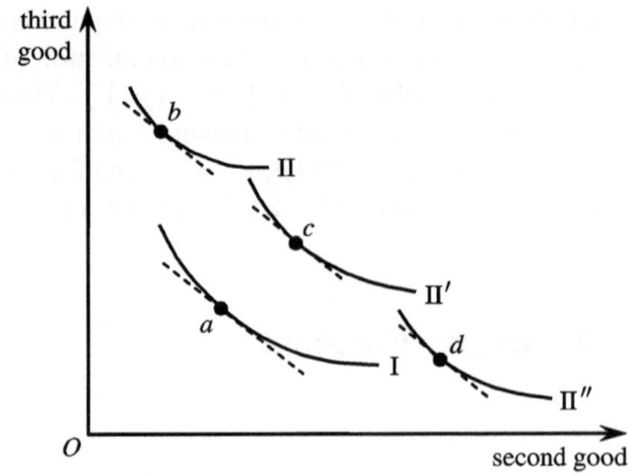

in view of Roy's identity (3.19), and the fact that $\dfrac{\partial h_j[p^*, V(p,Y)]}{\partial p_j} = \dfrac{\partial h_j}{\partial V}\dfrac{\partial V}{\partial p_j}$ and $\dfrac{\partial h_j}{\partial Y} = \dfrac{\partial x_j}{\partial Y}$ when $p = p^*$. The sign of the income effect depends, therefore, on whether the good is inferior or not, but its absolute value is small if the quantity purchased x_j is small.

More generally, the k-th part of (3.26) is

$$\frac{\partial x_k(p,Y)}{\partial p_j} = \frac{\partial^2 e(p, V(p^*,Y))}{\partial p_j \partial p_k} - x_j(p,Y)\frac{\partial x_k(p,Y)}{\partial Y}. \tag{3.30}$$

If $k \neq j$, the first term in the right-hand side gives the cross substitution effect of the change in the price of the j-th good on the demand for the k-th good. If it is denoted by S_{kj}, then it is obvious that $S_{kj} = S_{jk}$. We define that the j-th and k-th goods are substitutes when $S_{kj} = S_{jk}$ is positive and complements when it is negative. This is because S_{kk} and S_{jj} are negative and the consumption of the k-th good is increased with an increase in the consumption of the j-th good when they are complements, and the consumption of the k-th good is reduced with an increase in the consumption of the j-th good when they are substitutes.

From Fig. 3.4, it is clear that only the substitution between goods is possible in the two goods world. The complementarity is possible in the three goods case, but is dominated by the substitutability. To see this, consider the indifferent relations between the second and third goods in Fig. 3.7, when the level of utility and the amount of the first good is given. Suppose that the original equilibrium of the consumer is at a on the indifference curve I and the price of the first good is raised but the income is compensated so as to keep the level of utility unchanged. Since own substitution effect S_{11} is negative, the amount of the first good is reduced. This shifts the equilibrium to a point on the indifference curve II. If it is shifted to b, $S_{12} < 0$ and $S_{13} > 0$, i.e., the first and second goods are complements while the first and third goods are substitutes. If it is shifted to c, the first good is substitutable to both of second and third goods, since $S_{12} > 0$ and $S_{13} > 0$. Finally, if it shifts to d, $S_{12} > 0$ and $S_{13} < 0$, i.e., the first and second goods are substitutes and the first and third goods are complements.

For the general m goods case, note that the minimum expenditure $e(p, V)$ is homogeneous of degree 1 in p, so that $e(kp, V) = ke(p, V)$, and the compensated demand function $h(p, V)$ is homogeneous of degree 0 in p, so that $h(kp, V) = h(p, V)$, for any $k > 0$. The differentiation with respect to k at $k = 1$ gives

$$\sum_k \frac{\partial h_j}{\partial p_k} p_k = \sum_k S_{jk} p_k = 0 \quad (j = 1, \ldots, m). \tag{3.31}$$

Since $S_{jj} < 0$, it is possible that all goods are substitutes, i.e., $S_{jk} > 0$, for $j \neq k$, while it is impossible that all goods are complements, i.e., $S_{jk} < 0$, for $j \neq k$.

3.10 The Supply of Factors of Production

The household of the consumer supplies the factors of production as well as demands the consumables. Actually, the income of the consumer Y, which has been assumed as given, is earned by the supply of factors of production and varies as the prices of the factors are changed. To take this fact into consideration, denote the consumer's initial holdings of the j-th good by $\overline{x}_j$ and define the income of the consumer as

$$Y = \sum_j p_j \overline{x}_j. \tag{3.32}$$

If the j-th good is one of the consumables, $\overline{x}_j$ is either zero or very small, and the net demand for it, $x_j - \overline{x}_j$ is positive, where x_j is the gross demand. If the j-th good is a factor of production, however, even though x_j may be positive, $x_j - \overline{x}_j$ is negative, which implies that it is supplied by the consumer. In the case of labor, $\overline{x}_j$ is 24 h a day for a single individual, and x_j denotes his own demand for leisure time, say, 16 h a day, so that the supply of labor is $\overline{x}_j - x_j = 8$ h a day.

Since Y is now a function of p in Slutsky equation (3.26), the income effect is, instead of (3.29),

$$\frac{\partial h_j[p^*, V(p, Y)]}{\partial p_j} = \frac{x_j(p, Y)}{\partial Y}(\overline{x}_j - x_j(p, Y)) \tag{3.33}$$

in view of the fact that $\dfrac{\partial Y}{\partial p_j} = \overline{x}_j$. If the j-th good is supplied rather than demanded by the consumer, so that $\overline{x}_j - x_j$ is positive, then, the sign of the income effect is

Fig. 3.8

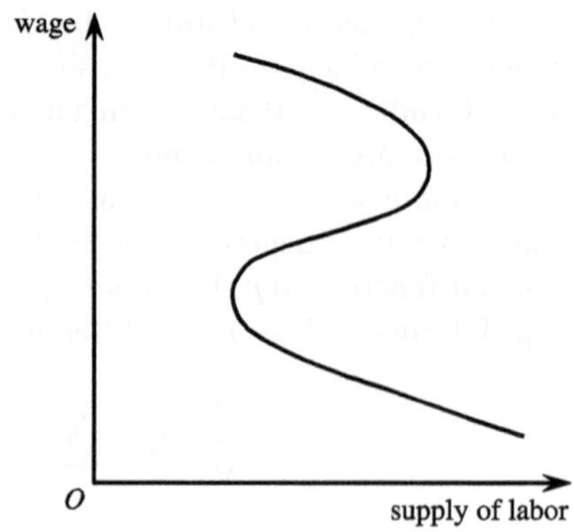

positive and different from that of substitution effect which is negative, when the good is not inferior so that $\frac{\partial x_j}{\partial Y}$ is positive. In the case of leisure and labor supply, a rise in the rate of wage decreases the demand for leisure as a substitution effect, but an increase in real income caused by higher wage increases the demand for leisure as an income effect. It is uncertain, therefore, whether a rise in wage increases or decreases the supply of labor. It is often admitted that the income effect is dominant when the rate of wage is already high so that a further rise in wage decreases the supply of labor. On the other hand, it is also insisted that the income effect is strong when the real income is too low and a reduction of the rate of wage causes the supply of labor to increase so as to earn money income to buy the necessaries of life. The supply curve of labor is, then, of inverse S shaped as is seen in Fig. 3.8.

3.11 Expected Utility

So far we have been considering that the utility is ordinal so that the taste of a consumer can be fully described by the preference relation on the consumption vectors without using the concept of utility function. Although it is convenient to work with a utility function U, any other function $V = f(U)$ such that f is an increasing function is also a utility function corresponding to the taste of the same consumer. It does not make sense, therefore, to use such concepts as the concavity of utility function and diminishing marginal utility, though the quasi-concavity of utility function and the convexity of indifference curves to the origin remain unchanged by the change of utility function from U to V. This is because we have been concerned with the behavior of the consumer under conditions of certainty. If we leave the world of certainty, however, such is not the case and we have to use the cardinal utility to describe the behavior of the consumer.

Fig. 3.9

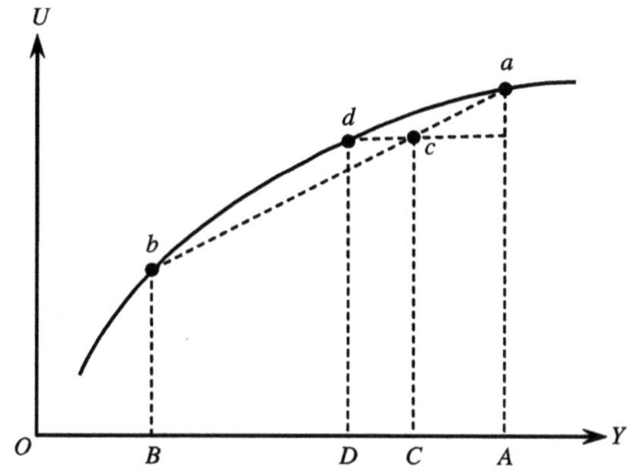

Consider the choice between money incomes which are not certain. First it may seem that the so-called principle of mathematical expectation applies and it is best to have the income with the highest expected money value. Many examples show, however, that this principle of mathematical expectation is not universally applicable. Consider, for example, the so-called paradox of the St. Petersburg game, considered by Daniel Bernoulli. A coin is to be tossed until heads turns up. You will be given \$ 1 if heads turns up on the first throw. If heads, having failed to turn up the first time, turns up the second time, \$ 2 will be given to you. You will receive \$ 4 if heads, having failed to turn up the first two times, turns up the third time, and so on. The series of your possible gains is hence $\$1, \$2, \$2^2, \$2^3, \ldots, \$2^{n-1}$. The mathematical expectation of this random income is derived by multiplying each of the possible gains by its probability, $1/2, 1/4, 1/8, \ldots, 1/2^n$. It is infinite, since $\sum_n 2^{n-1}\frac{1}{2^n} = \sum_n \frac{1}{2}$. Nevertheless, it is the fact that you prefer a certain income of a not very large amount, say, \$ 128 to this random income of the infinite mathematical expectation. This is because there is only 1 chance in 64 that the random income yields the amount over \$ 128.

A way to get rid of this paradox of the principle of mathematical expectation is, as was suggested by Bernoulli, to assume that people choose, not the highest expected money income, but the highest expected real income, i.e., the highest expected utility and that the marginal utility diminishes as the money value is increased. The law of diminishing marginal utility implies that utility as a function of money is a concave function and that a person to whom this law applies will always prefer a certain income to any random income of the identical expected value. In other words, such a person will always be willing to pay something for insurance against any risk to himself. In Fig. 3.9, money income Y is measured horizontally, and the utility is, vertically. Consider a person whose income is random so that it is OA with the probability $3/4$ and OB with the probability $1/4$. The curve ab indicates the utility of income, with the marginal utility of income being diminishing. The random income is indifferent to the certain income of OD, since the expected utility of the former is *Cc*, which is obtained as the utility *Aa* times $3/4$ plus the utility *Bb* times $1/4$. This person buys with a premium up to *AD* an insurance policy which guarantees the income *OA*. The expected profit of the insurance company is positive, since it will pay the insurance money *AB* with the probability $1/4$ while it can receive the premium higher than *AC*.

A person with the diminishing marginal utility is a risk averter who is always willing to insure against any risk to maximize the expected utility of his income. In other words, he will never participate even in a fair game of chance, for example, a game in which he has an equal chance of winning or losing a dollar, for the purpose of maximizing the expected utility, i.e., apart from enjoying the game itself. On the other hand, a person with the increasing marginal utility of income is a risk lover who prefers a random income to a certain one if both of them have the same expected value. He will not only engage in fair games of chance but also in such unfair games as lotteries, even if he does not enjoy the game itself. If the behavior of people facing risks can be described by the maximization of the expected utility, it make sense to assume that the marginal utility of income is diminishing or increasing, since the same person cannot buy an insurance policy and purchase a lottery ticket at the same time in the same situation. The utility is now cardinal in the sense that utility function is unique up to the increasing linear transformation. Consider any two utility functions which describe the behavior of the same person,

$$V(y) = V[U(y)] \tag{3.34}$$

where Y is the level of his money income. Since $\frac{dV}{dY}$ is diminishing (increasing) if $\frac{dU}{dY}$ is diminishing (increasing), $V = aU + b$, where a and b are constants.

Problems

3.1. Suppose the utility function is $U = x_1 x_2$ in the two goods case, where x_j denotes the amount of the j-th good consumed. Prove that this utility function is strictly quasi-concave. Is it also strictly concave?

3.2. In the programming model of Sect. 3.4 ((3.12)–(3.14)), demonstrate that the feasible set of $(U, x_1, \ldots, x_m)$ is convex and the utility function $U(x)$ is concave.

3.3. Discuss the difficulties we have if utility function is not strictly quasi-concave in Fig. 3.1.

3.4. By the use of assumptions on preference relation given in Sect. 3.5, explain why indifference curves do not intersect each other.

3.5. Define the compensation in income for the price change so that the consumer can buy exactly the unchanged quantity of goods if he wishes. Compare this definition with the definition of compensated income in Fig. 3.4 and show that two definitions coincide if the price change is infinitesimal.

3.6. The real income (the level of utility) is often approximated by deflating the money income with a price index. Show that the definition of compensated income in Problem 3.5 is the one to keep the real income unchanged, being based on this approximation of the real income.

3.7. Consider the maximization of utility $U(x) = U(x_1, \ldots, x_m)$ subject to the budget constraint $\sum_j p_j x_j \leq Y$. By eliminating, say, x_1, through substituting the constraint into the maximand, or by using Lagrange's method of multiplier, show that $\frac{\partial U/\partial x_1}{p_1} = \cdots = \frac{\partial U/\partial x_j}{p_j} = \cdots = \frac{\partial U/\partial x_m}{p_m}$. Show that this ratio is equal to the marginal utility of income, $\frac{\partial V}{\partial Y}$, where $V = V(p, Y) = U[x(p, Y)]$ is the indirect utility function defined in Sect. 3.7, by substituting $x(p, Y)$ into the budget constraint and differentiate it with respect to Y.

3.8. Solve the problem of utility maximization subject to the budget constraint, when the utility function is $U(x) = \sum_j a_j \log x_j$, where a_j's are positive constants.

3.9. Persons A, B and C have the identical taste (utility function) and are living, respectively, in cities a, b and c. Suppose the price of every good in city b is exactly the average of those in cities a and c. If A and C are enjoying the identical level of utility, is the average income of A and C enough for B to enjoy the same level of utility?

3.10. Consider the definition that the j-th good and the k-th good are substitutes (complements) if the marginal utility of the j-th good is decreased (increased) by an increase in the consumption of the k-th good. Does this definition make sense when the utility is ordinal?

3.11. Two goods are complete compliments if they are always used in the given unchanged proportion. Give some examples for them. Draw indifference curves between complete complements in Fig. 3.4 (the two goods world) and in Fig. 3.7 (the three goods world). Discuss the consistency with the definition of complementarity by the negative cross substitution effect, when the price of the first good is changed.

3.12. Using a figure similar to Fig. 3.9, explain that a person with increasing marginal utility of income is willing to buy a ticket of such unfair lotteries that the profit of the seller of tickets is positive.

Literature

For further studies in general, see Hicks, op. cit., pp. 303–314, Malinvaud, op. cit., pp. 12–42, and Varian, op. cit., pp. 80–117.
The use of programming model in the theory of the consumer (in Section 3.4) is suggested by G.S. Becker, "A Theory of the Allocation of Time," *Economic Journal* (1965), R.F. Muth, "Household Production and Consumer Demand Functions," *Econometrica* (1966), and K. Lancaster, "A New Approach to Consumer Theory," *Journal of Political Economy* (1966). See also K.J. Arrow, "An Extension of the Basic Theorems of Classical Welfare Economics," J. Neyman (ed.), *Proceedings of the Second Berkeley Symposium on Mathematical Statistics and Probability* (1950), W.M. Gorman, "Convex Indifference Curves and Diminishing Marginal Utility," *Journal of Political Economy* (1957), and ibid. "Intertemporal Choice and the Shape of Indifference Maps," *Metroeconomica* (1957), for the convexity assumption on utility function.
Slutsky equation was originally developed in E. Slutsky, "Sulla teoria del bilancio del consumotore," *Giornale degli Economisti* (1915) (English translation is "On the Theory of the Budget of the Consumer," AEA *Readings in Price Theory* (1952)). See also R.G.D. Allen and J.R., Hicks, "A Reconsideration of the Theory of Value," *Economica* (1934), and R.G.D. Allen, "Professor Slutsky's Theory of Consumer's Choice," *Review of Economic Studies* (1936). For substitutability and complementarity, see I.F. Pearce, *A Contribution to Demand Analysis* (1964), pp. 133–153.
For the expected utility, see M. Friedman and L.J. Savage, "The Utility Analysis of Choices involving Risk," *Journal of Political Economy* (1948), and L.J. Savage, *The Foundations of Statistics* (1954), pp. 91–104.

Chapter 4
Market Equilibrium (1)

4.1 General Equilibrium

In Chap. 2, we considered how firms supply the consumables and intermediate goods and demand factors of production and intermediate goods, when prices in the market are given. Chapter 3 was devoted to show how consumers demand the consumables and supply factors of production, taking market prices as given. Aggregate demand for each good and aggregate supply of each good are, therefore, functions of market prices which are taken by competitive firms and consumers as given and unchanged. These market prices are, then, to be determined so as to equate the aggregate demand and aggregate supply of all goods. The general equilibrium of a competitive economy is defined as a set of prices which clears all the markets.

Consider an economy of m goods which include the consumables, intermediate goods and the factors of production. Prices of goods are denoted by price vector $p = (p_1, \ldots, p_m)$, where p_j denotes the price of the j-th good. Let us review how demand and supply are determined by firms and consumers when prices p are given. Suppose there are r firms and denote by y_{kj} the output (if positive) or input (if negative) of the j-th good by the k-th firm, $j = 1, \ldots, m,\ k = 1, \ldots, r$. The k-th firm maximizes its profit $\pi_k = py_k = \sum_j p_j y_{kj}$, where $y_k = (y_{k1}, \ldots, y_{km})$, being subject to the production function $f_k(y_k) = 0$. As a result of this, the equilibrium y_k is given as a function of market prices p. Suppose there are n consumers and let x_{ij}, $\overline{x}_{ij}$ and d_{ki} denote, respectively, the gross demand (consumption) and the initial holding of the j-th good of the i-th consumer, and the distribution ratio of the profit of the k-th firm to the i-th consumer such that $\sum_i d_{ki} = 1$ ($i = 1, \ldots, n,\ j = 1, \ldots, m,\ k = 1, \ldots, r$). The i-th consumer maximizes his utility $U_i(x_i)$, where $x_i = (x_{i1}, \ldots, x_{im})$, being subject to the budget constraint

T. Negishi, *Elements of Neo-Walrasian Economics*, Advances in Japanese Business and Economics 5, DOI 10.1007/978-4-431-54535-4_4, © Springer Japan 2014

$px_i = \sum_j p_j x_{ij} = p\overline{x}_i + d_i \pi = \sum_j p_j \overline{x}_{ij} + \sum_k d_{ki} \sum_j p_j y_{kj}(p)$, where $\overline{x}_i = (\overline{x}_{i1}, \ldots, \overline{x}_{im})$, $d_i = (d_{1i}, \ldots, d_{ri})$ and $\pi = (\pi_1, \ldots, \pi_r)$. As a result of this, the equilibrium x_i is given as a function of market prices p.

The conditions for the general equilibrium p are

$$\sum_i x_{ij}(p) - \sum_k y_{kj}(p) - \sum_i \overline{x}_{ij} = 0 \quad (j = 1, \ldots, m) \tag{4.1}$$

where the left-hand side is the excess demand for the j-th good. If the j-th good is one of the consumables, (4.1) is rewritten as

$$\sum_i x_{ij}(p) - \sum_i \overline{x}_{ij} = \sum_k y_{kj}(p) \tag{4.2}$$

where the left-hand side is the aggregate net demand of consumers while the right-hand side is the aggregate supply from firms, since y_{kj}'s are positive. If the j-th good is an intermediate good, (4.1) is reduced to

$$\sum_k y_{kj}(p) = 0 \tag{4.3}$$

since some of y_{kj}'s are positive (supply) while some others are negative (demand). Finally, if the j-th good is (the service of) the factor of production, (4.1) is rewritten as

$$\sum_i \overline{x}_{ij} - \sum_i x_{ij}(p) = -\sum_k y_{kj}(p) \tag{4.4}$$

where the left-hand side is the aggregate net supply from consumers' household while the right-hand side is the aggregate demand from firms, since y_{kj}'s are negative.

We have m equations (4.1) which seem to be sufficient to determine m variables $p_1, \ldots, p_m$. In an m goods economy, however, what does matter is not the absolute level of prices of m goods, but the relative ratio of m prices, since demand and supply are unchanged if all the m prices are changed proportionally. In other words, we have only to determine $m - 1$ relative prices, say, $\frac{p_2}{p_1}, \ldots, \frac{p_m}{p_1}$. Fortunately, this does not mean that we have more equations than unknowns, since, as we shall see, not all the m equations (4.1) are independent.

4.2 Homogeneity and Walras' Law

The excess demand for all the goods, which are defined as functions of prices in the left-hand side of (4.1), are homogeneous of degree zero, since $x_{ij}(p)$ and $y_{kj}(p)$ are homogeneous of degree zero in the sense that $x_{ij}(kp) = x_{ij}(p)$ and $y_{kj}(kp) = y_{kj}(p)$ for all $k > 0$. In other words, demand and supply of all the goods remain unchanged if the prices of all the goods are changed proportionally. If we denote the excess demand for the j-th good by $E_j(p)$, then, (4.1) can be rewritten as

$$E_j(p) = E_j\left(1, \frac{p_2}{p_1}, \ldots, \frac{p_m}{p_1}\right) = 0 \quad (j = 1, \ldots, m) \tag{4.5}$$

since $E_j(kp) = E_j(p)$ for any $k > 0$, and, of course, for$k = \dfrac{1}{p_1}$, if p_1 is positive. The number of variables to be determined is, therefore, not m but $m - 1$, since all the m markets are cleared if $m - 1$ relative prices $\dfrac{p_2}{p_1}, \ldots, \dfrac{p_m}{p_1}$ are properly chosen.

The homogeneity of $y_{kj}(p)$ can be seen as follows. In addition to production functions, the equilibrium conditions for y_{kj}'s are

$$\frac{f_{kj}(y_k)}{f_{kh}(y_k)} = \frac{p_j}{p_h} \quad (j \neq h) \tag{4.6}$$

where f_{kj} denotes the partial derivatives of f_k with respect to y_{kj} and the like. In other words, the marginal rate of substitution between goods (the left-hand side) is equal to the price ratio (see Sect. 2.3 and Problem 2.2). Since the production function and marginal rate of substitution are functions of y_k only and independent of p, the equilibrium y_k remains unchanged if all the prices are proportionally changed, since the right-hand side remains unchanged in (4.6). Similarly, the homogeneity of $x_{ij}(p)$ can be seen as follows. In addition to the budget constraint, the equilibrium condition for x_{ij}'s are

$$\frac{U_{ij}(x_i)}{U_{ih}(x_i)} = \frac{p_j}{p_h} \quad (j \neq h) \tag{4.7}$$

where U_{ij} denotes the marginal utility of the j-th good for the i-th consumer, and the like. In other words, the marginal rate of substitution between goods (the left-hand side of (4.7)) is equal to the price ratio (see Sect. 3.3 and Problem 3.7). Since the marginal rate of substitution is a function of x_i only and independent of p, the unchanged equilibrium x_i can still satisfy (4.7), if all the prices are proportionally changed. As for the budget constraint, the equilibrium x_i need not to change to satisfy it, when all the prices are changed proportionally, since $\overline{x}_{ij}$ and d_{ki} are constants and $y_{kj}(p)$ remains unchanged.

Now we have m equations in (4.5) to determine $m-1$ unknowns. Since we have more conditions than unknowns, there is a possibility of overdeterminateness that it is impossible to satisfy all the conditions, if all the m equations in (4.5) are mutually independent conditions. Fortunately, however, they are not independent, in view of the so-called Walras' law

$$\sum_j p_j E_j \equiv 0 \tag{4.8}$$

which is not the equation but the identity in prices p. If any of $m-1$ equations in (4.5) are satisfied, (4.8) implies that the remaining one is also satisfied, so that there is no overdeterminateness. We have $m-1$ independent equations to determine $m-1$ unknowns.

Walras' law (4.8) can be derived from the budget constraints of consumers, which are identities in prices, since they have to be observed for any price vectors p, irrespective to whether it is the general equilibrium one or not. The summation of the budget constraints of all the consumers gives

$$\begin{aligned}
&\sum_i (px_i - p\overline{x}_i - d_i\pi)\\
&= \sum_i \sum_j p_j x_{ij} - \sum_i \sum_j p_j \overline{x}_{ij} - \sum_i \sum_k d_{ki} \sum_j p_j y_{kj}\\
&= \sum_j p_j \Big(\sum_i x_{ij} - \sum_k y_{kj} - \sum_i \overline{x}_{ij} \Big) \equiv 0.
\end{aligned} \tag{4.9}$$

The last part of which is nothing but Walras' law, since $\sum_i d_{ki} = 1$ by definition.

We have now $m-1$ equations to determine $m-1$ unknowns. The equality of the number of unknowns and that of equations does not, however, assure the existence of an economically meaningful solution, i.e., a general equilibrium price vector. For example, equilibrium relative prices have to be real numbers, and in general, positive numbers. Let us consider a simple case of two unknowns x and y and two equations $x^2 + y^2 = a$, and $y = bx + c$, where a, b and c are positive constants. Certainly, there are in general two solutions of complex numbers, but there exists no solution of real number unless $a(1+b^2) > c^2$. Figure 4.1 shows the case of no real solution where the circle ($x^2 + y^2 = a$) and the straight line ($y = bx + c$) do not intersect each other. The existence of a general equilibrium should be demonstrated, therefore, not by merely counting the numbers of unknowns and equations, but by more explicitly taking into consideration the conditions imposed on a general equilibrium price vector and corresponding quantity vectors of consumption and production.

Fig. 4.1

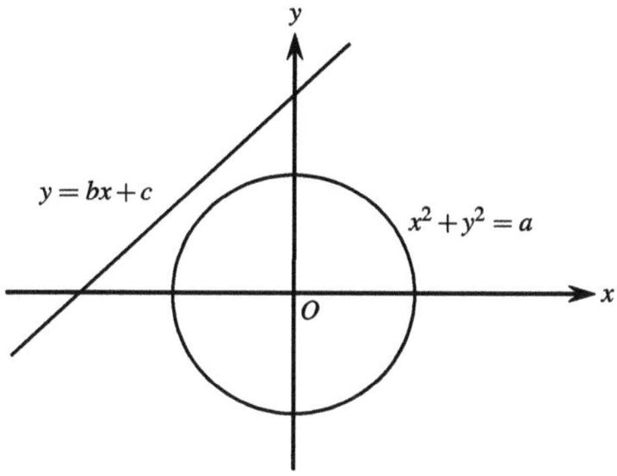

4.3 Edgeworth Box Diagram

Unfortunately, such a demonstration for the general m goods, n consumers and r firms case is highly technical and cannot be reproduced here in full details. We have to be satisfied by a proof of a simple case which, however, shows clearly the gist of the proof for the general case. The most simple economy we can imagine, which, however, is still meaningful for our problem, is the two goods two individuals of an exchange economy, where there is no production. To consider such a simple case, it is convenient to use the so-called Edgeworth box diagram.

Let us suppose that the first individual has an initial endowment of $\overline{x}_{11}$ units of the first good and $\overline{x}_{12}$ units of the second good. Similarly, suppose that the second individual has an initial endowment of $\overline{x}_{21}$ units of the first good and $\overline{x}_{22}$ units of the second good. Since there is no production, the total quantity of the first good in the economy before and after exchange is unchanged and given by $\overline{x}_1 = \overline{x}_{11} + \overline{x}_{21}$, and the total quantity of the second good is also unchanged and given by $\overline{x}_2 = \overline{x}_{12} + \overline{x}_{22}$. It follows that the only possible states of the economy are those represented by a set of points contained in a rectangle having dimensions $\overline{x}_1$ by $\overline{x}_2$ (shown in Fig. 4.2), where the quantity of the first good is measured horizontally, and that of the second good, vertically. Any point in the box represents a particular distribution of goods between two individuals. For example, if the distribution of goods is given by point A, the quantities of the first good and the second good obtained by the first individual, x_{11} and x_{12} respectively, are measured by the coordinates of A, using the south-west corner O as the origin; the quantities distributed to the second individual, x_{21} and x_{22}, are measured by the coordinates of point A, using the north-east corner O' as the origin.

The indifference curves I, II, III of the first individual are drawn, using O as the origin, and the indifference curves 1, 2, 3 of the second individual, using O' as the origin. The marginal rates of substitution between two goods of two individuals are equal when an indifference curve of the first individual is tangent to an indifference curve of the second individual. The locus of all such points is the contract curve ACB. The marginal rates of substitution are unequal at points

Fig. 4.2

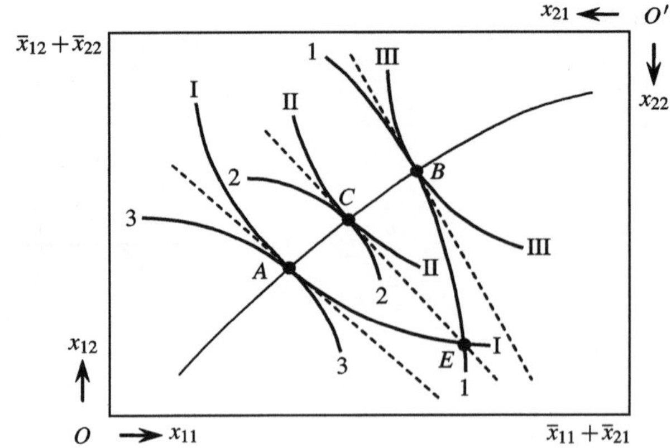

not on the contract curve, say point E of the initial endowments, $(\bar{x}_{11}, \bar{x}_{12})$ from O, or $(\bar{x}_{21}, \bar{x}_{22})$ from O', and it is possible to increase the utility level of both individuals by changing the existing distribution of goods. For example, if the final position after a redistribution of goods is in the inside of the area surrounded by two indifference curves passing E, both individuals would have gained, since both would be on higher utility indifference curves than at the point E. If a point on the contract curve is reached, it is not possible to improve further the position of either individual without a deterioration in the position of the other. In other words, points on the contract curve are Pareto optimal, which we shall discuss detailedly in Chap. 7.

If two individuals are rational, therefore, the exchange between them will result in a point on the contract curve, hence the term contract curve. Since any point on the contract curve between A and B can be the outcome of the exchange between two individuals who are initially located at the point E, the equilibrium of exchange between two individuals is indeterminate, if they behave rationally and freely. Let us suppose, however, that two individuals are acting as price takers or quantity adjusters to the given market prices. Such supposition may be rationalized that two goods are actually exchanged among $2n$ individuals for sufficiently large $n > 0$. Individuals are assumed to be grouped into two homogeneous groups of n individuals in the sense that individuals in the same group are completely identical each other, having the same taste (utility function, indifference map) and the same initial holdings of goods. Equilibrium of exchange among $2n$ individuals, then, can be described by the equilibrium of exchange between the representative individuals of two groups. In other words, we consider the equilibrium of exchange between two individuals, not isolated two individuals, but the two representative individuals arbitrary chosen respectively from different homogeneous groups of n individuals. Our model is a reduced one with the scale of one to n of the original $2n$ individual model of a competitive economy.

If we denote the price ratio, i.e., the price of the second good in terms of the first good by p, the first price taking individual will choose the best combination of two goods (x_{11}, x_{12}) being subject to his budget constraint, $x_{11} + px_{12} = \overline{x}_{11} + p\overline{x}_{12}$. Similarly, the second price taking individual will choose (x_{21}, x_{22}) being subject to $x_{21} + px_{22} = \overline{x}_{21} + p\overline{x}_{22}$. Equilibrium conditions for each individual are (1) the equality of the marginal rate of substitution and the price ratio (i.e., the tangency of indifference curve and the price line) and (2) the budget constraints. The market equilibrium is attained when demand and supply of two goods are equal, i.e., $x_{11} + x_{21} = \overline{x}_1$, $x_{12} + x_{22} = \overline{x}_2$. It should be noted that among two budget constraints and two market clearing conditions any one condition is implied by the remaining three conditions. In other words the so-called Walras' law holds.

At any point in the box diagram, market equilibrium conditions are satisfied. If the common tangent of two indifference curves is considered as the price line with the slope being equal to the price ratio, the condition (1) of the equilibrium of each individual is realized at any point on the contract curve *ACB*. Therefore, all the conditions for the competitive equilibrium are satisfied at such a point as point C on the contract curve, where the price line *CE* passes the initial endowment point E, i.e., the budget constraint is satisfied for each individual.

4.4 The Existence of an Exchange Equilibrium

Since markets are always cleared at all the points in the box diagram, to prove the existence of a general equilibrium for an exchange economy, we have only to show that there always exists a point like C on the contract curve *ACB* in Fig. 4.2, where a budget constraint is satisfied. Let us first consider the point A, i.e., the point of intersection of contract curve and the indifference curve of the first individual passing through the initial point E. Since indifference curves are drawn as strictly convex to the origin, we have

$$\begin{aligned} &F(x_{11}, x_{12}) \\ =&x_{11} + p(x_{11}, x_{12})x_{12} - \overline{x}_{11} - p(x_{11}, x_{12})\overline{x}_{12} < 0 \end{aligned} \tag{4.10}$$

at point A, where $p(x_{11}, x_{12})$ is the marginal rate of substitution of the first individual or the slope of the tangent of indifference curve I at point A, since point E, i.e., $(\overline{x}_{11}, \overline{x}_{12})$ is located above and to the right of such a tangent. In other words, budget constraint of the first individual is not satisfied, if p is considered to be the relative price in the market. Clearly, the point A is not an equilibrium. Similarly, we have at point B, i.e., the point of intersection of the contract curve and the indifference curve of the second individual passing the initial point E,

$$\begin{aligned} &F(x_{11}, x_{12}) \\ =&x_{11} + p(x_{11}, x_{12})x_{12} - \overline{x}_{11} - p(x_{11}, x_{12})\overline{x}_{12} > 0 \end{aligned} \tag{4.11}$$

Fig. 4.3

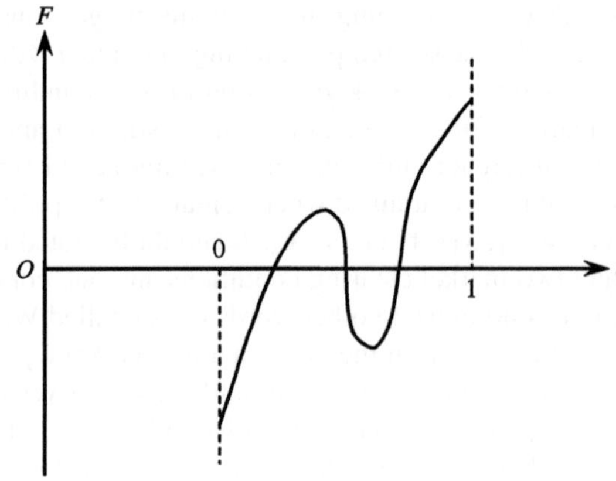

where $p(x_{11}, x_{12})$ is, of course, the marginal rate of substitution of the first individual or the slope of the tangent of indifference curve III at point B, since point E, i.e., $(\overline{x}_{11}, \overline{x}_{12})$ is located below and to the left of such a tangent. The budget constraint is not satisfied, and point B is again not an equilibrium.

If the marginal rate of substitution of the first individual p is assumed to be a continuous function of the quantity of two goods obtained by him, x_{11} and x_{12}, then $F(x_{11}, x_{12})$ defined in (4.10) and (4.11) is also a continuous function. The movement on the contract curve from A to B can be expressed as $x_{11} = x_{11}(t)$, $x_{12} = x_{12}(t)$ $(0 \leq t \leq 1)$, where $[x_{11}(0), x_{12}(0)]$ is the coordinates of the point A, $[x_{11}(1), x_{12}(1)]$ is the coordinates of the point B and x_{11} and x_{12} are continuous function of t. Then, $F[x_{11}(t), x_{12}(t)]$ is a continuous function of t such that $F < 0$ at $t = 0$ and $F > 0$ at $t = 1$. By the theorem of intermediate values of a continuous function (Fig. 4.3), we are sure that $F = 0$ at some $t = \overline{t}$ (possibly not unique) such that $0 < \overline{t} < 1$. The point whose coordinates from the origin O is $[x_{11}(\overline{t}), x_{12}(\overline{t})]$ is a competitive equilibrium of exchange, i.e., the point C in the box diagram of Fig. 4.2.

The gist of the above proof for the case of two goods two individuals (or two homogeneous group of individuals of the same size) exchange economy is to find a point with budget constraints satisfied (point C in Fig. 4.2) among Pareto optimal points (curve ACB) by interpreting identical marginal rate of substitution as the relative price. Essentially the same method of proof can be applied to the general case of m goods n individuals exchange economy, with more advanced mathematical theorems, i.e., fixed point theorems instead of the simple theorem of the intermediate valued of a continuous function. Consider the set of Pareto optimal distribution of consumption vectors $x_i = (x_{i1}, \ldots, x_{im})$ $(i = 1, \ldots, n)$, such that

$$\sum_i x_{ij} = \sum_i \overline{x}_{ij} \quad (j = 1, \ldots, m) \tag{4.12}$$

and that it is impossible to increase $U_i(x_i)$ without decreasing $U_h(x_h)$ for some $h \neq i$, where x_{ij} is the quantity of the j-th good to be given to the i-th individual,

$\overline{x}_{ij}$ is the i-th individual's given initial holding of the j-th good, and U_i is the utility of the i-th individual. Marginal rates of substitution, $\frac{U_{i2}}{U_{i1}}, \ldots, \frac{U_{im}}{U_{i1}}$, where U_{ij} is the partial derivative of U_i with respect to x_{ij}, are equalized among n individuals, i.e., for $i = 1, \ldots, n$, since otherwise it is possible to increase U_i without decreasing U_h, for all $h \neq i$. By interpreting such marginal rates of substitution as relative prices, i.e., $p_1 = 1, p_2 = \frac{U_{i2}}{U_{i1}}, \ldots, p_m = \frac{U_{im}}{U_{i1}}$, where p_j is the price of the j-th good in terms of the first good, consider the budget constraints,

$$\sum_j p_j x_{ij} = \sum_j p_j \overline{x}_{ij} \quad (i = 1, \ldots, n) \tag{4.13}$$

of n individuals. We have a mapping from the set of Pareto optimal distribution of consumption vectors to itself, by starting with a Pareto optimal distribution and by moving to another, if (4.13) is not satisfied by the first one. We are assured, then, by fixed point theorems that there exists, at least, one Pareto optimal distribution which satisfies (4.13) (see Problem 4.1).

4.5 Non-existence of Equilibrium

Looking at Fig. 4.2, some readers might wonder why it is necessary to prove the existence of an equilibrium at all, since it seems intuitively clear that the point like C exists always in Edgeworth's box diagram. To such readers we have to confess that so far we have been making implicit assumptions which are convenient to prove the existence of an equilibrium. For example, in Fig. 4.2, firstly, the initial point E is located, not on the boundary, but in the inside of the box, which implies that each individual has positive stock of all the goods. Secondly, indifference curves are drawn strictly convex to the origin so that the utility of every good is assumed to be not satiated. To show the necessity of the existence proof of an equilibrium, it may perhaps be useful to consider cases in which these convenient assumptions are not made.

Let us first consider the counter-example against the existence of equilibrium, which was given by A. Wald. In a three individuals three goods exchange economy, marginal utilities of the j-th good for the i-th individual U_{ij} $(i = 1, 2, 3,\ j = 1, 2, 3)$, are

$$U_{11}(x_{11}) = \frac{1}{x_{11}},$$

$$U_{12}(x_{12}) = \begin{cases} \dfrac{b - x_{12}}{x_{12}^2} & (\text{for } x_{12} \leq b) \\ 0 & (\text{for } x_{12} > b) \end{cases},$$

$$U_{13}(x_{13}) = \begin{cases} \dfrac{2(c - x_{13})}{x_{13}^2} & (\text{for } x_{13} \leq c) \\ 0 & (\text{for } x_{13} > c) \end{cases},$$

$$U_{21}(x_{21}) = \frac{1}{x_{21}^2},$$

$$U_{22}(x_{22}) = \frac{1}{x_{22}},$$

$$U_{23}(x_{23}) = 0,$$

$$U_{31}(x_{31}) = \frac{1}{x_{31}^2},$$

$$U_{32}(x_{32}) = 0,$$

$$U_{33}(x_{33}) = \frac{1}{x_{33}}$$

where x_{ij} signifies the amount of the j-th good held by the i-th individual after the exchange and the initial holding $\overline{x}_{ij}$ of the i-th individual of the j-th good is

$$\begin{aligned} &\overline{x}_{11} = a, \quad \overline{x}_{12} = 0, \quad \overline{x}_{13} = 0, \\ &\overline{x}_{21} = 0, \quad \overline{x}_{22} = b, \quad \overline{x}_{23} = 0, \\ &\overline{x}_{31} = 0, \quad \overline{x}_{32} = 0, \quad \overline{x}_{33} = c \end{aligned}$$

where a, b and c are given positive constants.

Suppose there is an equilibrium with positive prices, $p_1 = 1$, $p_2 > 0$ and $p_3 > 0$, where p_j is the equilibrium price of the j-th good. Since the second (third) individual does not want the third (second) good, in view of budget constraints and the equality of demand and supply, we have $x_{21} = p_2 x_{12}$, $x_{22} = b - x_{12}$, $x_{31} = p_3 x_{13}$ and $x_{33} = c - x_{13}$. Since the second individual's marginal rate of substitution between the first good and second good should be equal to p_2,

$$p_2 = \frac{(p_2 x_{12})^2}{b - x_{12}} \tag{4.14}$$

from which

$$p_2 = \frac{b - x_{12}}{(x_{12})^2}. \tag{4.15}$$

Similarly, the marginal rate of substitution between the first and third goods should be equal to p_3 for the third individual,

$$p_3 = \frac{c - x_{13}}{(x_{13})^2}. \tag{4.16}$$

Substitution of (4.15) and (4.16) into the equality of the first individual's marginal rate of substitution between the second and third goods and $\frac{p_2}{p_3}$,

$$\frac{(b - x_{12})(x_{13})^2}{2(c - x_{13})(x_{12})^2} = \frac{p_2}{p_3} \tag{4.17}$$

gives, however, a contradiction. It is easily seen that none of the equilibrium prices can be 0. Therefore, there exists no equilibrium.

Apparently, two implicit conditions we made in Fig. 4.2, i.e., non-satiation and positive initial holdings, are violated in this example of the non-existence of equilibrium. For some readers, however, it may not intuitively clear why such violation causes the non-existence of equilibrium in this example. It is recommended, then, to consider the following example of non-existence first, and to return to this one to solve Problem 4.2.

An example of the non-existence of equilibrium which is more directly related to our proof of existence in Fig. 4.2 was the one given by K.J. Arrow as an example of the case where the solution of the expenditure minimization for the given utility does not maximizes the utility subject to the budget equalized to the minimized expenditure. Consider Fig. 4.4, where indifference curves of the second individual are not strictly convex and the point A of the initial endowment is located on the boundary of the Edgeworth box. Curves and I_1 and I_2 are indifference curves of the first individual with the origin at O and curves J_1 and J_2 are those of the second individual with the origin at O'. Note that the utility of the first good is satiated for the second individual at points between O and A (including O and A) while it is not so for the first individual. Point A is clearly Pareto optimal and on the contract curve but not a competitive equilibrium, since there can be no price line which is tangent to both I_1 and J_2 at A. Suppose price of the first good in terms of the second is zero. Budget line through A is then horizontal and the first individual demands indefinitely large quantity of the first good. Suppose the price of the first good is positive. The second individual demands, then, larger quantity of the second good than at A, since his budget line is not tangential to indifference curve J_2 at A, so that it is again impossible to stay in the box. Since A is also the point of the initial endowments, it is evident that there is no equilibrium, if A cannot be one.

Fig. 4.4

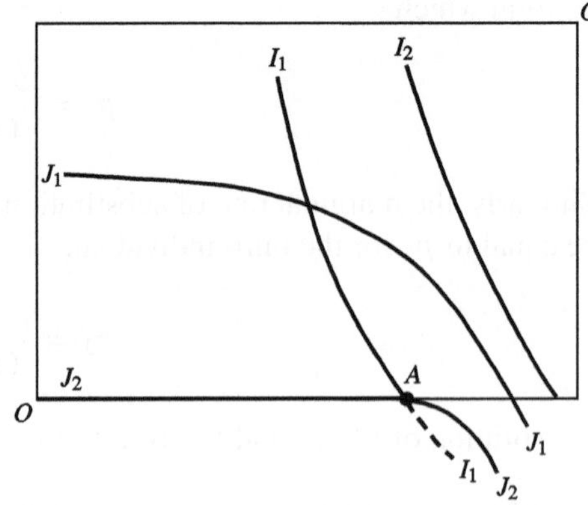

To avoid this anomalous case, we have to assume either that indifference curves are strictly convex (utility of no good is satisfied) or that the point of initial endowments is not located on the boundary of the box (every individual has strictly positive quantity of every good), so that the value of goods distributed to every individual at Pareto optimal points can be positive. If the relative price of the first good is zero, the expenditure is minimized at point A in Fig. 4.4 for the utility level of indifference curve I_1. Since the minimum expenditure, i.e., the value of goods given to the first individual is zero, however, the utility is not maximized subject to the budget line which is the horizontal line through A. Generally, the expenditure is minimized for the given utility at Pareto optimal points, if marginal rates of substitution are considered as relative prices. Unless the minimized expenditure is positive, however, this does not imply that the utility is maximized subject to the budget constraint equalized to it (see Problem 4.3).

4.6 Equilibrium with Production

The proof of the existence of equilibrium for an economy of exchange, explained in Sect. 4.4, can be extended to the case of an equilibrium with production. Consider the set of Pareto optimal allocation of consumption vectors $x_i = (x_{i1}, \ldots, x_{im})$ $(i = 1, \ldots, n)$, and production vectors $y_k = (y_{k1}, \ldots, y_{km})$ $(k = 1, \ldots, r)$, such that

$$\sum_i x_{ij} = \sum_i \overline{x}_{ij} + \sum_k y_{kj} \quad (j = 1, \ldots, m) \tag{4.18}$$

and

$$f_k(y_k) = 0 \quad (k = 1, \ldots, r) \tag{4.19}$$

where y_{kj} is the output (if positive) or input (if negative) of the j-th good by the k-th firm. By interpreting marginal rates of substitution as relative prices, i.e., $p_1 = 1, p_2 = \frac{U_{i2}}{U_{i1}}, \ldots, p_m = \frac{U_{im}}{U_{i1}}$, consider the budget constraints,

$$\sum_j p_j x_{ij} = \sum_j p_j \overline{x}_{ij} + \sum_k d_{ki} \sum_j p_j y_{kj} \quad (i = 1, \ldots, n) \tag{4.20}$$

where d_{ki} is the distribution ratio of the profit of the k-th firm to the i-th individual. Then, we can find a Pareto optimal allocation which satisfies (4.20). It is also a competitive equilibrium, since marginal rates of substitution for firms, $\frac{f_{k2}}{f_{k1}}, \ldots, \frac{f_{km}}{f_{k1}}$, where f_{kj} is the partial derivative of f_k with respect to y_{kj}, are equalized among r firms and also to relative prices, $p_2, \ldots, p_m$, so that the profit $\sum_j p_j y_{kj}$ is maximized subject to $f_k(y_k) = 0$ $(k = 1, \ldots, r)$, at Pareto optimal allocations.

For example, suppose two firms are producing different single products by using identical two factors of production. Reinterpret box diagram in Fig. 4.2 that the first factor of production is measured horizontally, the second factor, vertically, and that the input of factors by the first firm are measured from the origin O, and those of the second firm, from the origin O'. Curves I, II, and III are isoquants for the first product of the first firm, and curves 1, 2, 3 are isoquants for the second product of the second firm. The allocation of factors of production at the point I, where isoquants are crossing each other, is certainly not Pareto optimum, since the output of both products can be increased by moving to C, so that the utility of an individual can be increased without reducing that of others. Pareto optimum allocations are represented by points on the curve ACB, where isoquants of two products are tangent each other so that marginal rates of substitution of different firms are equalized.

To see that marginal rates of substitution of firms are also equalized to relative prices defined by marginal rates of individual consumers, consider a two goods one individual one firm (or n identical individuals n identical firms) production economy. In Fig. 4.5, the quantity of one of two goods, the service of labor (time) is measured vertically, and that of the other good, a labor product horizontally. The curves I and J are indifference curves of the individual. The initial quantity of labor service held by the individual is represented by OA. It is assumed that there is no economy of scale and that the possibility of production of the firm is shown by the curve AB, expressing the relation between input of labor service measured downward from A and the output of the product measured to the right from O. The consumer's utility is maximized at C, where the indifference curve I is tangent to the curve AB. If the marginal rate of substitution of the individual, expressed by the slope of the curve I at C, is interpreted as the relative price of the product and labor service, the firm's profit is maximized at C, where its marginal rate of substitution,

Fig. 4.5

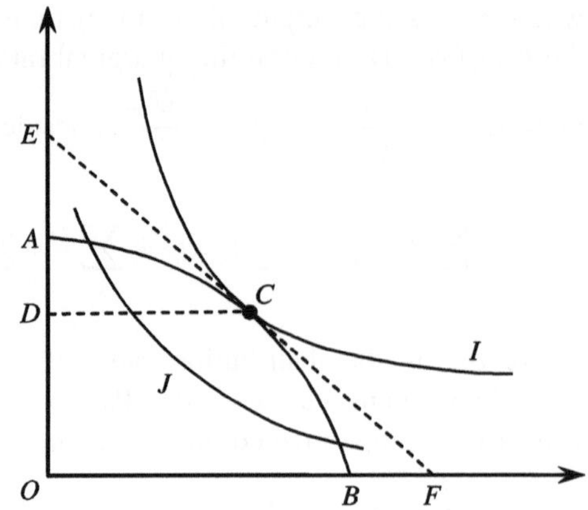

the slope of the curve *AB*, is equalized to the relative price. The maximum profit, the difference between *ED* and *AD*, i.e., *EA* in terms of labor service, is distributed to the individual. The budget line of the individual is, therefore, *EF*, on which the utility is maximized at C.

4.7 Economy of Scale

If the economy of scale is introduced, there is a difficulty for the case of an economy with production to prove the existence of a competitive equilibrium. In Fig. 4.6, which is similar to Fig. 4.5, it is assumed that an overhead cost is incurred to produce the product (measured horizontally), which is represented by the input *AG* of labor service for a firm. The variable cost of production is, on the other hand, by the curve *GB*. Since the marginal variable cost is increasing, the average cost (measured in terms of labor input) is expressed by a typical U-shaped curve. If a positive quantity of the product is produced in a competitive equilibrium, the marginal rate of substitution of individual and that of firm must be equal, as they are at C, to the price ratio. The price ratio of the produced good and labor service at D is equal to the slope of the common tangent *ECF* of curves *GB* and I. The profit of the firm is negative, however, since the value, in terms of labor, of the product *DC* produced from the inputs *AD* of labor is merely *ED*. If the point of no production A is a trivial equilibrium, on the other hand, the price ratio is equal to the slope of the tangent *AH* to the indifference curve J at A. The point A cannot, however, be an equilibrium, since it is profitable again for the firm to produce a positive quantity under the price ratio *AH*.

To get rid of this difficulty, let us suppose that the trade of a firm is distributed equally to n individuals in our model of an economy consist of n identical individuals and n identical firms and that the number n is infinitely large. Consider Fig. 4.7, which is a reproduction of Fig. 4.6. Since the number of firms is infinite, the

Fig. 4.6

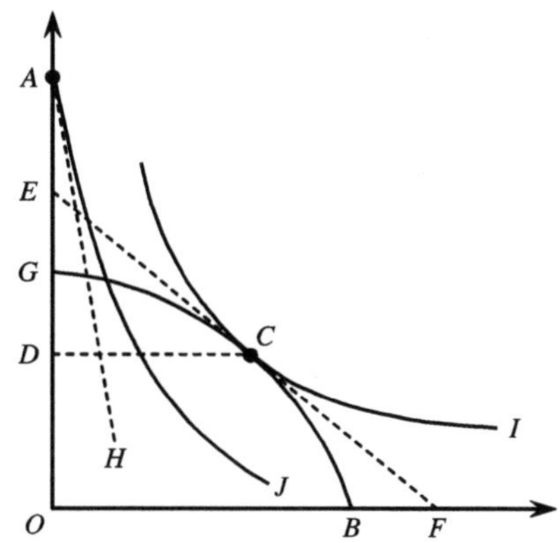

Fig. 4.7

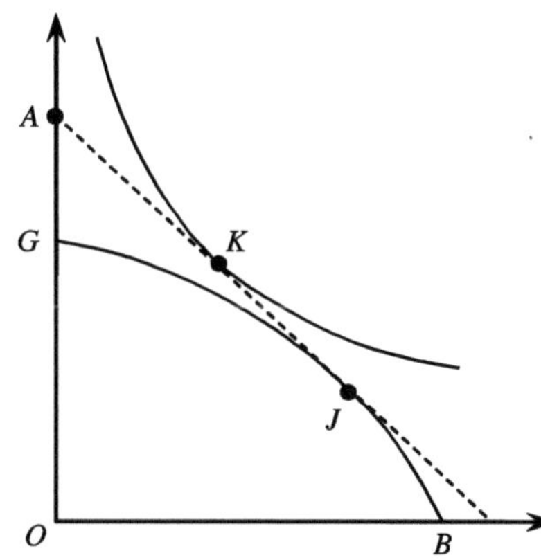

input of labor and the output of product per firm can be at any point on the line *AJ* which is tangent to the curve *GC* representing the variable cost, if we suppose some firms are at *A* (no production) and the rest of firms are at *J*. Then, an equilibrium exists at *K*, where an indifference curve of every identical individual is tangent to the line *AJ*. Since the price ratio of the product and labor service is equal to the slope of *AJ*, the profit of firm at *J* is also zero. The income of each individual is wage income only, so that *AJ* is his budget line. Each individual's utility is maximized at *K*, and aggregate demand and supply of the product as well as of the labor service are equalized, since the number of individuals is equal to that of firms.

In other words, if we suppose a firm trades with an individual as in Fig. 4.6, the feasible set of production for a firm *AEGCBODG* is not convex, which is the source of the difficulty there. If infinitely many firms trade with every individual equally, and therefore infinitely many individuals trade with every firm equally, however, the aggregate feasible set, and therefore the average feasible set of production for a firm are convexificated as *AKJBOG* in Fig. 4.7. The assumption that the number of firms and individuals is infinitely large seems to be reasonable, since we are assuming that influence of single individual and of single firm on market prices can be negligible and that individuals and firms are taking market prices constant.

An alternative solution for the non-convex case is perhaps to introduce the possibility of the so-called nonlinear prices which are quantity dependent. A well-known case of nonlinear prices is the two-part tariffs. In Fig. 4.6, suppose that consumers have to pay the entrance fee to the market *AG* first so as to obtain the right to purchase the products, and then pay the uniform unit price which is equal to the marginal cost, expressed by the slope of the line *ECF* in terms of labor service. Although the marginal price is constant, the average price for consumer is not, since the constant fee *AG* is to be distributed to each unit purchased. Since firm's constant overhead cost is covered now by the lump sum entrance fee paid by the consumers, it can make the positive profit *EG*, which is distributed to consumers so that the income of each consumer is *OE* in terms of labor service. A more indirect way is to collect taxes from consumers and subsidize firms for their overhead cost *AG*.

Problems

4.1. Consider the maximization of a weighted sum of utilities of n individuals, $\sum_i a_i U_i(x_{i1}, \ldots, x_{im})$ being subject to conditions of the equality of demand and supply, $\sum_i x_{ij} = \sum_i \overline{x}_{ij}$ $(j = 1, \ldots, m)$, where a_i is the given positive constant. Interpret Lagrangean multipliers as prices and discuss the Pareto optimality of the solution. Show that the solution is also a general equilibrium if weights of individuals happen to be in inverse proportion to the equilibrium marginal utility of income for them.

4.2. In Wald's example in Sect. 4.5, find a Pareto optimal distribution in which budget constraints are satisfied if marginal rates of substitution are interpreted as relative prices. Discuss why such a case cannot be an equilibrium.

4.3. Suppose that $\sum_j p_j x_j \geq \sum_j p_j \overline{x}_j > 0$ for all x such that $U(x) \geq U(\overline{x})$, where U is quasi-concave and increasing and $x = (x_1, \ldots, x_m)$ and $\overline{x} = (\overline{x}_1, \ldots, \overline{x}_m)$. Show that $\overline{x}$ maximizes $U(x)$ subject to $\sum_j p_j x_j \leq \sum_j p_j \overline{x}_j$.

4.4. Read M. Morishima, *Walras' Economics* (1977), pp. 100–122, and discuss his solution of the overdeterminancy problem.

4.5. Give some examples of two-part tariffs. From the fact that most of examples are those in the service industries, consider the conditions for the successful introduction of two-part tariffs.

Literature

For further studies in general, see Malinvaud, op. cit., pp. 105–136, and Varian, op. cit., pp. 136–175.
A complete discussion on the existence of general equilibrium is given in G. Debreu, *Theory of Value* (1959), pp. 74–89, and in K.J. Arrow and F.H. Hahn, *General Competitive Analysis* (1971), pp. 107–128. See also T. Negishi, *General Equilibrium Theory and International Trade* (1972), pp. 11–27.
Examples of non-existence of equilibrium cited in the text are found in A. Wald, "On Some Systems of Equations of Mathematical Economics," *Econometrica* (1951), and in Arrow, op. cit. (see Chap. 3, Bibliography). See also L. Hurwicz, "Optimality and Informational Efficiency in Resource Allocation Processes," Arrow, Karlin and Suppes (eds.), *Mathematical Methods in the Social Sciences* (1959, 1960).
An advanced discussion of the convexification of non-convex economy is given in Arrow and Hahn, op. cit., pp. 169–182, while the problem of nonlinear prices is explained in L. Philips, *The Economics of Price Discrimination* (1983), pp. 158–175.

Chapter 5
Market Equilibrium (2)

5.1 The Input–Output Analysis

The nature and significance of input–output analysis or interindustry analysis, which was initiated by W. Leontief, can be interpreted in many different ways. It can be seen as the generalization of Keynesian multiplier theory, or as the modern version of Quesnay's Tableau économique or Marx's reproduction scheme, or as a degenerated linear programming model. From our point of view, however, it can be considered as an empirically oriented simplified version of the general equilibrium theory. While the importance of the analysis of interindustry input–output relations is duly emphasized, consumer demands are assumed to be given by outside information. The optimization and substitutability in production are assumed away by the use of the no-joint-output constant-coefficient production functions which are, however, numerically estimated by the data available from input–output tables. The input–output analysis can, therefore, provide numerical answers for a number of interesting problems of the general equilibrium of an economy.

Suppose there are n industries and let us denote by X_i the gross output of the i-th industry, $i = 1, \ldots, n$. A part of the output of the i-th industry X_{ij} is distributed to the j-th industry and consumed there to produce the output X_j $(i, j = 1, \ldots, n)$. In addition to such inter-industry demands, there is the final demand c_i for the output of the i-th industry, which includes consumers' demand, government's demand, and demand from foreign countries, i.e., the difference between exports and competing imports. The balance between demand and supply of outputs of industries can, therefore, be expressed as

$$X_i = \sum_j X_{ij} + c_i \quad (i = 1, \ldots, n) \tag{5.1}$$

which are, however, not sufficient to determine $n(n + 1)$ unknowns, i.e., X_i's and X_{ij}'s, even if c_i's are given exogenously.

T. Negishi, *Elements of Neo-Walrasian Economics*, Advances in Japanese Business and Economics 5, DOI 10.1007/978-4-431-54535-4_5, © Springer Japan 2014

Table 5.1

	Industry 1	Industry 2	Industry 3	Final demand	Total output
Industry 1	X_{11}	X_{12}	X_{13}	c_1	X_1
Industry 2	X_{21}	X_{22}	X_{23}	c_2	X_2
Industry 3	X_{31}	X_{32}	X_{33}	c_3	X_3

To reduce the number of unknowns, let us define input coefficients $a_{ij} = \dfrac{X_{ij}}{X_j}$ $(i, j = 1, \ldots, n)$, and assume that these are technological constants. Actually, these coefficients can be empirically estimated from input–output tables which describe interindustry flows of the economy at certain base year. Table 5.1 shows the input–output tables of three industries economy. By using these coefficients, we can reduce (5.1) into

$$X_i = \sum_j a_{ij} X_j + c_i \quad (i = 1, \ldots, n) \tag{5.2}$$

where unknowns are the gross outputs of n industries, X_i $(i = 1, \ldots, n)$. The gross output X_i's of any year can be calculated from (5.2), if the final demands c_i's for the year are given and input coefficients a_{ij}'s are estimated from the input–output table for the base year.

The output of the j-th industry X_j requires not only the input of the product of the i-th industry X_{ij} $(i = 1, \ldots, n)$, but also the input of the primary factors of the production like labor and the input of the intermediate goods which are non-competingly imported. Assuming that prices and input coefficients of these factors of production and of these imported goods are constant, and that the rate of per unit tax is also constant, we have

$$p_j = \sum_i a_{ij} p_i + v_j \quad (j = 1, \ldots, n) \tag{5.3}$$

where p_j and v_j denote, respectively, the price and value-added coefficient of the product of the j-th industry. The reason for (5.3) is that the competition makes the price equalized with the marginal cost which is identical to the average cost if input coefficients are constants. If v_j's are given, we can calculate p_j's from (5.3).

There is a symmetric relation called duality between (5.2) and (5.3). To see it more clearly, let us denote by A the $n \times n$ matrix composed by a_{ij} and rewrite (5.2) as

$$(I - A)X = c \tag{5.4}$$

where, I, X and c are, respectively, $n \times n$ identity matrix, output vector $X = (X_1, \ldots, X_n)$ and the final demand vector $c = (c_1, \ldots, c_n)$. The matrix $(I - A)$ is called Leontief matrix. Assuming $(I - A)$ is nonsingular so that it has its inverse, (5.4) can be solved for X required to produce a given c,

$$X = (I - A)^{-1}c \tag{5.5}$$

where $(I - A)^{-1}$ is called Leontief inverse (matrix) such that $(I - A)(I - A)^{-1} = I$. Similarly, (5.3) can be rewritten as

$$(I - A)'p = v \tag{5.6}$$

where $(I - A)'$, p and c are, respectively, the transposed matrix of $(I - A)$, price vector $p = (p_1, \ldots, p_n)$ and the value-added coefficient vector $v = (v_1, \ldots, v_n)$. It is solved for p if v is given,

$$p = (I - A)'^{-1}v \tag{5.7}$$

where, of course, $(I - A)'^{-1}$ is also the transposed matrix of Leontief inverse.

5.2 Leontief Inverse

We can calculate, by the use of Leontief inverse in (5.5) and (5.7), the effect on prices and outputs of changes, for example, in the final demands, the rate of wage or the price of non-competingly imported intermediate goods. If all the n^2 elements of Leontief inverse are positive, the output of all the goods X are increased by an increase in the final demand of a good c_i. Similarly, the price of all the goods p are reduced, when the labor productivity rises in an industry, but the rate of wage remains unchanged, or at least does not rise as much as the productivity. In the case of $n = 3$, we can easily see that such is the case, if input coefficients a_{ij}'s are all positive.

Firstly, let us note that $(1 - a_{ii})$ is positive for any i. This is because we can assume away such a highly inefficient industry that it cannot produce a positive net output of its product. In (5.6), then, we can see that $(I - A)'$ has positive diagonal elements $(1 - a_{ii})$ $(i = 1, \ldots, n)$, and negative non-diagonal elements, $-a_{ji}$ $(i = 1, \ldots, n,\ j = 1, \ldots, n,\ i \neq j)$. Since $p > 0$ and $v > 0$ in a base year, i.e., when a_{ij}'s are calculated, (5.6) implies

$$(1 - a_{ii})p_i > a_{ji}p_j \quad (j \neq i). \tag{5.8}$$

Now let us define the minor of the element a_{ij} of $n \times n$ matrix A as the determinant of a $(n - 1) \times (n - 1)$ matrix obtained by striking out the i-th row and the j-th column of the original matrix A. Let us further define the cofactor of a_{ij} as its minor multiplied $(-1)^{(i+j)}$. Then, (5.8) implies that the cofactor of all the elements of $(I - A)'$ are positive.

In the case of $n = 3$, (5.6) is actually

$$\begin{array}{rrr} +(1-a_{11})p_1 & -a_{21}p_2 & -a_{31}p_3 = v_1 \\ -a_{12}p_1 & +(1-a_{22})p_2 & -a_{32}p_3 = v_2 \\ -a_{13}p_1 & -a_{23}p_2 & +(1-a_{33})p_3 = v_3 \end{array}$$

and $(I - A)'$ is

$$(I-A)' = \begin{bmatrix} (1-a_{11}) & -a_{21} & -a_{31} \\ -a_{12} & (1-a_{22}) & -a_{32} \\ -a_{13} & -a_{23} & (1-a_{33}) \end{bmatrix}. \tag{5.9}$$

For example, the cofactor of $(1-a_{33})$ is $(1-a_{11})(1-a_{22})-a_{21}a_{12}$, which is positive in view of (5.8). The cofactor of $-a_{21}$ is $a_{12}(1-a_{33}) + a_{13}a_{32} > 0$. The cofactor of $-a_{31}$ is $a_{12}a_{23} + a_{13}(1-a_{22}) > 0$.

The element b_{ij} of the inverse B of a matrix A, i.e., $B = A^{-1}$, is the cofactor of the element a_{ij} of A divided by the determinant of A. Since the cofactor of all the elements of $(I - A)'$ are positive, therefore, all the elements of Leontief inverse are positive if the determinant of $(I - A)'$ is positive. The determinant of $(I - A)'$ cannot be negative, however, since (5.7) has to be satisfied by $p > 0$ and $v > 0$ of the base year. Since $1-a_{ii} > 0$ and $(1-a_{ii})(1-a_{jj})-a_{ij}a_{ji} > 0$ in (5.9), $(I-A)$ satisfies Hawkins–Simon condition that all principal minors of $I - A$ are positive.

Diagonal elements of Leontief inverse are all larger than one. For example, the numerator of the element b_{11} of Leontief inverse $B = (I - A)^{-1}$ in the case of $n = 3$ is the cofactor of $(1 - a_{11})$ of $I - A$, $(1 - a_{22})(1 - a_{33}) - a_{23}a_{32} > 0$ while the denominator of b_{11} is the determinant of $I - A$, which can be evaluated by expansion by its cofactors as

$$\begin{aligned} |I-A| &= (1-a_{11})[(1-a_{22})(1-a_{33}) - a_{23}a_{32}] \\ &\quad + a_{12}[(1-a_{33})(-a_{21}) - a_{31}a_{23}] \\ &\quad - a_{13}[a_{21}a_{32} + a_{31}(1-a_{22})] > 0. \end{aligned} \tag{5.10}$$

While the first term in the right-hand side of (5.10) is positive but smaller than the numerator of b_{11}, the second and third terms of the right-hand side of (5.10) are negative. Since the numerator is larger than the denominator, therefore, b_{11} is larger than one.

The reason why diagonal elements of Leontief inverse are larger than one is explained as follows. An increase in the final demand for the i-th industry causes firstly the same amount of increase in the output of the i-th industry. This requires, however, increases in the output of other industries, which in turn require additional increase in the output of the i-th industry. The sum of direct and indirect effects on the output of the first industry is, therefore, larger than the original increase in the final demand. Similarly, an increase in labor productivity in the i-th industry, which causes firstly a direct reduction in the unit cost of the product of the i-th industry, subsequently induces larger reduction in the cost, and therefore in the price, through the reduction of costs and prices in the other industries. Therefore, Leontief inverse is sometimes called as matrix multiplier.

5.3 (Non) Substitution Theorem

As was explained in Chap. 2, the locus of the combinations of two different inputs to produce a given amount of an output is called an isoquant and is generally drawn as a curve convex to the origin in Fig. 2.1. The curve *AB* in Fig. 5.1 is the reproduction of the isoquant drawn in Fig. 2.1. In input–output analysis, however, it is assumed that an isoquant is L shaped like *DCE* in Fig. 5.1, which has a kink at C. This is because the substitution between inputs is assumed away and input coefficients are assumed to be constant. In Fig. 5.1, the slope of the line *OF*, which is the locus of kinks of isoquants for different level of output, is given by the ratio of input coefficients of two inputs. It is this simplifying assumption that makes numerical computations possible in input–output analysis. Fortunately, this assumption seems to be empirically justifiable, since it has been known that input coefficients are not much different if they are computed from input–output tables of different years and of different countries.

In terms of linear programming, the assumption of L shaped isoquants implies that there is only one production process in each industry, while a traditional smooth isoquant corresponds to the case in which there are infinitely many processes in each industry so that inputs are continuously substitutable. From the point of view of technology of production in factories, shops, farms and firms, it is incredible that each industry has only one process and inputs are not substitutable at all. This question can be answered, at least partly, by the so-called (non) substitution theorem, which insists that in a competitive economy actually only one process is always utilized in each industry, even though technologically there are infinitely many different processes available. The condition necessary for this theorem is, in addition to constant returns to scale, and no-joint-output, that there exists only one primary factor of production, say, labor, which is supplied to industries from non-industrial exogenous sector of the economy.

The theorem in the two good case is explained in Fig. 5.2, where the first good is measured horizontally, and the second good, vertically. The dotted line *OC* shows a process in the first industry, which produces the net output $(1 - a_{11})$ of the first good from the input a_{21} of the second good. If all the labor supply of the economy is allocated to this process, the net output of the first good and the input of the second good is indicated by the coordinates of point G. Similarly, the dotted line *OD* shows a process in the second industry, and point H indicates output and input

Fig. 5.1

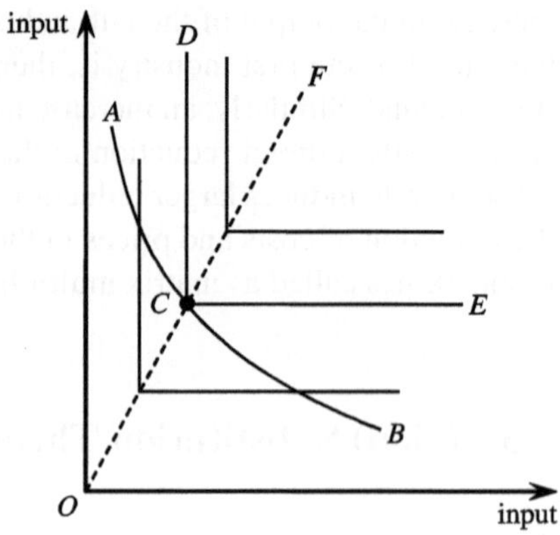

Fig. 5.2

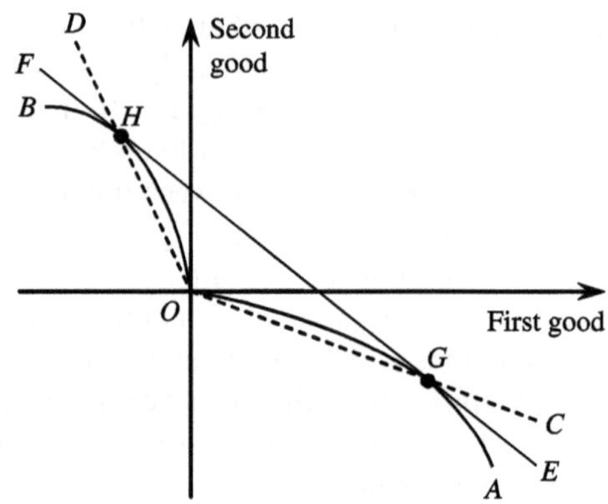

when all the labor supply is allocated. The locus of point G for infinitely many different processes in the first industry is the curve OA, and the similar locus for the second industry is the curve OB. Since the labor input is given, these curves show the diminishing productivity of non-labor input. If labor supply is divided between two processes OC and OD, the resulted net output of two goods, which can be supplied to the final demands, are indicated by points located between H and G on the line EF.

Since the line EF is tangent to both of curve OA and curve OB, it is clear that only the net output of two goods resulted from the combination of two processes OC and OD is Pareto optimal, in the sense that it is impossible to increase the net output of a good without reducing that of the other, by using the other combination of processes. As was suggested in the previous chapter, and to be explained fully in Chap. 7, the perfect competition generates the Pareto optimal resources allocation. In a competitive economy, therefore, only the processes OC and OD are actually utilized to produce any Pareto optimal combinations of two goods, i.e., to supply for any pattern of final demands, even though there are infinitely many technologically possible processes available. In other words, technologically isoquants are like AB

in Fig. 5.1, but only the point C is realized so that it looks as if isoquants are L shaped like DCE.

5.4 Tâtonnement Process

In the previous chapter, we demonstrated the existence of a general equilibrium in which demand and supply are equalized for all goods. It is, however, one thing to show the existence of such an equilibrium, but it is quite another to assure that an equilibrium can really be reached through some adjustment processes even if markets are in disequilibria in the beginning. The stability analysis of a competitive equilibrium is concerned with the problem whether an equilibrium can be approached through adjustments following the law of supply and demand that the price of a good is raised (reduced) if demand exceeds (falls short of) supply. Tâtonnement process is an example of such adjustment processes, which is simplified by the assumption that no exchange transactions are carried out at disequilibria so that demand and supply are expressed as functions of prices only. In other words, it is a preliminary process of adjustments in prices carried out before exchange transactions take place, which can sometimes be seen in some well organized markets like stock exchanges. The assumption of tâtonnement can be justified if the speed of adjustment in prices is high so that the effect, if any, on demand and supply of exchange transactions in disequilibria can safely be ignored.

Consider an $m + 1$ goods economy, where the $m + 1$-th good is the numeraire so that its price $p_{m+1} = 1$. A modern version of tâtonnement process, which was originally considered by Walras in a more unsophisticated way, is

$$\frac{dp_i}{dt} = d_i E_i(p_1, \ldots, p_m) \quad (i = 1, \ldots, m) \tag{5.11}$$

where p_i is the price of the i-th good, t is time, d_i is a positive constant indicating the speed of the adjustment in the i-th market, E_i is the excess demand, i.e., the difference between demand and supply, of the i-th good. In other words, (5.11) implies that the instantaneous rate of change in price is proportional to the excess demand. We can imagine an auctioneer who changes the price according to the excess demand from demanders and suppliers, who in return take the price as given. The behavior of prices through time can be obtained as $p_i(t)$ $(i = 1, \ldots, m)$, by solving (5.11). If prices converge to a set of general equilibrium prices $\overline{p}_1, \ldots, \overline{p}_m$ which satisfies

$$E_i(\overline{p}_1, \ldots, \overline{p}_m) = 0 \quad (i = 1, \ldots, m) \tag{5.12}$$

i.e., if $p_i(t) \to \overline{p}_i$ as $t \to \infty$, $i = 1, \ldots, m$, then the general equilibrium is stable.

The fact that the tâtonnement assumption of no disequilibrium trade is implicit in (5.11) can easily be seen as follows. Consider an exchange economy without

Fig. 5.3

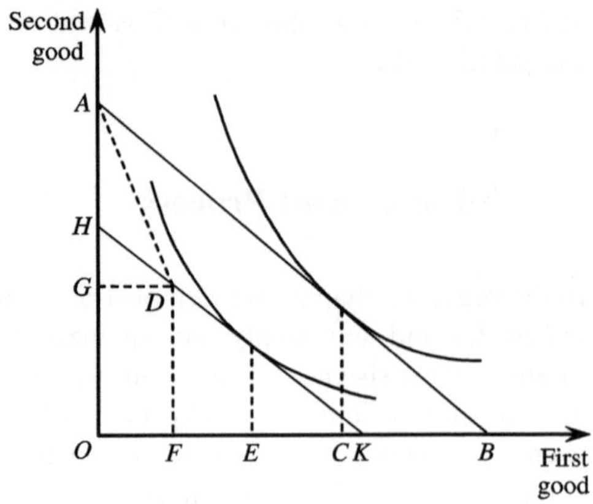

production. Suppose an individual supplies the first good and demands the second. Indifference curves and budget lines of the individual are shown in Fig. 5.3, where the first good is measured horizontally, and the second good, vertically. Originally, the individual possesses *OA* of the second good, and demands *OC* of the first, if the price of the first good is indicated by the slope of *AB*, while the second good is taken as numeraire. Suppose, however, that the price of the first good was initially higher, and the individual actually purchased at this higher disequilibrium price *OF* of the first good. He now possesses only *OG* of the second good, and demand only *OE* of the first good in all, if the price of the first good is indicated by the slope of *AB*, since his budget line is now *HK*. Demand cannot, therefore, be expressed as a function of price only, if exchange transactions are permitted at disequilibrium prices. The possibility of such disequilibrium trade is assumed away in (5.11) and (5.12), where excess demands are considered as functions of prices only. For the sake of simplicity, we shall make this tâtonnement assumption in this chapter, until the so-called non-tâtonnement processes are considered in Sect. 5.10 below.

5.5 Hicksian Stability

Before to solve (5.11) generally, let us consider an interesting special case in which the speed of adjustment d_i's are infinitely large except in one market. Although similar discussion can be made in general cases, for the sake of simplicity we confine ourselves in the case of $m = 3$. Suppose d_2 and d_3 are infinitely large in (5.11) for $m = 3$. Now (5.11) is reduced to (5.13)

$$\frac{dp_1}{dt} = d_1 E_1(p_1, p_2, p_3),$$
$$0 = E_2(p_1, p_2, p_3),$$
$$0 = E_3(p_1, p_2, p_3) \tag{5.13}$$

since the second and third markets can be considered as always in equilibrium. To discuss the stability, i.e., the convergence of the solution $p_1(t)$, $p_2(t)$, $p_3(t)$ of (5.13) to a general equilibrium $\overline{p_1}$, $\overline{p_2}$, $\overline{p_3}$ at which E_1, E_2 and E_3 vanish, consider a linear system approximated at $\overline{p_1}$, $\overline{p_2}$, $\overline{p_3}$,

$$\frac{dp_1}{dt} = d_1(E_{11}q_1 + E_{12}q_2 + E_{13}q_3),$$
$$0 = E_{21}q_1 + E_{22}q_2 + E_{23}q_3,$$
$$0 = E_{31}q_1 + E_{32}q_2 + E_{33}q_3 \tag{5.14}$$

where $q_i = p_i - \overline{p}_i$ and $E_{ij} = \frac{\partial E_i}{\partial p_j}$, evaluated at the general equilibrium, $i, j = 1, \ldots, 3$. The solution of (5.13) can be approximated by the solution of (5.14), provided that it remains in the neighborhood of the general equilibrium. In other words, the stability of the latter solution implies the local stability of the former.

If the solution of (5.14) is $q_1 = c_1 e^{rt}$, $q_2 = c_2 e^{rt}$, $q_3 = c_3 e^{rt}$, where c_i and r are unknown constants, q_i's converge to 0 as $t \to \infty$, if $r < 0$. To obtain the condition for the negative r, substitute $q_i = c_i e^{rt}$ into (5.14). Since $e^{rt} \neq 0$, we have

$$(d_1 E_{11} - r)c_1 + d_1 E_{12} c_2 + d_1 E_{13} c_3 = 0,$$
$$E_{21} c_1 + E_{22} c_2 + E_{23} c_3 = 0,$$
$$E_{31} c_1 + E_{32} c_2 + E_{33} c_3 = 0 \tag{5.15}$$

which has a non-zero solution for c_i's only if

$$\begin{vmatrix} (d_1 E_{11} - r) & d_1 E_{12} & d_1 E_{13} \\ E_{21} & E_{22} & E_{23} \\ E_{31} & E_{32} & E_{33} \end{vmatrix} = 0. \tag{5.16}$$

By solving (5.16) for r, the condition for the negative r is

$$r = \frac{d_1 |A|}{A_{11}} < 0 \tag{5.17}$$

where A is a 3×3 matrix of E_{ij} and A_{11} is the cofactor of E_{11} of A. This is a dynamic interpretation of Hicksian (imperfect) stability condition, which was originally obtained by Hicks rather statically.

Since one cannot tell easily whether the condition (5.17) is satisfied or not, it is convenient to have some sufficient conditions for (5.17). One such condition is the assumption of the gross substitutability that $E_{ij} > 0$ for all $i \neq j$. In view of substitutability and complementarity among goods discussed in Chaps. 2 and 3, we can assume the gross substitutability if all the goods are substitutes and consumers' income effects are not so strong.

To show that the gross substitutability is sufficient for Hicksian stability, let us remember that there are actually four goods in our $m = 3$ case and the excess demand $E_i(p_1, p_2, p_3, p_4)$ is homogeneous of degree zero with respect to p_1, p_2, p_3 and p_4. From Euler's theorem on homogeneous function,

$$E_{i1}p_1 + E_{i2}p_2 + E_{i3}p_3 + E_{i4}p_4 = 0 \quad (i = 1, \ldots, 4) \tag{5.18}$$

from which we know that $E_{ii} < 0$ and $p_i|E_{ii}| > p_j E_{ij}$ for all $i \neq j$, if gross substitutability $E_{ij} > 0$ $(i \neq j)$ is assumed. At the general equilibrium $(\overline{p}_1, \overline{p}_2, \overline{p}_3, 1)$, therefore,

$$Ap = u \quad \text{or} \quad p = A^{-1}u \tag{5.19}$$

where $p = (\overline{p}_1, \overline{p}_2, \overline{p}_3) > 0$ and $u = (-E_{14}, -E_{24}, -E_{34}) < 0$. All the cofactors of A are positive, since $p_i|E_{ii}| > p_j E_{ij}$ and $E_{ij} > 0$. For example, the cofactor of E_{11} is $E_{22}E_{33} - E_{32}E_{23} > 0$, that of E_{12} is $-E_{21}E_{33} + E_{31}E_{23} > 0$, and that of E_{13} is $E_{21}E_{32} - E_{31}E_{22} > 0$. All the elements of A^{-1} are negative, therefore, if $|A|$ is negative. In (5.19), however, $|A|$ cannot be positive, since $p > 0$ and $u < 0$. From (5.17), then, Hicksian stability is demonstrated.

The concept of Hicksian stability is convenient for the study of comparative statics, which compares two equilibria statically, i.e., ignoring what happens in dynamic passage between them. If a is a parameter indicating consumers' taste concerning the choice between the first and fourth goods, general equilibrium prices are determined by

$$\begin{aligned} E_1(p_1, p_2, p_3, a) &= 0, \\ E_2(p_1, p_2, p_3) &= 0, \\ E_3(p_1, p_2, p_3) &= 0 \end{aligned} \tag{5.20}$$

where we assume $\dfrac{\partial E_1}{\partial a} = E_{1a} > 0$ without losing the generality. To compare two equilibria before and after a change in a, let us differentiate (5.20) with respect to a and obtain $\dfrac{dp_i}{da}$. By solving

$$E_{11}\frac{dp_1}{da} + E_{12}\frac{dp_2}{da} + E_{13}\frac{dp_3}{da} = -E_{1a},$$
$$E_{21}\frac{dp_1}{da} + E_{22}\frac{dp_2}{da} + E_{23}\frac{dp_3}{da} = 0,$$
$$E_{31}\frac{dp_1}{da} + E_{32}\frac{dp_2}{da} + E_{33}\frac{dp_3}{da} = 0 \tag{5.21}$$

we have

$$\frac{dp}{da} = A^{-1}v \tag{5.22}$$

where $\frac{dp}{da} = \left(\frac{dp_1}{da}, \frac{dp_2}{da}, \frac{dp_3}{da}\right)$ and $v = (-E_{1a}, 0, 0)$.

From Hicksian stability, therefore, $\frac{dp_1}{da} > 0$. This is because $\frac{A_{11}}{|A|}$, i.e., the first row and the first column of A^{-1} is negative from (5.17). The use of stability condition here is justified, since the comparison of two equilibria does not make sense unless the new equilibrium can be reached through the adjustment process (5.13). If the gross substitutability is assumed, furthermore, $\frac{dp_i}{da} > 0$ for all i, since all the elements of A^{-1} are negative. An increase in the demand for a good raises not only the price of that good but also the prices of all the other goods. Let us note the formal similarity between input–output analysis and more traditional general equilibrium analysis under gross substitutability.

5.6 Frobenius Theorem

To discuss the stability of the solution of the linearly approximated version of not (5.13) but (5.11), it is convenient to have some knowledge on the so-called Frobenius theorem on positive matrices. A matrix composed of all positive elements is called a positive matrix. The solution s of

$$|sI - B| = 0 \tag{5.23}$$

where I, B and s are identity matrix, a square matrix and a scalar unknown, is called a characteristic root of the matrix B. Frobenius theorem assures that a positive matrix B has a positive real characteristic root. Although the theorem can be proved for the general case, we confine ourselves to confirm it for the case of 3×3 matrix.

Consider an equation is s,

$$\begin{vmatrix} s-b_{11} & -b_{12} & -b_{13} \\ -b_{21} & s-b_{22} & -b_{23} \\ -b_{31} & -b_{32} & s-b_{33} \end{vmatrix} = 0 \tag{5.24}$$

where b_{ij}'s are all positive. Assuming without the loss of generality that $b_{33} > b_{22} > b_{11}$, define $s_1 = b_{33} > 0$. Since b_{32} and b_{23} are positive, $F(s) = (s-b_{22})(s-b_{33}) - b_{23}b_{32} < 0$ if $s = s_1$. $F(s) = 0$ has, therefore, a solution $s_2 > s_1 > 0$. The left-hand side of (5.24) can be written as

$$\begin{aligned} G(s) &= (s-b_{11})[(s-b_{22})(s-b_{33}) - b_{23}b_{32}] \\ &\quad - (-b_{12})[(-b_{21})(s-b_{33}) - b_{31}b_{23}] \\ &\quad + (-b_{13})[b_{21}b_{32} + b_{31}(s-b_{22})] \end{aligned} \tag{5.25}$$

which is negative at $s = s_2$, since $s_2 > b_{33} > b_{22}$. $G(s) = 0$ has, therefore, a largest positive solution $s_3 > s_2 > 0$. This is the Frobenius root of the positive 3×3 matrix B composed of b_{ij}'s.

It can also be shown that this Frobenius root is larger than the real part of any other solutions s of (5.24). To see this, rewrite $G(s) = 0$ as

$$G(s) = (s-s_3)(s^2 + as + b) = 0 \tag{5.26}$$

where a and b are constants. The solutions of $(s^2 + as + b) = 0$ are generally two conjugate complex numbers and their identical real part is $-\dfrac{a}{2}$. Comparing the coefficients of s^2 terms in (5.24) and (5.26), we have$3s_3 > \sum_i b_{ii} = s_3 - a$ and $s_3 > -\dfrac{a}{2}$, from which we can conclude that s_3 is larger than the real part of any other solutions.

Finally, consider a matrix C with positive non-diagonal elements $c_{ij} > 0 (i \neq j)$, which has negative diagonal elements $c_{ii} < 0$. This matrix can be transferred into a positive matrix $cI + C$, where a positive real number c is properly chosen. It is clear that the real part of all the characteristic roots of $cI + C$ are larger by c than the real part of the corresponding characteristic root of C. In the case of 3×3 matrix,

$$|sI - cI - C| = (s-c)^3 + a(s-c)^2 + b(s-c) + d = 0 \tag{5.27}$$

where a is the sum of $-c_{ii}$, b is the sum of 2×2 principal minors of C, $c_{ii}c_{jj} - c_{ij}c_{ji}$, and d is $(-1) \times$ the determinant of C. If all the 2×2 principal minors are positive and the determinant of C is negative, then, $(s_3 - c)$ should be negative, where s_3 is the Frobenius root of $cI + C$ which satisfies (5.27). Since s_3 is larger than the real part of any other characteristic roots of $cI + C$, and the real part of characteristic root of C is smaller by c than the real part of the corresponding root of $cI + C$, this implies that the real part of all the characteristic roots of C are negative.

5.7 The Local Stability

We are now ready to discuss the local stability of a competitive equilibrium through the adjustment process (5.11), for which the study of the behavior of the solution of

$$\frac{dq_i}{dt} = d_i(E_{i1}q_1 + E_{i2}q_2 + E_{i3}q_3) \quad (i = 1, \ldots, 3) \tag{5.28}$$

is sufficient. In (5.28), $q_i = p_i - \overline{p}_i$ and $E_{ij} = \dfrac{\partial E_i}{\partial p_j}$, evaluated at the general equilibrium $\overline{p}_1, \overline{p}_2, \overline{p}_3 \quad (i, j = 1, \ldots, 3)$. By substituting particular solution $q_i(t) = c_i e^{rt}$ $(i = 1, \ldots, 3)$ into (5.28) we have

$$\begin{bmatrix} d_1E_{11} - r & d_1E_{12} & d_1E_{13} \\ d_2E_{21} & d_2E_{22} - r & d_2E_{23} \\ d_3E_{31} & d_3E_{32} & d_3E_{33} - r \end{bmatrix} \begin{bmatrix} c_1 \\ c_2 \\ c_3 \end{bmatrix} = \begin{bmatrix} 0 \\ 0 \\ 0 \end{bmatrix} \tag{5.29}$$

since $e^{rt} \neq 0$. This has a non-zero solution for c_i's only if the determinant of the matrix in the left-hand side of (5.29) is zero,

$$|rI - D| = 0 \tag{5.30}$$

where D is 3×3 matrix composed by $d_i E_{ij}$'s. In other words, the unknown constant r can be obtained as characteristic roots of the matrix D.

The general solution of (5.28) is given by

$$q_i(t) = \sum_{p=1}^{s} Q_{ip}(t) \exp(r_p t) \quad (i = 1, \ldots, 3) \tag{5.31}$$

where $s \leq 3$ is the number of simple roots of D and $Q_{ip}(t)$ is a polynomial in t of degree at most one less than the number of times the p-th characteristic root of D is repeated and r_p is the p-th simple root of D. Because exponential terms dominate polynomials, the existence of Q_{ip}'s in (5.31) has no effect on the asymptotic behavior of $q_i(t)$ as $t \to \infty$. Generally, some characteristic roots may be complex numbers. If $r_p = a_p + b_p i$, however, $\exp(r_p t) = \exp(a_p t b_p i t) = \exp[a_p t(\cos b_p t + i \sin b_p t)]$. Since $\cos b_p t$ and $\sin b_p t$ are bounded, then, the asymptotic behavior of $q_i(t)$ is determined by the real parts of the characteristic roots of D, and necessary and sufficient condition for the local stability is that the real parts of all characteristic roots of D are negative.

This stability condition is satisfied if we assume that all the goods are gross substitute so that $d_i E_{ij} > 0$ for $i \neq j$. As we discussed in Sect. 5.5, from the homogeneity of excess demand functions $E_i(p_1, p_2, p_3, p_4)$ $(i = 1, \ldots, 3)$, the gross substitutability implies that $d_i E_{ii} < 0$ and that $d_i p_i |E_{ii}| > d_i p_j E_{ij}$ for all $i \neq j$. The latter result implies further that all the 2×2 principal minors of 3×3 matrix D, $d_i E_{ii} d_j E_{jj} - d_i E_{ij} d_j E_{ji}$, are positive. Finally, again as was shown in Sect. 5.5, the determinant $|A|$ of 3×3 matrix A of E_{ij} is negative, so that the determinant $|D|$ of the matrix D is also negative. In other words, the principal minors of the matrix D alternate in sign, if all the goods are gross substitutes.

Now let us consider a positive matrix $cI + D$, where c is a positive constant larger than the absolute value of all the diagonal elements of D, i.e., $d_i E_{ii}$. The real part of the characteristic roots of D is smaller by c than the real part of the corresponding characteristic roots of $cI + D$. Since the principal minors of D alternate in sign, the Frobenius root of $cI + D$ is smaller than c, as was shown in Sect. 5.6. This implies the stability condition that the real part of all the characteristic roots of D are negative, since Frobenius root of a positive matrix is larger than the real part of all the characteristic roots.

5.8 The Global Stability

So far we have been considering an $m + 1$ goods economy, where prices are normalized by making the $m + 1$-th good numeraire so that $p_{m+1} = 1$. In this case, actually, the equilibrium set of prices is unique, if all the goods are gross substitutes. Suppose not. Let $p = (\overline{p}_1, \overline{p}_2, \overline{p}_3, \overline{p}_4)$ and $p' = (\overline{p}'_1, \overline{p}'_2, \overline{p}'_3, \overline{p}'_4)$ $(\overline{p}_4 = \overline{p}'_4 = 1)$, are both equilibrium prices in the case of $m = 3$. Since prices are normalized, p' is not a scalar multiple of p, so that $p' \neq sp$ for any positive constant s. Without loss of generality, suppose that $\dfrac{p_1}{p'_1} = \min_i \left(\dfrac{p_i}{p'_i}\right)$ $(i = 1, \ldots, 4)$. From the homogeneity of excess demand functions, $E_1(p'') = E_1(p')$, where $p'' = \dfrac{p_1}{p'_1} p'$. Since $p''_i < p_i$ for $i \neq 1$, $E_1(p'') < E_1(p) = 0$ from the gross substitutability, which is, however, a contradiction with our supposition that p' is an equilibrium. Since the equilibrium set of prices is unique, we can consider the local stability of the solution of (5.11) in the neighborhood of the equilibrium, by using (5.28) which is a linear approximation to (5.11) at the equilibrium.

The different goods are, however, treated asymmetrically in the adjustment process (5.11), since the relative price of a non-numeraire good and the numeraire good is changed according only to the excess demand for the former, while there is no role for the excess demand for the numeraire good. Unless a special role is assigned to a particular good in the process of exchange (like money), it is desirable to treat all the goods symmetrically in the adjustment process. Instead of (5.11), then, we have to consider a non-normalized process

$$\frac{dp_i}{dt} = d_i E_i(p_1, \ldots, p_{m+1}) \quad (i = 1, \ldots, m+1) \tag{5.32}$$

for the $m + 1$ goods economy, where E_i's are homogeneous of degree zero in $p_1, \ldots, p_{m+1}$. Equilibrium set of prices $(\overline{p}_1, \ldots, \overline{p}_{m+1})$ are not unique, since prices are not normalized by the choice of numeraire and any positive scalar multiple of an equilibrium set of prices is also an equilibrium from the homogeneity of excess demand functions. Now it does not make sense to consider the local stability in the neighborhood of a particular equilibrium, and we have to consider more globally whether the solution of (5.32) converges to any equilibrium set of prices or not.

First of all, we can show that the solution of (5.32) remains bounded in the sense that $\sum_i \frac{p_i(t)^2}{d_i}$ remains unchanged through time, since

$$\frac{d\left[\sum_i \frac{p_i(t)^2}{d_i}\right]}{dt} - 2\sum_i p_i E_i = 0 \tag{5.33}$$

in view of (5.32) and Walras' law. In addition to this, to show the stability, we have to demonstrate that a kind of distance to equilibrium is always decreasing through time. Several examples of such distance, which is called Liapounoff function, have been found for the case in which all the goods are gross substitutes. Among them, what is most interesting is the one suggested by M. Allais, $V(t) = \sum_i p_i(t)|E_i(p_1(t), \ldots, p_{m+1}(t))|$, since we can intuitively grasp the economic significance of this distance to equilibrium. To show that $V(t)$ is always decreasing through time, let us first note that $V(t) = \sum_i p_i|E_i| = 2\sum_i p_i \max(0, E_i)$ $= (-2)\sum_i \min(0, E_i)$, in view of Walras' law $\sum_i p_i E_i \equiv 0$. In other words, the sum of absolute value of excess demands is equal to twice the sum of positive excess demands and also to twice the absolute value of the sum of negative excess demands.

For the sake of simplicity, consider the four goods case and, without losing the generality, suppose that the first and second goods have positive excess demand and the third and fourth goods have negative excess demand at a certain point of time, i.e., $V(t) = 2(p_1E_1 + p_2E_2) = -2(p_3E_3 + p_4E_4)$, at $t = t_0$. By differentiating $V(t)$ at $t = t_0$, we have

$$\begin{aligned}\frac{dV(t)}{dt} &= \sum_i \frac{\partial V}{\partial p_i}\frac{dp_i}{dt} \\ &= \frac{\partial(-2p_3E_3 - 2p_4E_4)}{\partial p_1} d_1 E_1 \\ &+ \frac{\partial(-2p_3E_3 - 2p_4E_4)}{\partial p_2} d_2 E_2 \\ &+ \frac{\partial(2p_1E_1 + 2p_2E_2)}{\partial p_3} d_3 E_3 \\ &+ \frac{\partial(2p_1E_1 + 2p_2E_2)}{\partial p_4} d_4 E_4 < 0 \end{aligned} \tag{5.34}$$

in view of (5.32) and the assumption of gross substitutability, $\frac{\partial E_i}{\partial p_j} > 0 \ (i \neq j)$, since E_1 and E_2 are positive and E_3 and E_4 are negative at $t = t_0$. Similarly, we can show that $V(t)$ is always decreasing through time, though the composition of groups of goods with positive and negative excess demands changes as prices change through time. Although we have to clear some mathematical problems like the fact that $V(t)$ cannot be differentiated everywhere to prove the stability rigorously, it is intuitively evident that prices converge to equilibrium, since the sum of absolute value of excess demands always decreases through time.

5.9 Instability of an Equilibrium

A question remains is whether the tâtonnement adjustment process (5.32) is generally stable without any restrictions such as gross substitutability. Unfortunately, the answer is no, because we have an example of instability due to Scarf. Consider the case of three goods three individuals exchange economy, i.e., $m = 2$, in (5.32). Let the utility function of the first, second and third individuals, respectively, be $U_1(x_{11}, x_{12}, x_{13}) = \min(x_{11}, x_{12})$, $U_2(x_{21}, x_{22}, x_{23}) = \min(x_{22}, x_{23})$ and $U_3(x_{31}, x_{32}, x_{33}) = \min(x_{33}, x_{31})$ and the initial holding of goods be $\overline{x}_{ij} = 1$ for $i = j$, and $\overline{x}_{ij} = 0$ for $i \neq j$. In other words, each individual desires only two goods, which are perfectly complementary, i.e., desired only in the fixed ratio (one to one in this case). For example, the indifference curves of the first individual for the first two goods are L shaped as is shown in Fig. 5.4, and the first individual has no desire for the third good.

Fig. 5.4

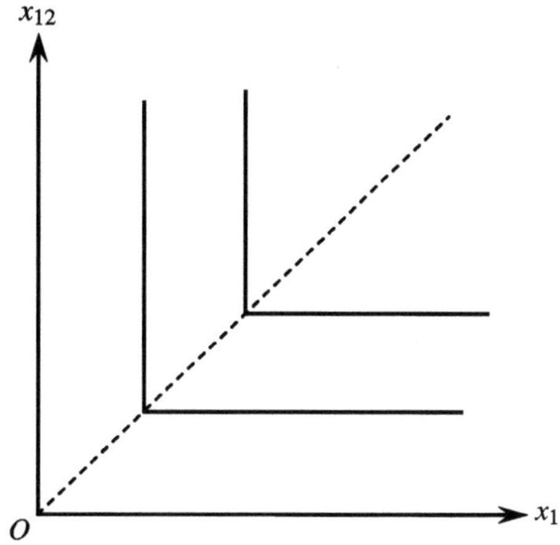

Routine calculations show that the excess demand for each good is

$$E_1 = -\frac{p_2}{p_1 + p_2} + \frac{p_3}{p_3 + p_1},$$
$$E_2 = -\frac{p_3}{p_2 + p_3} + \frac{p_1}{p_1 + p_2},$$
$$E_3 = -\frac{p_1}{p_3 + p_1} + \frac{p_2}{p_2 + p_3} \tag{5.35}$$

and that $p_1 = p_2 = p_3$ is the only equilibrium possible. For the sake of simplicity, let us assume that $d_1 = d_2 = d_3 = 1$ in (5.32) for $m = 2$. As was already confirmed in Sect. 5.8, then, $\sum_i p_i(t)^2$ remains unchanged through time. Consider a solution of (5.32) for $m = 2$ and (5.35) which starts with initial prices $p_1(0)$, $p_2(0)$, $p_3(0)$ such that $p_1(0)^2 + p_2(0)^2 + p_3(0)^2 = 3$ and $p_1(0)p_2(0)p_3(0) \neq 1$. Since the only possible equilibrium is such that $p_1 = p_2 = p_3$ and $\sum_i p_i^2 = 3$, the equilibrium to which this solution can ever converge is $p_1 = p_2 = p_3 = 1$. By differentiating with respect to time, however, it can also be shown that $p_1(t)p_2(t)p_3(t)$ remains unchanged through time along with this solution. This implies that generally the equilibrium cannot be approached by solution of (5.32) where excess demands are given as (5.35).

What is the implication of the existence of this counter-example to the stability of a competitive equilibrium? Unless some restrictions like the gross substitutability are imposed on the form of excess demand functions, it is generally impossible for the adjustment process (5.32) to approach a competitive equilibrium. Does this imply the inability of the law of supply and demand to establish a competitive equilibrium? Not necessarily. As was pointed out in Sect. 5.4, the adjustment process like (5.11) and (5.32) are constructed on the basis of a very special assumption of tâtonnement that no exchange transactions take place until an equilibrium is reached. In other words, the effect of exchange transaction at disequilibria is ignored in tâtonnement processes. This assumption can be justified if the process is stable and an equilibrium is quickly established. If the process is not stable, however, the effect of disequilibrium transactions cannot be ignored and the relevancy of tâtonnement processes is greatly reduced. In the above example of the instability, the result is dependent not only on the assumption on the form of utility functions but also on the assumption on the distribution of the initial holdings which is assumed to be unchanged through time by the tâtonnement assumption. If disequilibrium transactions are not ruled out, the distribution of goods among individuals, i.e., $\overline{x}_{ij}$'s are changed through time and the assumption that $\overline{x}_{ii} = 1, \overline{x}_{ij} = 0$ is not assured. Excess demands are not like (5.35) and the instability might not be demonstrated. In other words, we have to consider the adjustment process in which effects of disequilibrium transactions are duly introduced, before we conclude whether the law of supply and demand can establish a competitive equilibrium.

5.10 Non-tâtonnement Process

Now let us leave the world of tâtonnement process and consider non-tâtonnement process, i.e., an adjustment process in which exchange transactions are actually carried out at disequilibrium prices. While recontract is possible in tâtonnement in the sense that all the contracts made at disequilibria are preliminary and can be cancelled without the agreement of the other parties, recontract is not possible in non-tâtonnement process and disequilibrium exchange transactions are effective and cannot be cancelled after prices are changed. Consider an $m + 1$ goods n individuals exchange economy without production, where each individual is endowed with initial holdings of goods. Unlike in the case of tâtonnement, however, current stock of goods held by individuals can be made different from their initial holdings by exchange transactions carried out among individuals at disequilibria. Even though such transactions themselves do not change the value of stocks held by individuals at the prices prevailing at the time of exchange transactions, the current value of individuals' stock of goods can be different from that of initial holdings, since prices are changed in disequilibria. Demand for goods are, therefore, no longer the functions of prices only, and must depend on the current distribution of goods among individuals.

We have to extend (5.32), for example, into

$$\frac{dp_j}{dt} = d_j E_j(p_1, \ldots, p_{m+1}, \overline{x}_{11}, \ldots, \overline{x}_{n,m+1}) \quad (j = 1, \ldots, m + 1) \qquad (5.36)$$

where $\overline{x}_{ij}$ is the current stock of the j-th good held by the i-th individual, since $\overline{x}_{ij}$'s are functions of time t and generally different from their initial value $\overline{x}_{ij}(0)$, i.e., the given initial holdings, and E_j's are defined as $E_j = \sum_i x_{ij} - \sum_i \overline{x}_{ij}(0)$, where x_{ij}'s are obtained by the maximization of the utility being subject to the budget constraint $\sum_j p_j x_{ij} = \sum_j p_j \overline{x}_{ij}$ $(i = 1, \ldots, n,\ j = 1, \ldots, m+1)$. Even though $\sum_i \overline{x}_{ij} = \sum_i \overline{x}_{ij}(0)$ in an exchange economy, it is clear that an individual demand x_{ij} depends on his current stock of goods $x_{i1}, \ldots, x_{i,m+1}$ and the excess demand E_j depends on the current distribution of goods among individuals.

The process of exchange at disequilibria can generally be described by

$$\frac{d\overline{x}_{ij}}{dt} = F_{ij}(p_1, \ldots, p_{m+1}, \overline{x}_{11}, \ldots, \overline{x}_{n,m+1}) \quad (i = 1, \ldots, n,\ j = 1, \ldots, m+1) \tag{5.37}$$

where F_{ij}'s are some unknown functions incorporating rules of exchange transactions out of equilibrium. For example, $\sum_i F_{ij} = 0$ $(j = 1, \ldots, m+1)$, in an exchange economy. Furthermore, since to get something one must offer something else of the same value in return,

$$\sum_j p_j F_{ij} = 0 \quad (i = 1, \ldots, n) \tag{5.38}$$

has to be satisfied.

By solving (5:36) and (5.37), we obtain the dynamic behavior of prices p_j's and the distribution of goods $\overline{x}_{ij}$'s as functions of time in a non-tâtonnement process. The concept of equilibrium with respect to such process is very wide. Any Pareto optimal distribution of goods can be an equilibrium, if the marginal rates of substitution between any goods, which are identical for all the individuals, and prices are proportional. The question remains is whether the solution of non-tâtonnement process converges to such a set of equilibria, even if no restrictive assumptions are made on che form of excess demand functions.

Suppose chat the so-called short-side principle, i.e., demand or supply whichever is smaller is realized in the market, prevails in exchange transaction out of equilibrium so that

$$\text{sign}(x_{ij} - \overline{x}_{ij}) = \text{sign}\Big(\sum_i x_{ij} - \sum_i \overline{x}_{ij}\Big), \quad \text{if} \quad x_{ij} - \overline{x}_{ij} \neq 0. \tag{5.39}$$

The implication of this condition is as follows. If there is an aggregate excess supply in the market of the j-th good, all individual demanding the j-th good will be able to satisfy their demand, while some supplying individuals will be left with unsold goods. Therefore, after exchange, there remain only negative individual excess demands (positive excess supplies). If there is an aggregate excess demand in the market of the j-th good, all supplying individuals will find they can supply all they had planned, while some demanding individuals will have their demands unsatisfied, with the result that all the remaining individual excess demands are positive.

Differentiating the budget constraint of the i-th individual, we have

$$\sum_j p_j\left(\frac{dx_{ij}}{dt} - \frac{d\overline{x}_{ij}}{dt}\right) + \sum_j \frac{dp_j}{dt}(x_{ij} - \overline{x}_{ij}) = 0. \tag{5.40}$$

From (5.37) to (5.40), then, we have $\sum_j p_j \frac{dx_{ij}}{dt} < 0$ in disequilibrium. Now consider $\sum_i U_i(x_{i1}, \ldots, x_{i,m+1})$, i.e., the sum of utilities, as a Liapounoff function. By differentiating it with respect to time, we have

$$\sum_{i,j} \frac{\partial U_i}{\partial x_{ij}} \frac{dx_{ij}}{dt} = \sum_i \lambda_i \sum_j p_j \frac{dx_{ij}}{dt} < 0 \tag{5.41}$$

in disequilibrium, where λ_i is the marginal utility of income, a positive function of time t. From (5.41) we can show that the non-tâtonnement process is stable. At disequilibria, individuals are expecting the level of utilities higher than can be realized at equilibria, but disequilibrium level of utilities are always decreasing through time, which explains intuitively that the system is approaching to equilibria.

There is a possibility, however, that the short-side principle (5.39) conflicts with another plausible rule for disequilibrium transactions, the voluntary exchange principle that no one can oblige any agent to exchange more than he wants, or in the other direction. A way to get rid of this difficulty is to introduce a medium of exchange, i.e., money, and to require the voluntary exchange principle only for nonmonetary goods. This requirement is plausible, since we often have more money than we wanted to keep ultimately, temporarily after the sale and before purchase. It is interesting to see that a non-tâtonnement process requires the introduction of money as a medium of exchange while such a role of money does not exist in a tâtonnement process in which transactions are carried out simultaneously and instantaneously only at equilibrium.

Problems

5.1. In Sect. 5.2, we utilized the fact that $p > 0$ and $v > 0$ in the base year rather than $x > 0$ and $c > 0$. Discuss the possibility of the case in which some c_i is negative.

5.2. In Fig. 5.2, explain that the combination of net output of two goods corresponding to the mid-point between H and G is produced by allocating half the labor supply to the first industry and other half, to the second industry.

5.3. Suppose that the price of a good is adjusted according to the difference between demand and supply and that the supply of the good is adjusted according to the difference between price and marginal cost. In terms of the slope of demand and supply curves, derive (Walrasian) stability condition for the case where the latter adjustment is instantaneous and (Marshallian) stability condition for the case where the former adjustment is instantaneous.

5.4. From the point of view of Hicksian stability and gross substitutability, discuss the stability of foreign exchange by the use of four goods model composed of the exportables, the importables, the domestic currency and the foreign currency.

5.5. Demonstrate that the gross substitutability is sufficient for Hicksian stability by using not homogeneity but Walras' law.

5.6. Explain that the stability of the solution of a linearly approximated system like (5.14) is sufficient but not necessarily necessary for the stability of the solution of the original non-linear system like (5.13).

5.7. If r_p is a complex number in (5.31) in Sect. 5.7, does it mean that $q_i(t)$ cannot be a real number? Consider the role of initial conditions to determine $Q_{ip}(t)$.

5.8. From the point of view of non-tâtonnement process, discuss the implications of two examples of non-existence of equilibrium given in Sect. 4.5.

5.9. Prove that the non-tâtonnement process (5.36) and (5.37) is stable if the assumptions (5.37) and the gross substitutability are assumed.

Literature

For further studies in input–output analysis, see R. Dorfman, P.A. Samuelson and R.M. Solow, *Linear Programming and Economic Analysis* (1958), pp. 204–264, and R.R. Cornwall, *Introduction to the Use of General Equilibrium Analysis* (1984), pp. 93–140.
See Hicks, op. cit., pp. 315–319, Malinvaud, op. cit., pp. 138–143, Varian, op. cit., pp. 188–196 for further studies in general on the stability problem. Also useful are J. Quirk and R. Saposnik, *Introduction to General Equilibrium Theory and Welfare Economics* (1968), pp. 149–216, A. Takayama, *Mathematical Economics* (1974), pp. 295–358, and G. Gandolfo, *Economic Dynamics: Methods and Models* (1980), pp. 263–299, 395–412. Frobenius and related theorems are explained in Takayama, op. cit., pp. 359–409.

For tâtonnement and non-tâtonnement processes in particular, see Arrow and Hahn, op. cit., pp. 324–346, and Negishi, op. cit., pp. 207–227. See also Negishi, *Microeconomic Foundations of Keynesian Macroeconomics* (1979), pp. 20–24.

Chapter 6
Perfect and Imperfect Competition

6.1 Market Structure

So far we have been assuming that markets are perfectly competitive and consumers and firms are taking market prices as given. The assumption is justified by the supposition that there are very large number of consumers and firms so that market prices are not much affected by the actions of any single consumer or firm. As a result of perfect competition, equilibrium prices are equalized to marginal costs. Perfect competition is, however, an exceptional polar case, which should be regarded as an idealistic or limiting situation, since many firms are not taking prices as given and prices are, in general, different from marginal costs in the real world. While perfectly competitive markets are homogeneous and resemble one another as happy families, imperfectly competitive markets are heterogeneous and imperfect, like unhappy families, in many different ways.

Traditionally, such diversified cases of imperfect competition are firstly classified according to the numbers of sellers and buyers in the markets. A market with a large number of buyers and a single seller is a monopoly, while one with a large number of sellers and a single buyer is a monopsony. The case with one seller and one buyer is called bilateral monopoly. Having a large number of buyers, a market with two sellers is called a duopoly while one with several sellers is called an oligopoly. If the situations of buyers and sellers are interchanged, duopoly and oligopoly become, respectively, duopsony and oligopsony. Any combination of different cases in different markets is possible for a single firm. A firm might be a monopolist in the market for a product, a perfect competitor in the market for another product, and a duopsonist in a factor market.

Imperfect markets are further classified with regard to product differentiation. In the case of perfect competition, all firms in the same industry produce a single homogeneous product and buyers are indifferent between the outputs of the various firms. In duopoly and oligopoly, however, the products of different firms may be close substitutes but differentiated in the eyes of buyers. Monopolistic competition has, like perfect competition, a large number of firms, but each small firm sells

T. Negishi, *Elements of Neo-Walrasian Economics*, Advances in Japanese Business and Economics 5, DOI 10.1007/978-4-431-54535-4_6, © Springer Japan 2014

a differentiated product so that it is a monopolist as far as its own product is concerned. The difference between monopoly and the monopolistic competition is that in the latter case entry is free and excess profit disappears in the long run.

An effect of the product differentiation is to reduce the number of sellers effectively to one for a product. Traditional approach, which classifies markets according to the number of firms and product differentiation, therefore, seems to emphasize that the small number of firms makes the price of a product different from its marginal cost. There are, however, some arguments, as we shall see, which insist that prices are equalized to marginal costs even if the number of firms is small. This may suggest that what makes the competition imperfect is not so much the small number of competitors as the cost of information and communication and the cost of organizing cooperation.

6.2 Monopoly

Traditional theory of imperfect competition starts with the case of a monopoly, a polar case directly opposite to that of the perfect competition. The theory of monopoly was essentially worked out by A. Cournot in 1838. The demand function for the product of a monopolist is the demand function for the industry, which is an aggregate of the demand functions of individual consumers. If we assume that the corresponding demand curve is downward sloping,

$$q = D(p) \quad \left(\frac{dq}{dp} < 0\right) \tag{6.1}$$

where p is the price consumers take as given and q is the aggregate quantity demanded by them. Then, the inverse demand function

$$p = p(q) \quad \left(\frac{dp}{dq} < 0\right) \tag{6.2}$$

is obtained from (6.1). This implies that if the monopolist supplies q of the product, the price which clears the market is p. The profit of the monopolist to be maximized with respect to q is

$$p(q)q - C(q) \tag{6.3}$$

where $p(q)q$ is the revenue from the sales of q and $C(q)$ is the total cost of producing q. The condition for the maximization is

$$p\left(1 + \frac{q}{p}\frac{dp}{dq}\right) = \frac{dC}{dq} \tag{6.4}$$

Fig. 6.1

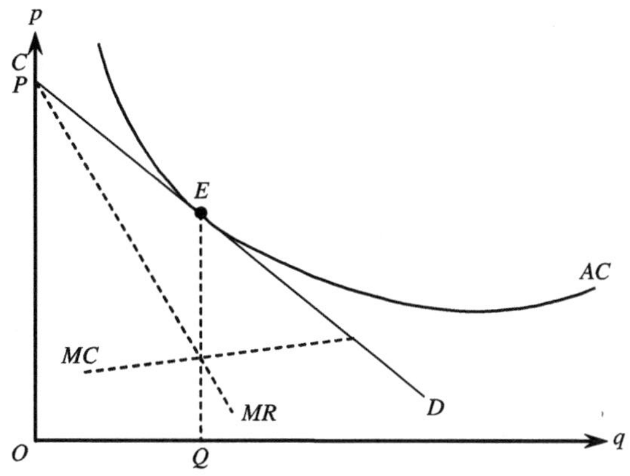

where the left-hand side is the marginal revenue and the right-hand side is the marginal cost. Since the elasticity of demand $-\dfrac{(dq/q)}{(dp/p)}$ is positive and less than 1, the marginal revenue is less than p. In other words, the price of the monopolistic product is higher than the marginal cost.

The condition for the equilibrium of a firm in monopolistic competition is also (6.4), if we interpret (6.1) as the demand function of a differentiated product of the firm, when the price of products of all the other firms in the industry are assumed to be given and unchanged. Unlike in the case of monopoly, however, the entry of new firms to the industry is free in the case of monopolistic competition. If the level of profit is higher in the industry than the general or normal level of profit elsewhere in the economy, the number of firms is increased with the result that the demand curve for the firm is shifted downward. Figure 6.1 shows the long-run equilibrium of a firm in monopolistic competition, when the industry is in equilibrium so that the number of firms remains unchanged. The curve *AC* shows the average cost which include the normal profit. The equilibrium level of supply q is *OQ* at which the marginal revenue *MR* is equalized with the marginal cost *MC*. The corresponding equilibrium price p is *QE* at which the firm's demand curve *D* is tangent to the *AC* curve so that the maximized profit is just equal to the normal profit. The demand curve *D* is drawn on the assumption that all the other firms in the industry charge the same price *QE* respectively for their differentiated products.

The theory of monopolistic competition is a hybrid of the theory of monopoly and the theory of perfect competition. In perfect competition, the number of firms is sufficiently large so that each small firm assumes that it has no perceptible influence on market prices. In monopolistic competition, the number of firm is sufficiently large so that each small firm assumes that its actions have no perceptible influence on each of his competitors and draws its demand curve on the assumption of unchanged prices of products of other firms. There is, however, an important difference between perfect competition and monopolistic competition. In the former, the average cost should be non-decreasing so as to make the maximized profit non-negative at the level of output at which price is equalized to marginal cost. In the latter, however, the average cost should be decreasing at the long-run equilibrium, as is seen in Fig. 6.1, since it must be tangent to the downward sloping demand curve.

6.3 Cournot's Oligopoly Theory

Unlike in the case of perfect competition and monopolistic competition, the number of firms is sufficiently small so that the actions of any individual firm have a perceptible influence on its rivals in the case of duopoly and oligopoly. In other words, the situation is the one for the theory of games, since the outcome depends upon the actions of participants with mutually conflicting interests. As a matter of fact, the classical solution of the problem of duopoly and oligopoly suggested by Cournot is the one called Nash solution in the modern theory of games. The strategy combination $s^* = (s_1^*, \ldots, s_n^*)$ in a n-person non-cooperative game, where s_i is a strategy available to the i-th player, is called a Nash solution, if it is impossible that any single player can obtain a higher payoff through the use of different strategy, given the strategy choices of the other $n - 1$ players. If p_i denotes the payoff to the i-th player, s^* is a Nash solution, if

$$p_i(s^*) \geq p_i(s_1^*, \ldots, s_{i-1}^*, s_i^*, s_{i+1}^*, \ldots, s_n^*) \tag{6.5}$$

for any possible s_i and for $i = 1, \ldots, n$.

Consider the case of a duopoly. The condition for the equality of demand and supply is $q_1 + q_2 = D(p)$, where D is the demand for the industry given as a decreasing function of the price p in (6.1), and q_1 and q_2 are respectively quantities to be supplied from two firms. It is convenient to consider the inverse demand function $p = f(q_1 + q_2)$ as in (6.2). The profit of the first firm is

$$f(q_1 + q_2)q_1 - C(q_1) \tag{6.6}$$

and that of the second firm is

$$f(q_1 + q_2)q_2 - C(q_2). \tag{6.7}$$

In other words, the profit of a firm is a function not only of its own supply but also of the supply of the other firm. Cournot considered the Nash solution that each firm will independently maximize its profit, assuming that the supply of the other is unchanged. The conditions for it are obtained by the differentiation of (6.6) and (6.7) respectively with respect to q_1 and q_2,

$$f(q_1 + q_2) + q_1 f'(q_1 + q_2) - C'(q_1) = 0 \tag{6.8}$$

and

$$f(q_1 + q_2) + q_2 f'(q_1 + q_2) - C'(q_2) = 0 \tag{6.9}$$

where f' and C' denote the derivatives of f and C.

Since two firms are enjoying the entirely identical conditions, we should have $q_1 = q_2$ at equilibrium. By adding (6.8) and (6.9) together, therefore, we have

$$2f(q) + qf'(q) - 2C'\left(\frac{q}{2}\right) = 0 \tag{6.10}$$

where $q = q_1 + q_2$.

Similarly, in the case of oligopoly of n firms, the i-th firm's profit is

$$f\left(\sum_i q_i\right)q_i - C(q_i) \quad (i = 1, \ldots, n) \tag{6.11}$$

where q_i $(i = 1, \ldots, n)$ is the supply of the i-th firm. The condition to maximize (6.11) with respect to q_i is given as

$$f\left(\sum_i q_i\right) + q_i f'\left(\sum_i q_i\right) - C'(q_i) = 0 \quad (i = 1, \ldots, n) \tag{6.12}$$

if the other firms' supplied q_j $(j \neq i)$ are considered unchanged. Conditions are identical for all firms, and we should have $q_1 = q_2 = \cdots = q_n$ in (6.12). Adding n conditions together in (6.12), then, we have

$$nf(q) + qf'(q) - nC'\left(\frac{q}{n}\right) = 0 \tag{6.13}$$

where $q = \sum_i q_i$.

Being based on (6.13), Cournot insisted that the price p is equalized to the marginal cost C' when the number of firms is infinitely large and the competition is unlimited, i.e., the case of the perfect competition. To see this, let us simplify the story by assuming that the demand function is linear and that the marginal cost is constant. By substituting $p = f(q) = a - bq$ and $C'\left(\frac{q}{n}\right) = c$, where a, b and c are positive constants, into (6.13), we obtain

$$q = \frac{n(a - c)}{b(n + 1)}. \tag{6.14}$$

The substitution of (6.14) into $p = a - bq$ yields

$$p = \frac{a + nc}{n + 1}. \tag{6.15}$$

If n is infinitely large, then, the price p approaches to the marginal cost c. The competitive price is a limit of oligopoly prices when the number of oligopoly firms is infinitely large. This limit theorem of Cournot is a pioneering contribution to the theory of a large economy (an economy with infinitely large number of participants) which is a central topic of modern mathematical economics.

6.4 Post-Cournot Theories

In view of Cournot's limit theorem, we have to admit that the existence of infinitely many firms is a sufficient condition for the perfect competition in which a single firm perceives an infinitely elastic demand curve. It is, however, by no means a necessary condition. Even for the case of $n = 2$, that is, a duopoly, Bertrand argued in 1883 to the effect that the price will be equalized to the marginal cost if each duopolist assumes that the other will keep its price (not supply) unchanged and identical average as well as marginal costs are constant. If the price is higher than the cost, each firm will undercut its rival by a very small margin because it will monopolize the market and obtain maximum profit by undercutting infinitesimally. This process continues until the price is equalized to the marginal cost. In other words, a Bertrand-type duopolist behaves as if he perceived an infinitely elastic demand curve. Bertrand's assumption can be criticized, of course, since duopolists will know, when they are out of equilibrium or when they decide to test their assumption, that their assumption are incorrect; their rival do not keep their prices constant. But Cournot's assumption of unchanged supplies from rivals is also subject to the same criticism, and we cannot accept Cournot and at the same time reject Bertrand.

The basic assumption of Cournot's theory of duopoly is that each firm changes its supply assuming that the supply of the other firm is unchanged. In other words, each firm adjust its supply to the given supply of the other. In Bowley's terminology, conjectual variations are zero for both firms. Stackelberg called such a behavior of firms as followership. If a firm acts as a follower, however, the other firms can make a larger profit by taking advantage of it. Suppose the first firm chooses q_1 in accordance with (6.8) when q_2 is given. The second firm can consider q_1 as a function of q_2 and make its conjectual variation

$$\frac{dq_1}{dq_2} = \frac{f' + q_1 f''}{C'' - q_1 f'' - 2f'} \tag{6.16}$$

by differentiating (6.8), where f'' and C'' are second derivatives of f and C. The second firm's supply to maximize its profit is then obtained by the substitution of (6.16) into

$$f(q_1 + q_2) + q_2 f'(q_1 + q_2) + q_2 f'(q_1 + q_2)\frac{dq_1}{dq_2} - C'(q_2) = 0 \tag{6.17}$$

and by the replacement of (6.9) with (6.17). Stackelberg called such an active behavior of a firm as leadership. While Cournot's duopoly equilibrium is follower–follower equilibrium, a leader–follower equilibrium is certainly a possible alternative. If both firms act as leader, however, there is no equilibrium. This is the problem of Stackelberg disequilibrium.

A recent development is to consider a multi-period model of duopoly which allows for collusion without requiring the firms to make binding agreements. Consider the maximization of joint profit of two identical firms. The condition for it is

$$f(2q^m) + 2q^m f'(2q^m) - C'(q^m) = 0 \tag{6.18}$$

where q^m signifies the supply of each single firm, f is the inverse demand function (6.2) and C is a common cost function. Let us denote Cournot solution which satisfies (6.8) and (6.9) by $q_1 = q_2 = q^c$. Obviously $\frac{p^m}{2} > p^c$, where p^m and p^c denote, respectively, the maximized joint profit and the profit of each single firm corresponding to q^c. Suppose the time horizon of two firms is infinite and the second firm openly announces the following strategy. In the first period, the second firm supplies q^m, and it continues to do so in the future provided that the first firm also supplies q^m in each period. If the first firm does not supply q^m in a period, the second firm supplies q^c in the future. For the first firm, there are two alternative reactions possible. Firstly, it can supply q^m in the first period and also in the future, so that it can enjoy profit $\frac{p^m}{2}$ in all periods. Secondly, given the supply q^m of the second firm in the first period, the first firm may maximizes its profit in the first period, the condition for which is

$$f(q_1 + q^m) + q_1 f'(q_1 + q^m) - C'(q_1) = 0. \tag{6.19}$$

The profit of the first firm corresponding to q_1 which satisfies (6.19) is larger than $\frac{p^m}{2}$. The first firm can expect, however, no more profit than p^c in the future since the second firm supplies q^c in this case. Unless the rate of the time preference of the first firm is very high, therefore, it is possible to have the case of tacit collusion of duopoly firms or self-enforcing agreements between them.

6.5 Edgeworth's Limit Theorem

It is interesting to compare Cournot's limit theorem (Sect. 6.3) and Edgeworth's limit theorem. The former starts with monopoly, which is extended to duopoly and oligopoly, and describes the perfect competition as the limit of oligopoly, where the

Fig. 6.2

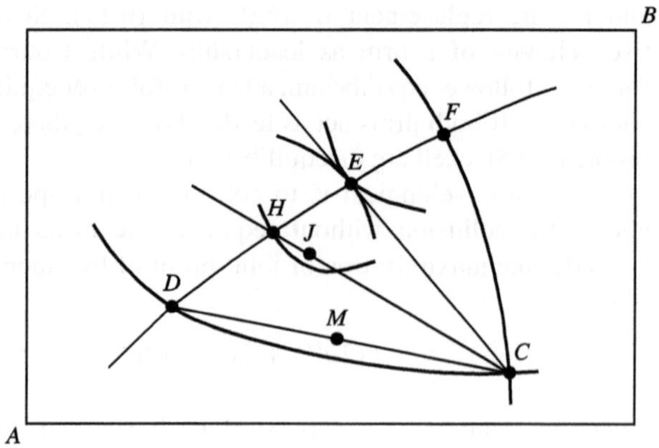

number of firms is infinitely large. Edgeworth's starting point is the case of bilateral monopoly in an exchange economy, where two traders exchange two goods between them, and the perfect competition is explained as the limiting case where two goods are exchanged between two infinitely large homogeneous groups of traders. The latter theorem is demonstrated by the so-called Edgeworth Box Diagram, i.e., Fig. 6.2 which is a reproduction of Fig. 4.2 in Sect. 4.3. The quantity of the first good is measured horizontally, and that of the second good, vertically. Goods to be distributed to trader A is measured from the origin A, while those distributed to trader B, from the origin B. The curve $DHEF$ is the contract curve, the locus of points where indifference curves of two traders are tangent to each other. The point C is the initial point, which indicates the distribution before exchange. In the case of two traders, A and B, the equilibrium is indeterminate, since it can be any point on the contract curve between D and F in Fig. 6.2.

Suppose then that there are four traders, two identical (in taste and initial holding) traders in each group, i.e., trader A_1 and trader A_2 of type A and trader B_1 and trader B_2 of type B. It is evident that equal quantities of goods should be allocated to identical traders of the same type, after, for example, A_1 traded with B_1 and A_2 traded with B_2. Suppose not. If two identical traders are not equally favoured, such a distribution is blocked by the coalition of two traders who are less favoured in each group, since they can be better off by themselves. If two identical traders are equally favoured, the distribution is again blocked by the coalition of two traders of the same group. We can, therefore, still use Fig. 6.2 to consider the exchange between four traders, by interpreting the figure that it describes the trade between the representative traders of each homogeneous group of identical traders.

Distribution D on the contract curve, which can be an equilibrium in the case of two traders, can now be blocked by a coalition of A_1, A_2 and either one of B_1 and B_2. Suppose A_1 and, say, B_1 who joins the coalition keep the trade contract D between them while A_2 cancels the contract D with B_2 who does not join the coalition and returns to C. Thus, A_1, A_2 and B_1 can arrange by themselves in such a way that, whilst B_1 remains at point D, A_1 and A_2 reach the mid-point M between

D and C, thereby achieving a higher level of utility than at D. With some further redistribution among themselves, all the traders joining coalition A_1, A_2 and B_1, can be better off by themselves than they are at D, and the all distribution D is blocked. Any distribution on the contract curve and close to D can be blocked similarly by the same coalition. Similarly, distribution F or those distributions on the contract curve and close to F can be blocked by a coalition of both B_1 and B_2, and any one of A_1 and A_2. Thus, the range of possible equilibria is less indeterminate in the case of four traders than in the case of two traders. Distributions like H in Fig. 6.2, however, cannot be blocked by the coalitions of three traders among four traders, and belong to the core, i.e., the set of distributions which cannot be blocked by coalitions of traders. The reason why H cannot be blocked is that at the mid-point between H and C traders of type A cannot achieve a higher level of utility than at H.

Let us now consider the case where there are infinitely many identical traders of type A and infinitely many identical traders of type B. In this case, any distribution on the contract curve, except that of the perfect competition E, can be blocked by a coalition of traders. For example, consider the distribution H in Fig. 6.2. This distribution can be blocked by a coalition formed by all the A traders and more than half but less than all the B traders. In the coalition some A traders still continue trade with B traders in the coalition and are located at H, while the rest of A traders having no trade partners in the coalition are located at C. By increasing the number of B traders joining the coalition sufficiently and therefore increasing the number of A traders located at H, we can make the average distribution to A traders (some at H, some at C) sufficiently close to H, on the line CH, that it is located like J above the indifference curve of A passing through H. By redistribution among themselves, therefore, all the traders joining the coalition can be better off than they are at H, so that H is blocked by such a coalition. Similarly, any point between D and F where the common tangent to two indifference curves does not pass through C can be blocked by a coalition of traders, if necessary, by changing the role of A traders and B traders from those in the case of H. Only the distribution E of the perfect competition can belong to the core in this case.

6.6 A Cooperative Theory of Duopoly (1)

Both Cournot's theorem and Edgeworth's theorem insist that the perfect competition is a limiting case where the number of participants of the market is infinitely large. There are, however, several important differences between two theorems. While oligopolists act independently and non-cooperatively in Cournot's theorem, traders cooperate to organize coalitions and to block unfavourable distributions in Edgeworth's theorem. Unless the number of firm is infinite, Cournot's oligopoly equilibrium is not Pareto optimal, since the price is not equalized to marginal cost. Even in the case of bilateral monopoly, however, indeterminate equilibria are Pareto optimal in Edgeworth's cooperative game, since they are on the contract curve. While the law of indifference, i.e., one price for one good, is assumed in Cournot's

Fig. 6.3

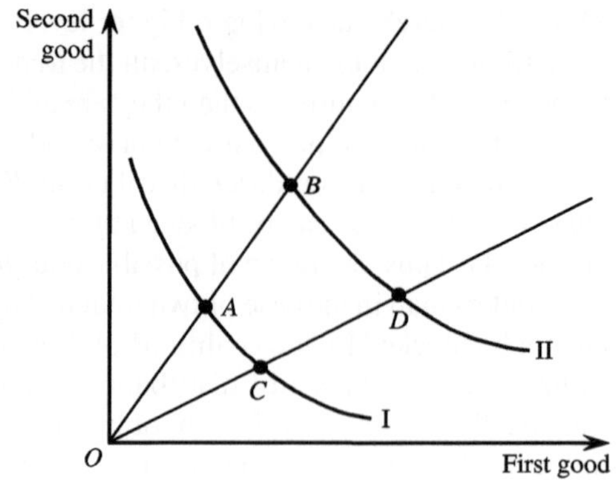

oligopoly theory, it is not required in Edgeworth's game of exchange, except for the case of perfect competition where it is not assumed but demonstrated. Traders are not assumed to be price takers, therefore, in Edgeworth's explanation of the perfect competition. Finally, as we shall see, the duopoly equilibrium can be shown to be equivalent to the equilibrium of the perfect competition in Edgeworth's cooperative game, which is absolutely impossible in Cournot's non-cooperative game.

Suppose there are only two traders of one type and infinitely many traders of another type, though the total quantities of two goods are finite. Since equal quantities of goods should be distributed to identical traders of the same type, we can still use Edgeworth box diagram, Fig. 6.2, which now describes the half of the economy, one of the duopolists and its infinitely many customers. We have to, however, assume that identical indifference curves of infinitely many traders are homothetic so that the marginal rate of substitution between two goods depends only on the ratio of the quantities of goods, as is shown in Fig. 6.3. Since the slope of indifference curves are identical at A and B, and at C and D, we can aggregate indifference curves I of two identical traders into aggregate indifference curve II which is also an indifference curves of individual traders when quantities of two goods are doubled. In general, homothetic indifference curves of infinitely many identical traders can be interpreted as aggregate indifference curves as well as indifference curves of individual traders.

Let us suppose first that there are two B traders, B_1 and B_2 and infinitely many traders of type A. In Fig. 6.2, C seen from B indicates the quantity of two goods initially held by a B trader, and, seen from A, indicates the aggregate quantity of two goods initially held by the half of A traders. A distribution H can now be blocked by a coalition of one B trader and more than half but less than all of infinitely many A traders. All the A traders currently trading with B_1 trader which joins the coalition also join the coalition and keep the trade contract H with B_1. Some A traders currently trading with B_2 which does not join the coalition join the coalition and cancel the contract with B_2 to return to the initial holdings. Suppose, for the moment, indifference curves and points H and C are not aggregate but individual. By decreasing the number of the latter type A traders joining the coalition sufficiently and therefore increasing the number of A traders located at H, relative to those A traders located at C, we can make the average distribution to individual A traders in the coalition sufficiently close to that at the point H, on the line *CH*, so that it is like the distribution at J located above the indifference curve passing through H. By redistribution among themselves, therefore, all the traders joining the coalition can be better off than they are at H, so that H is blocked.

Suppose next that there are two A traders, A_1 and A_2 and infinitely many traders of type B. In Fig. 6.2, C indicates initial holdings of one A traders and those of half the B traders, respectively. In this case, the distribution H can be blocked by a coalition of one A trader and the less than half of infinitely many B traders. Suppose A_1 joins the coalition. Those B traders also joining the coalition can keep trade with A_1 unchanged so that they can keep the same level of utility as enjoyed at the distribution H. A_1 cancels trade with those B traders who are not permitted to join the coalition, so that A_1 moves on *HC* from H toward C. Unless it cancels too many contracts with B traders, A_1 can be located like at J above the indifference curve passing through H. By the redistribution among themselves, then, all the traders joining the coalition can be made better off than they are at H, so that H is blocked.

Similarly, any point between D and F on the contract curve where the common tangent to two indifference curves does not pass through the point C can be blocked by a coalition of traders, if necessary, by changing the role of A traders and B traders from those in the case of H. Again, it is only the point E which belongs to the core. In other words, in Edgeworth's exchange game, even a duopoly market ends up with an equilibrium identical to that of the perfect competition, if customers are infinitely many and free to organize coalitions.

6.7 A Cooperative Theory of Duopoly (2)

Since the model of a duopoly discussed in the previous section is the case of pure exchange economy, it may be desirable to transform it into the model of duopoly with production. Let us start with Cournot's duopoly, where infinitely many identical customers are equally divided between two identical firms. Assume that marginal cost is constant. Figure 6.4 describes a duopolist and its customers, i.e., a half of infinite consumers. Duopolist's product is measured horizontally, and money, vertically. An aggregate indifference curve is drawn with two aggregate budget lines *AB* and *FG*. The marginal cost is indicated by the slope of line *CD*. The equilibrium of Cournot duopoly is at *D*, where the price of the product is higher than the marginal cost, since the slope of *AB* is steeper than that of *CD*. Since consumers' aggregate money income is *AO*, and the marginal cost is constant and equal to the average cost, the profit of a duopolist is *AC*, which is assumed not to be distributed to the customers of this duopolist.

Firstly, Cournot equilibrium D is converted into a marginal cost pricing equilibrium E, where the price of the product is equalized to the marginal cost, since the line *FG* is parallel to the line *CD*. In other words, D can be blocked by a coalition

Fig. 6.4

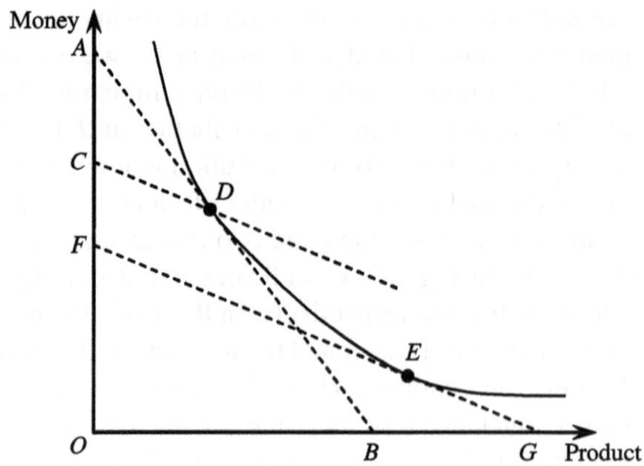

of a duopolist and its customers. While consumers are indifferent between D and E, the profit of the firm is increased by CF, since the firm collects the entrance fee to its market AF from its customers, in addition to the unit price equalized to the marginal cost. The entrance fee is the price for the right to purchase the product of the firm and constant for a consumer irrespective of the quantity of the product to be purchased. The marginal cost pricing equilibrium with the entrance fee is not unique. There are many others than E, which are more favourable to consumers but less favourable to the firm with the entrance fee less than AF but more than AC. Identical consumers have to achieve, of course, the same level of utility, and identical firms have to make the same amount of profit, at any marginal cost pricing equilibrium with entrance fee. We can show, however, that any such marginal cost pricing equilibria can be blocked by a coalition of consumers and a firm, provided that the entrance fee is positive.

Figure 6.5 shows indifference curves of an individual consumer, from which the aggregate indifference curve of Fig. 6.4 is constructed. Having money income AO initially, a consumer pays the lump sum entrance fee AB first, and then purchases OF of the product of a duopolist at the unit price equalized to the constant marginal cost, which is indicated at the slope of the line BD. The point C in Fig. 6.5 corresponds to the point E in Fig. 6.4, i.e., a marginal cost pricing duopoly equilibrium with positive entrance fee. Such an equilibrium can be blocked by a coalition of a duopolist and more than half but less than all of infinitely many consumer. In other words, the coalition is made by a duopolist and all of its current customers and some of customers of the other firm.

A duopolist and its current customers, who join the coalition, keep the current trade unchanged, so that the duopolist makes the profit AF in Fig. 6.4 while each current customer is located at C in Fig. 6.5. The consumers who are customers of other duopolist but join the coalition terminate their current trade with the other duopolist, so that each of them is located at point A in Fig. 6.5. If the number of consumers of the latter type is chosen properly, then, the average position of consumers in the coalition can be made, like the point E in Fig. 6.5, on the line

Fig. 6.5

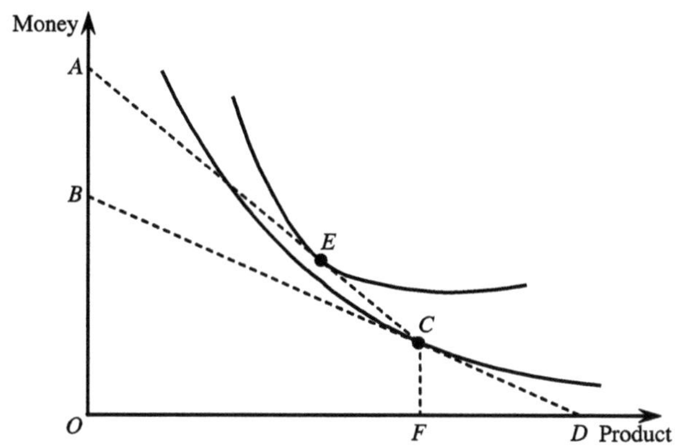

AC and on an indifference curve higher than the one passing C. By redistribution among themselves, therefore, a duopolist and consumers joining the coalition can be made better off than at the original equilibrium by themselves. This can be done, for example, in the following way. Consumers located at C in Fig. 6.5 make resale CE of the product to consumers located at A at the average, not the marginal, price at which they purchased from the duopolist, i.e., the price indicated by the slope of the line AC. Then, all the consumers located at E pay some amount of money to the duopolist (an entrance fee for the coalition?). Alternatively, a duopolist joining the coalition cancels old traders with current customers and newly offers such a contract to all the consumers in the coalition that the unit price is equal to old average price but the entrance fee is very low. In other words, a duopolist can organize the coalition to block the old equilibrium by attracting larger number of consumers through very low entrance fee which is compensated by higher marginal price.

Thus, even the equilibrium of a duopoly market is equivalent to that of the perfect competition, if each duopolist can freely communicate with customers of other firm and attract them by more favourable conditions so as to make its own profit larger, since it is only the case where A equalized with B in Fig. 6.5 that cannot be blocked by coalitions considered above. Of course, the assumptions of perfect information and free communication are very unrealistic in many industries. In this sense, the theory of non-cooperative duopoly and oligopoly may be more realistic than that of cooperative ones. This suggests, however, that what makes the competition imperfect is not so much the small number of firms in industries as the cost of information, communication, negotiation and organization.

6.8 Kinked Demand Curve

If information is not perfect, and communication is difficult so that cost of organizing coalitions is large, the competition is imperfect and the price of the product is not equalized with the marginal cost, even if the number of firms in the

Fig. 6.6

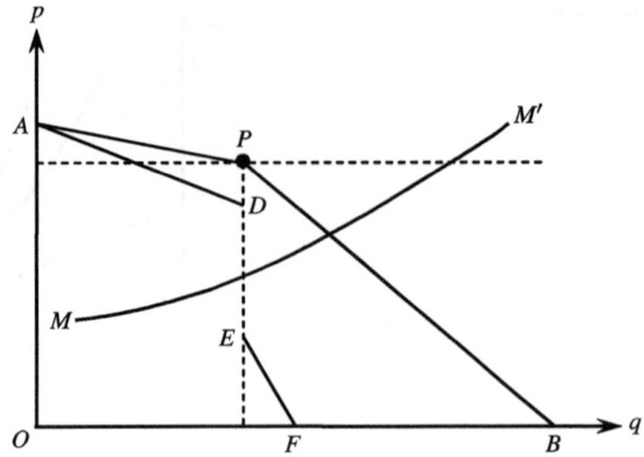

market is large. In the perfect competition, price taking firms perceive infinitely elastic demand curves for their products. Since information is perfect, demand can be increased infinitely by a slight reduction of the price. If information is not perfect, however, an increase in demand is limited, since lower price asked by a firm may not be fully informed to consumers who are currently buying from other firms. Even if it is informed, some of such consumers, who are not informed of the quality of the product of price cutting firm, may not shift their demand to the firm, unless the reduction of price is considerable. Firms have to perceive, then, downward sloping demand curves for the reduction of prices. On the other hand, a higher price charged by a firm necessarily induces present customers to leave in search of lower price firms, even if such search activities involve some costs. Firms have to perceive, therefore, fairly elastic demand curves for higher prices. In other words, firms perceive kinked demand curves which are due to the asymmetric behavior of consumers.

Traditionally, kinked demand curves are considered, not in the case of large number of firms as in the above, but in the case of small number of firms, with asymmetric behavior of rival firms in their oligopolistic mutual interdependence. P. Sweezy insisted that an oligopolist's perceived demand curve can only be thought of with reference to a given starting point, that is, a price–output combination that depends upon the history of the case. In Fig. 6.6, where the quantity q is measured horizontally and the price p vertically, the point P is such a starting point, that is, the point of currently realized price and the sale of output of an oligopolistic firm. The firm perceives a subjective demand curve from this starting point. It is pointed out that rival firms react asymmetrically according to whether a price change is upward or downward. If the firm raises its price it must expect to lose business to its rivals who will not raise their price, while if the firm cuts its price it has no reason to believe that it will succeed in taking business away from its rivals who will retaliate by cutting their prices so as to avoid the loss. The perceived demand curve tends to be elastic going up and inelastic going down from the starting point P. In other words, it has a corner, or a kink, at P, like APB in Fig. 6.6.

The marginal revenue curve derived from APB is $ADEF$, which has a discontinuity at the level of output where the perceived demand curve has a kink. If the marginal cost curve MM' passes, as in Fig. 6.6, between the two parts of the discontinuous marginal revenue curve, the starting point P is also the point of profit maximization. Sweezy pointed out that any disturbance that affects only the position of the marginal cost curve may leave the equilibrium price and output entirely unaffected. More important for oligopolistic price rigidity is, however, the fact that, as Sweezy stated any shift in demand will clearly first make itself felt in a change in the quantity sold at the current price. In other words, a shift in demand changes the position of the starting point P at which the kink occurs to the right or left without affecting the price. If the marginal cost is not increasing rapidly, the equilibrium price will remain unchanged while shifts in demand are absorbed by changes in the level of output.

A possible application to a recent economic problem may be the inefficacy of changes in rate of foreign exchange to solve the problem of the balance of trade. Suppose that international trade is carried out almost exclusively by specialized firms, i.e., exporters and importers. In other words, the domestic and foreign markets are separate and related only by the activities of domestic and foreign exporters and importers. In the case of perfect competition, changes in the rate of foreign exchange are reflected in the relative price of home and foreign goods in domestic and foreign markets, so that trade deficits or surpluses are cleared by flexible rate of exchange, unless the elasticity of the demand for the goods is very small (see Problem 6.7). Suppose, however, that foreign exporters and domestic importers face kinked demand curves in domestic markets, either because of asymmetric behaviour of consumers or because of asymmetric behaviour of rival firms. The effect of kinked demand curve is the possible rigidity of the price in domestic currency of the foreign goods in the face of changing rate of exchange, since shifts in the marginal cost curves of domestic importers and foreign exporters who buy in foreign markets and sell in domestic markets, are very likely to keep the price of foreign goods charged to domestic consumers unchanged. A changing rate of exchange has, at least in short-run, no price effect and can affect the economy merely through the income effects which are due to foreign exchange gains and losses accrued to exporters and importers, arising from the fact that domestic exporters buy at the price given in terms of home currency and sell at the price given in terms of foreign currency, and domestic importers buy at the price given in terms of foreign currency and sell at the price given in terms of home currency. Similar effects occur also in the foreign markets, and the adjustability of trade balance by the flexible rate of exchange is much reduced, since price effects cannot be expected and income effects are mutually conflicting.

Problems

6.1. Suppose the utility function of identical consumers is log-linear with respect to quantities of goods. Derive the aggregate demand function for a good, and solve for the level of output of identical Cournot duopoly firms with the constant marginal cost.

6.2. Assuming linear demand function, obtain reaction functions of duopolists, which give the level of the output of a duopolist as a function of that of the other. Discuss whether a pair of outputs of two firms converges to Cournot duopoly equilibrium, if two firms determine successively their level of output by reaction functions.

6.3. In the model of tacit collusion of duopoly discussed in Sect. 6.4, the time horizon of firms has to be infinite. Why?

6.4. Explain why the law of indifference cannot be observed in Edgeworth's exchange game of four traders (in Sect. 6.5), if the exchange process starts from C and terminates at H in Fig. 6.2.

6.5. Limit theorems are also called equivalence theorems, since the limiting cases are equivalent to the equilibrium of perfect competition with price taking consumers and firms. Discuss the implications of equivalent theorems for the theory of perfect competition. Do they make the assumptions of price taking behavior and price setting auctioneer unnecessary? Do they make the assumptions more significant?

6.6. By using kinked demand curve, explain the fact that increases in demand and in marginal cost are likely to raise prices while decreases in them are likely to keep prices unchanged (*EF* in Fig. 6.6 may be located below the horizontal axis).

6.7. Define the balance of trade as the difference between the aggregate value of exports and that of imports in terms of domestic currency. The quantity of exports is an increasing function of the relative price of foreign and home goods as the foreign demands of home goods, and the quantity of imports is a decreasing function of the same relative price as the home demands of foreign goods. Derive the condition in terms of demand elasticities for the trade surplus (deficit) to be reduced by a relative rise of the price of home (foreign) goods.

Literature

For further studies in general, see Malinvaud, op. cit., pp. 144–183, and Varian, op. cit., pp. 52–79. See also J. Friedman, *Oligopoly and the Theory of Games* (1977), pp. 15–43, 69–84, and ibid., *Oligopoly Theory* (1983), pp. 19–49, 104–114.
The theory of games is discussed with reference to oligopoly in Friedman (1977), op. cit., pp. 139–172, and ibid. (1983), pp. 207–226. For tacit collusion of duopoly,

see Friedman (1893), op. cit., pp. 123–134. Edgeworth box diagram with unequal numbers is discussed in Friedman (1977), op. cit., pp. 283–285.
The literature on kinked demand curve is nicely surveyed by G.C. Reid, *The Kinked Demand Curve Analysis of Oligopoly* (1981). See also M. Itoh and T. Negishi, *Disequilibrium Trade Theories* (1987), pp. 89–93.

Chapter 7
Optimal Allocation of Resources

7.1 Welfare Economics

Up to now we have been concerned with the description and the analysis of how a market economy, composed of consumers and firms, actually behaves to allocate resources to produce products and to distribute incomes to be spent on them. Our study aims, of course, to consider basic principles of an abstract economy under ideal conditions rather than to describe the details of actual economies. However abstract it is, nevertheless, what we have studied is to be called the positive economics, since it is ultimately to be judged by facts. Ideal or perfect conditions are assumed merely from the point of view of the simplification of the consideration, and not meant to be desirable from some ethical point of view. Theory of perfect competition is, therefore, similar to the law of motion in vacuum.

While the positive economics tries to explain how an economy of the real world works, the welfare economics is a normative study which aims to design and control an economy so that it works ideally or optimally from a certain ethical point of view. In welfare economics, the problem of value judgement cannot be avoided, since it is concerned not with true-or-false problems but with good-or-bad problems. Still, however, it is possible and also necessary to do scientific studies. Firstly, we can consider that a certain value judgement on the aim of an economy is assumed to be given. We have to, then, discuss technically how such an aim can be achieved optimally by using what kind of means available, since a modern economy is a complicated system so that the effect of a policy measure cannot necessarily be found out easily. Secondly, we can and should study how a social decision on the aim of economic policies can be formed from mutually conflicting individual value judgements on it. Welfare economics gives, therefore, a foundation of the study of such economic policies as fiscal, monetary and industrial policies.

It is convenient to divide the problems of welfare economics into two groups, those of optimal (efficient) resource allocation and those of optimal income distribution. In the latter problems individual value judgements are sharply in conflict with each other while for the former problems the problem of value judgement

T. Negishi, *Elements of Neo-Walrasian Economics*, Advances in Japanese Business and Economics 5, DOI 10.1007/978-4-431-54535-4_7, © Springer Japan 2014

is less serious in the sense that they can be considered by the use of an optimal criteria which may be supported unanimously. The so-called fundamental theorem of welfare economics insists that a competitive economy can solve the problems of optimal allocation of resources, provided certain conditions are satisfied. More detailedly, first, a perfectly competitive equilibrium is Pareto optimal, and second, any Pareto optimal allocation of resources can be created by the use of a perfectly competitive market mechanism and a proper redistribution of income. Markets fail, of course, to allocate resources optimally, if the required conditions are not met. While the fundamental theorem of welfare economics is discussed in this chapter, the next chapter will be devoted to consider various market failures. Problems of optimal income distribution will be left to be discussed in Chap. 9.

7.2 The Concept of Consumers' Surplus

Perhaps the oldest and simplest way of demonstrating the optimality of competition is to use the concept of consumers' surplus. Even in the case of an equal value exchange, generally both parties gain in utility. The theory of consumers' surplus is an attempt to measure the gains from exchange in terms of money. Since money is used to measure utility, each unit of money must be assumed to have identical utility, just as the length of a measure has to be unchanged to be able to measure the length of other things. In other words, the marginal utility of money should be constant and not be diminishing as the amount of money is increased. Intuitively, the plausibility of this assumption can be explained as follows. The utility of money signifies here not the utility of money itself but the utility of goods in general which can be purchased with money. The marginal utility of a single good diminishes if its quantity is increased relative to those of other goods. The marginal utility of money remains, however, constant if the quantity of money is increased, since it implies that all the goods are increased in the same proportion.

In Fig. 7.1, we measure the quantity of a certain good horizontally, and the quantity of money, vertically. Curves like *AG* and *BH* are indifference curves of an individual consumer. Since prices of all the goods other than the one measured horizontally are assumed to be given and unchanged, what is measured vertically is the real quantity of money or the purchasing power of money. Suppose the individual has initially *OA* amount of money, and the price in terms of money of the good in question is shown by the slope of the budget line *AF*. The individual chooses the point *C* where an indifference curve is tangent to *AF*. He buys *OE* amount of the good by paying *AK* amount of money. The corresponding consumers' surplus is the difference expressed in terms of money of utility level between the indifference curve *BH* which passes *C* and the indifference curve *AG* which passes *A*. In other words, it is the vertical distance between two indifference curves, which, like *AB* and *DC*, is indeterminate in general, unless the marginal utility of money is constant.

Let us denote by x the quantity of a good measured horizontally in Fig. 7.1, by M the quantity of money measured vertically, and by U the utility of an individual as

Fig. 7.1

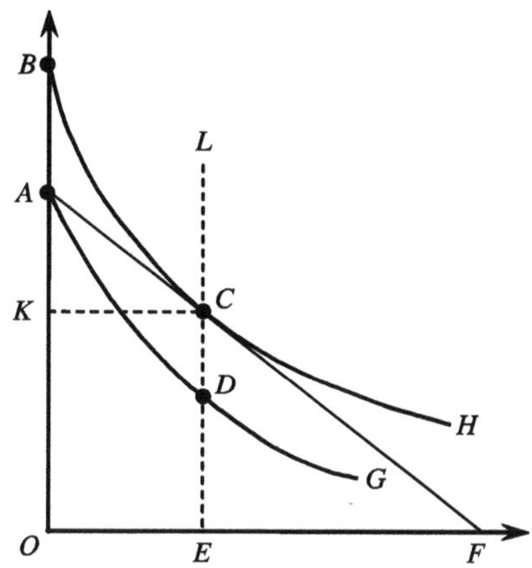

a function of x and M. The constancy of the marginal utility of money $\frac{\partial U}{\partial M}$ implies that $\frac{\partial^2 U}{\partial M \partial x} = 0$ and $\frac{\partial^2 U}{\partial x \partial M} = 0$. In other words, the marginal utility of the good in question $\frac{\partial U}{\partial x}$ remains unchanged when M is changed but x is kept constant. The slope of the indifference curves between x and M remains unchanged if M only is changed, since it is the ratio of the marginal utility of money to the marginal utility of the good. In Fig. 7.1, the slope of the indifference curves at the points, like A and B, or D and C, which have equal abscissas, are identical. Therefore, $AB = CD$, and more generally, the vertical distance between two indifference curves is the same at anywhere. If the marginal utility of money is constant, therefore, U can be expressed in terms of M and the consumers' surplus is determinate.

When the initial amount of money OA is changed, the equilibrium point C moves vertically on EL and there is no changes in the amount of the good purchased OE, provided that the price of the good is unchanged. In other words, the income elasticity of demand for the good is zero and there is no income effect, if the marginal utility of money is constant. This implies that the good in question is not important in the budget of consumers and the proportion of income spent on it is very small in the total income.

To use the concept of the consumers' surplus for the demonstration of the optimality of competition, it is convenient to express it by the use of the demand curve. In Fig. 7.2, the quantity of the good in question is measured horizontally, and the price in terms of money is, vertically. Suppose the curve DD' is the demand curve of the individual in question. Then, the consumers' surplus $AB = CD$ in Fig. 7.1 can be expressed as the area DFA in Fig. 7.2, if the price of the good in terms of money, i.e., the slope of AF in Fig. 7.1, is equal to OF in Fig. 7.2. To show this fact, consider the so-called Roy's identity

Fig. 7.2

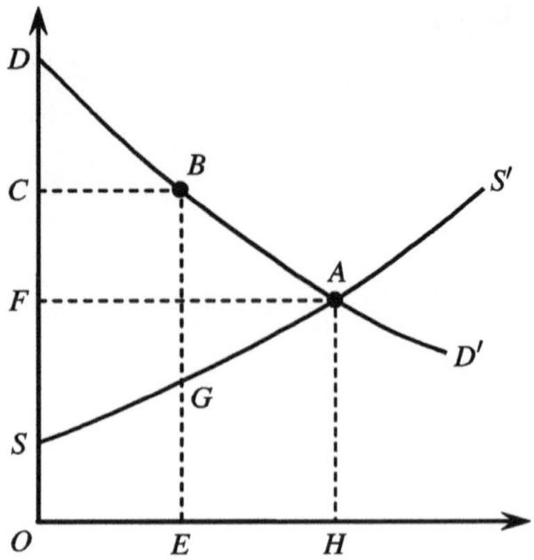

$$x(p) = -\frac{\dfrac{\partial V(p, Y)}{\partial p}}{\dfrac{\partial V(p, Y)}{\partial Y}} \tag{7.1}$$

which we explained in Sect. 3.7, where p, Y, x and V are, respectively, the price of the good in terms of money, the initial amount of money (i.e., *OA* in Fig. 7.1), the demand for the good and the indirect utility function defined in Sect. 3.7. If we integrate (7.1) between from $p_1 = OF$ to $p_0 = OD$ in Fig. 7.2,

$$\int_{p_1}^{p_0} x(p)\, dp = [V(p_1, Y) - V(p_0, Y)] \frac{\partial V(p, Y)}{\partial Y} \tag{7.2}$$

since the marginal utility of money $\frac{\partial V}{\partial Y}$ is constant. The left-hand side of (7.2) is the area *DFA* in Fig. 7.2 while the right-hand side is the consumers' surplus multiplied by the constant marginal utility of money, since x is zero at p_0.

7.3 Consumers' Surplus Analysis

Now let us consider that the curve *DD'* in Fig. 7.2 is the aggregate demand curve of all the consumers in the economy. Since consumers' surplus of each individual is expressed in terms of money and can be added or subtracted, the sum of consumers' surplus of all the consumers can be expressed by the area *DFA*, if the curve *DD'* is the aggregate demand curve. This represents the sum of gains in utility accrued to consumers from the purchase of the good in question up to *OH* at the price *OF*.

In addition to this, however, there is another surplus which is accrued to consumers from the supply of the good.

Suppose the good in question is produced from the inputs of other goods including factors of production. Since prices of such goods are assumed to be given, we can calculate for each firm the minimum cost of production for any level of output. If the price and the level of output of the good in question are specified, then, the difference between their product and the minimum cost of production is the profit of the firm, which is to be distributed to the household of consumers. The curve SS' in Fig. 7.2 is the aggregate supply curve of the industry, which is the industry's marginal cost curve obtained as the horizontal sum of the marginal cost curve of individual firms. The area *FSA* represents the sum of the profit of firms and is called the producers' surplus, when the price and output of the good are respectively *OF* and *OH*, and the fixed cost is assumed away.

The producers' surplus is also a surplus accrued to consumers, since the profit of firms are distributed to the household of consumers. There is no possibility, however, of the shift of aggregate demand curve DD' caused by this distribution of the producers' surplus to consumers. The reason is, as we noted in the previous section, the constancy of the marginal utility of money which makes the income elasticity of demand for the good in question zero. In other words, there is no problem of counting the same thing twice between the consumers' surplus and the producers' surplus. To consider the gains accrued to consumers from the industry in question, therefore, we have to add the producers' surplus to the consumers' surplus.

Suppose that the industry is perfectly competitive, so that the equilibrium price is equalized to the marginal cost. In Fig. 7.2, the good in question is supplied up to *OH* and the price is *OF*. The consumers' surplus is *DFA* and the producers' surplus is *FSA*, so that the total surplus created in the industry is *DAS*. If this competitive industry does not exist and the good in question is not supplied at all, the loss to consumers in utility is represented by the area of *DAS* in terms of money.

Suppose next that the industry is now monopolized so that the supply is reduced to *OE* to make the profit of the monopolistic firm maximized. Now the consumers' surplus is reduced to *DBC* since the price is *OC*, while the producers' surplus is *CBGS* which is, by definition, larger than *FAS*. The total surplus is *DBGS*, which is definitely smaller than the surplus in the competitive case, i.e., *DAS*. The triangle *BAG* is now in the hands of a devil. It is impossible to increase the total surplus by reducing the output from the level of the perfect competition.

Finally, suppose that the industry is competitive but the supply of the good in question is subsidized up to *BG* for a unit in Fig. 7.3, which is a reproduction of Fig. 7.2. The level of output is increased from the *laissez-faire* competitive level *OH* to *OE*. Though the price is *OJ*, the revenue for a unit of the producers is *OC*, including the subsidy *CJ*. The producers' surplus is, therefore, represented by the area *CBS*, which is larger by *CBAF* than the producers' surplus *FAS* of the level of output *OH*. The total subsidy *CBGJ* must be financed by a tax imposed on consumers so that the consumers' surplus is not *DGJ* but smaller than *DGJ* by *CBGJ*. This is smaller than the consumers' surplus *DAF* of the level of output *OH* by the difference between *CBGJ* and *FAGJ*. From the comparison of the decrease

Fig. 7.3

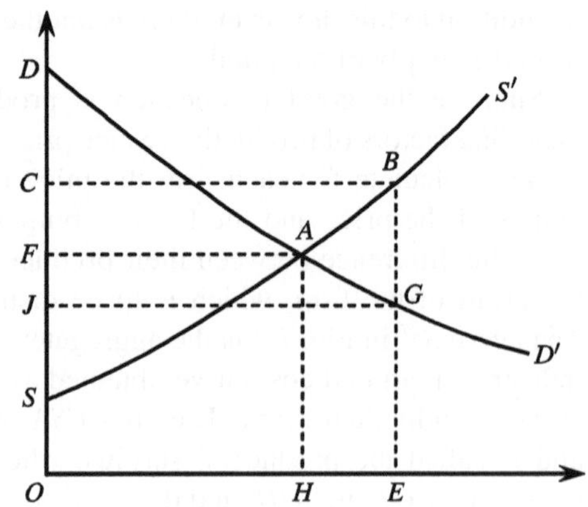

in consumers' surplus *CBGAF* and the increase in producers' surplus *CBAF*, we see that the total surplus is smaller than the one at the level of output *OH* by the triangle *ABG*. It is impossible to increase the total surplus by increasing the output from the level of the perfect competition under *laissez-faire*.

Is the above demonstration of the maximization of the total surplus sufficient for the demonstration of the optimality of competition in which the price is equalized to the marginal cost? Apart from a limiting assumption of the constant marginal utility of money which makes the income elasticity of demand for the good in question zero, there are two fundamental difficulties inherent in the consumers' surplus analysis.

Firstly, it is only a partial equilibrium analysis and not a general equilibrium analysis. The maximization of the total surplus accrued to consumers from an industry is demonstrated when prices of all the goods other than the product of the industry are assumed to be given constants. Generally it is impossible to demonstrate that the total surplus accrued from an entire economy is maximized by the iteration of such a partial equilibrium analysis of surplus from a single industry. At best, it merely shows the local maximization that the perfect competition maximizes surplus of an economy in a small neighborhood of a perfectly competitive general equilibrium point. Although we are the last to deny the consumers' surplus as a useful heuristic tool, the result obtained has to be reconsidered by the general equilibrium analysis.

Secondly, a very strong value judgement is inherent in the consumers' surplus analysis. Individual utilities are assumed to be cardinal and measured in terms of money. They are, then, added or subtracted. It is one thing, however, to assume cardinality of the utility, but it is quite another to make interpersonal comparison of utility. Even if one admits the assumption of the constant marginal utility of money, he can rightly object against the comparability of the consumers' surplus and the producers' surplus, for example, in Fig. 7.2. The value judgement of the consumers' surplus analysis may not be supported unanimously. The owner of the monopolistic firm has a right to reject the conclusion derived from our consumers' surplus analysis in Fig. 7.2. It is desirable, therefore, to base our analysis on a weaker value judgement which may be supported more unanimously.

7.4 General Equilibrium Model of Allocation

To deal with the first difficulty of consumers' surplus analysis mentioned in the above, let us construct a general equilibrium model of allocation of resources, which is very much similar to the general equilibrium model of a market economy considered in previous chapters. Consider an m goods, n consumers and r firms economy. Resources to be optimally allocated are the initial stocks of m goods, to be denoted by $\overline{x}_1, \ldots, \overline{x}_m$, which are, if necessary to be transformed in the production processes of r firms, and eventually to be allocated to n consumers, so as to satisfy some optimal criteria of economic welfare.

The role of r firms is to transform inputs of some goods (including factors of production) into outputs of other goods. Technological restrictions on such transformation is summarized in the production functions of each firm. The k-th firm's production function is

$$f_k(y_{k1}, \ldots, y_{km}) = 0 \tag{7.3}$$

where y_{kj} denotes the output of the j-th good if it is positive, and input of the j-th good if it is negative, $j = 1, \ldots, m$, $k = 1, \ldots, r$. The nature of production function was discussed detailedly in Chap. 2. Since we do not presuppose the market economy, the production vector or input–output vector of each firm $y_k = (y_{k1}, \ldots, y_{km})$ $(k = 1, \ldots, r)$ is not to be chosen so as to maximize profit, but to be determined so as to allocate resources optimally.

Goods to be allocated to the i-th consumer are denoted by the consumption vector $x_i = (x_{i1}, \ldots, x_{im})$, where x_{ij} signifies the quantity of the j-th good to be allocated to the i-th consumer, $i = 1, \ldots n$, $j = 1, \ldots, m$. Each consumer has his utility function $U_i(x_i)$ $(i = 1, \ldots, n)$, the implication of which was discussed detailedly in Chap. 3. Unlike in the market economy, there is no budget constraints for consumers. Allocating f goods to consumers should be done so as to maximize the social welfare which is defined from the point of view of a given value judgement.

An allocation of resources in our general equilibrium model is given by consumption and production vectors, i.e., $(x_1, \ldots, x_n,\ y_1, \ldots, y_r)$. The condition for feasible allocations is, in addition to (7.3),

$$\sum_i x_{ij} = \overline{x}_j + \sum_k y_{kj} \quad (j = 1, \ldots, m). \tag{7.4}$$

In the case of a two goods two consumers economy with no production, any point in the Edgeworth box diagram (Fig. 4.2) is a feasible allocation. For more general cases, however, it is convenient to consider the feasibility in terms of

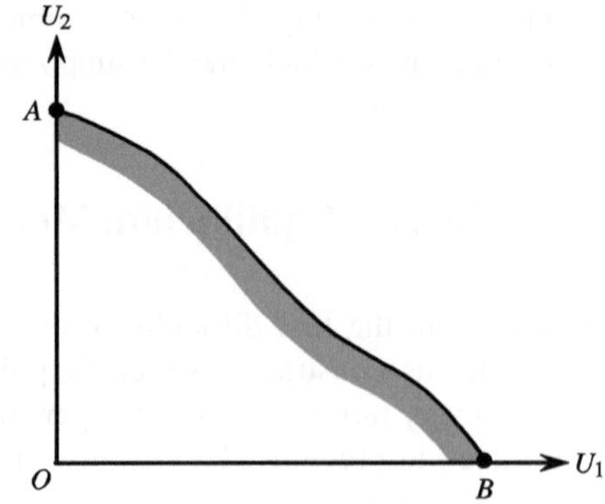

Fig. 7.4

utility of consumers. Consider the set of utilities, $U_1(x_1), \ldots U_n(x_n)$, which satisfies feasibility conditions (7.3) and (7.4). This utility possibility set is bounded, in view of the given initial stocks $\overline{x}_1, \ldots, \overline{x}_m$, and the nature of production and utility functions. In the case of two consumers economy, the set is the shaded area in Fig. 7.4 (see Problem 7.4). The curve AB is called the utility frontier.

Suppose we are given a value judgement on social welfare called consumer sovereignty which may be supported unanimously in a modern democratic society. The problem of optimal resource allocation is then reduced to choose some points in the utility possibility set, from the point of view of some welfare criteria which do not appeal to strong value judgements. In the case of consumers' surplus analysis, utilities are measured in terms of money and the maximization of the sum of utilities is the criterion, which is certainly too strong to be supported unanimously.

7.5 Pareto Optimality

A welfare criterion much weaker than that of consumers' surplus analysis is the Pareto optimality, which was already used in the previous chapters on the general equilibrium. An allocation is Pareto optimal if it is impossible to increase the utility of any consumer without decreasing those of others. In the case of two goods two consumers economy without production, any points on the contract curve are Pareto optimal in Edgeworth box diagram (Fig. 4.2). In the case of two consumers economy, any points on the utility frontier AB are Pareto optimal in Fig. 7.4. Since the point like A in Fig. 7.4, which is much favorable to the second consumer and unfavorable to the first, is also Pareto optimal, it is unlikely that this criterion is supported as the sufficient condition of the optimality. One has to admit, however, that Pareto optimality is generally a necessary condition for the optimality which is based on almost any reasonable stronger value judgements on welfare. In this sense, Pareto optimality can be used as a criterion for the optimal allocation of resources.

Whether to exclude the allocation like A in Fig. 7.4 or not is not the problem of resource allocation but the problem of income distribution.

As is easily conjectured from the consideration of the case of a two goods two consumers economy without production, i.e., Edgeworth box diagram, a necessary condition for Pareto optimality is that the marginal rates of substitution between any two goods are identical for all the consumers and for all the firms. To see this, consider a feasible allocation of resources $(x_1, \ldots, x_n, \; y_1, \ldots, y_r)$ and an infinitesimally small change from it, i.e., $(dx_1, \ldots, dx_n, \; dy_1, \ldots, dy_r)$, which keeps feasibility conditions (7.3) and (7.4) satisfied, so that

$$\sum_j f_{kj} dy_{kj} = 0 \quad (k = 1, \ldots, r) \tag{7.5}$$

and

$$\sum_i dx_{ij} = \sum_k dy_{kj} \quad (j = 1, \ldots, m) \tag{7.6}$$

where f_{kj} denotes the partial derivative of f_k with respect to y_{kj}. If the marginal rates of substitution are different among consumers and firms, it can be shown that the allocation is not Pareto optimal and the utility of some consumers can be increased by such a change in the allocation without reducing the utility of other consumers.

Suppose the marginal rates of substitution are different among consumers. Without loss of generality, let us assume that the marginal rate of substitution between the first two goods is different between the first two consumers, i.e.,

$$\frac{U_{11}}{U_{12}} > \frac{U_{21}}{U_{22}} \tag{7.7}$$

where U_{ij} denotes the marginal utility of the j-th good for the i-th consumer. Consider a change in the allocation such that $dx_{11} = -dx_{21} > 0$, $dx_{12} = -dx_{22} < 0$, $dx_{ij} = 0$ for $i \neq 1, 2$, or $i = 1, 2$ and $j \neq 1, 2$, and $dy_{kj} = 0$ for all $k, \; j$. By making dx_{ij} $(i = 1, 2, \; j = 1, 2)$ to satisfy

$$\frac{U_{11}}{U_{12}} > -\frac{dx_{12}}{dx_{11}} = -\frac{dx_{22}}{dx_{21}} > \frac{U_{21}}{U_{22}} \tag{7.8}$$

then, we can increase U_1 and U_2 without decreasing U_i $(i \neq 1, 2)$, since from (7.8), $dU_1 = U_{11}dx_{11} + U_{12}dx_{12} > 0$ and $dU_2 = U_{21}dx_{21} + U_{22}dx_{22} > 0$. In other words, we can make both individuals better off in Edgeworth box diagram if two indifference curves are not tangent, through an exchange of two goods at the rate of exchange which lies between two different marginal rates of substitution.

Suppose next that the marginal rate of substitution is different between consumers and firms. Without losing the generality, let us assume that

Fig. 7.5

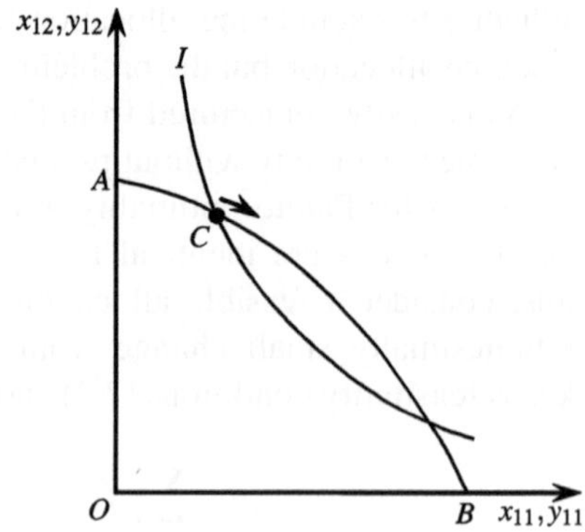

$$\frac{U_{11}}{U_{12}} > \frac{f_{11}}{f_{12}} \tag{7.9}$$

i.e., the marginal rate of substitution between the first two goods is different between the first consumer and the first firm. Consider a change in the allocation such that $dx_{11} = dy_{11} > 0$, $dx_{12} = dy_{12} < 0$, $f_{11}dy_{11} + f_{12}dy_{l2} = 0$, and all the other dx_{ij}'s and dy_{kj}'s are zero. Since

$$\frac{U_{11}}{U_{12}} > -\frac{dx_{12}}{dx_{11}} = -\frac{dy_{12}}{dy_{11}} = \frac{f_{11}}{f_{12}} \tag{7.10}$$

from (7.9), we can see that U_1 is increased. Figure 7.5 shows an example, where the first two goods are produced by the first firm and allocated to the first consumer. The curve *AB* signifies the production function when the input and output of all the other goods are given. The curve *I* is an indifference curve when the consumption of all the other goods are given. The allocation *C* is not Pareto optimal, since the utility can be increased by moving from *C* toward *B* on the curve *AB*. See Sect. 4.6 for another example.

Finally, let us suppose that the marginal rate of substitution is different between firms. Again without loss of generality, we can assume that

$$\frac{f_{11}}{f_{12}} < \frac{f_{21}}{f_{22}} \tag{7.11}$$

i.e., the marginal rate of substitution between the first two goods is different between the first two firms. Consider a change in the allocation such that $dx_{11} = dy_{11} + dy_{21}$, $dy_{12} = -dy_{22} < 0$, $f_{11}dy_{11} + f_{12}dy_{12} = 0$, $f_{21}dy_{21} + f_{22}dy_{22} = 0$, and all the other dx_{ij}'s and dy_{kj}'s are zero. Since $dy_{11} > 0$, $dy_{21} < 0$, and

$$\frac{f_{11}}{f_{12}} = -\frac{dy_{12}}{dy_{11}} < \frac{f_{21}}{f_{22}} = -\frac{dy_{22}}{dy_{21}} \tag{7.12}$$

Fig. 7.6

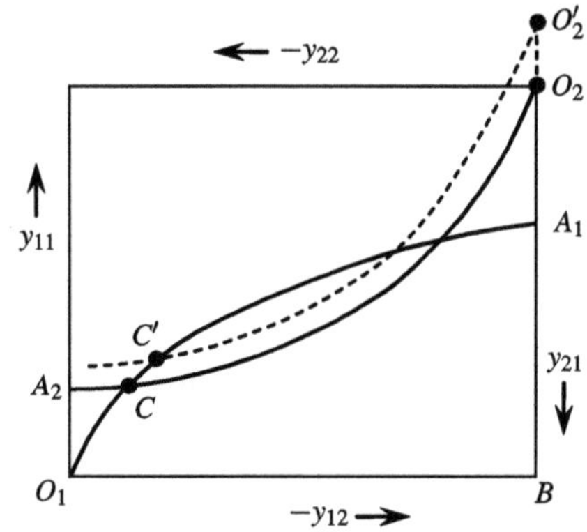

from (7.11), it follows that $dx_{11} = dy_{11} + dy_{21} > 0$ and U_1 is increased by the change in the allocation. Figure 7.6 shows an example of this case, where both firms produce the first good from the input of the second good. Input and output of the first firm are measured from the origin O_1 and those of the second firm, from O_2. The curves O_1A_1 and O_2A_2 signify the production functions of two firms. The quantities of the second good are measured horizontally and O_1B is the sum of input of the second good of two firms while the quantities of the first good are measured vertically and BO_2 is the sum of output of the first good of two firms. The allocation C is not Pareto optimal. The transfer of input from the second firm to the first firm shifts C to C'. Then O_2 is shifted vertically upward to O_2' and increases the sum of output of the first good. See Sect. 4.6 for another example.

7.6 Fundamental Theorem (1)

It is intuitively clear that a perfectly competitive equilibrium is Pareto optimal, since the marginal rate of substitution is equalized to relative price and therefore identical among all consumers and firms in the perfect competition. Equal marginal rate of substitution is, however, merely a necessary condition for the Pareto optimality. The first half of the fundamental theorem of welfare economics should, therefore, be proved more rigorously by the use of *reductio ad absurdum*. Let us suppose that a perfectly competitive equilibrium is not Pareto optimal and show that this supposition leads to a contradiction.

Suppose $(x_1, \ldots, x_n,\ y_1, \ldots, y_r,\ p)$ is a perfectly competitive equilibrium (see Sect. 4.1) but not Pareto optimal, where x_i, y_k and p are, respectively, consumption vector of the i-th consumer, production vector of the k-th firm and price vector. Since it is not Pareto optimal, there is another feasible allocation $(x_1', \ldots, x_n',\ y_1', \ldots, y_r')$ which satisfies (7.3) and (7.4) such that

$$U_i(x_i') \geq U_i(x_i) \quad (\text{for all } i) \tag{7.13}$$

and

$$U_i(x_i') > U_i(x_i) \quad \text{(for some } i\text{)} \tag{7.14}$$

where, of course, $U_i(x_i)$ is the utility function of the i-th consumer.

Since the utility is maximized being subject to the budget constraint in a competitive equilibrium,

$$U_i(x_i) \geq U_i(x_i') \quad \text{for any } x_i' \text{ such that} \quad \sum_j p_j x_{ij} \geq \sum_j p_j x_{ij}' \tag{7.15}$$

and therefore

$$\sum_j p_j x_{ij}' > \sum_j p_j x_{ij} \quad \text{for any } x_i' \text{ such that} \quad U_i(x_i') > U_i(x_i). \tag{7.16}$$

From the continuity of the utility function, then,

$$\sum_j p_j x_{ij}' \geq \sum_j p_j x_{ij} \quad \text{for any } x_i' \text{ such that} \quad U_i(x_i') \geq U_i(x_i). \tag{7.17}$$

Nextly, since the profit is maximized being subject to production function in a competitive equilibrium,

$$\sum_j p_j y_{kj} \geq \sum_j p_j y_{kj}'. \tag{7.18}$$

Finally,

$$\sum_j p_j \left(\sum_i x_{ij} - \sum_k y_{kj} - \sum_i \overline{x}_{ij} \right) i = 0 \tag{7.19}$$

since all the market are cleared in a competitive equilibrium.

In view of (7.16), (7.17) and (7.18), however, (7.19) implies that

$$\sum_j p_j \left(\sum_i x_{ij}' - \sum_k y_{kj}' - \sum_i \overline{x}_{ij} \right) > 0. \tag{7.20}$$

Since $p_j \geq 0$ and $\sum_i \overline{x}_{ij} = \overline{x}_j$, (7.20) is clearly in contradiction to (7.4). Our original supposition that there is a feasible allocation which satisfies (7.3), (7.4), (7.13) and (7.14) is wrong and every perfectly competitive equilibrium is proved to be Pareto optimal.

The fact that a perfectly competitive equilibrium is Pareto optimal is particularly welcome since the allocation through a competitive market is a decentralized allocation in the sense that decisions on consumption are left to individual consumers and decisions on production are left to individual firms. Such a decentralization is desirable because information on individual utility functions or individual production functions generally reside in the relevant household of consumers or in the relevant firms and may not be available or may be available only at high cost elsewhere. If the numbers of consumers and firms are very large and the effects on prices of individual behavior are negligible, furthermore, there is incentive compatibility for price taking maximizing behavior and there is no incentive for price manipulating strategic behavior. As we saw in Sect. 6.7, this argument can be extended even to the case where the number of firms is small. There is no need of auditing or inspection and we can rely on Adam Smith's invisible hands of markets.

We do not need particular assumptions on utility functions, production functions, etc. to prove the first half of the fundamental theorem of welfare economics. There are, of course, several implicit assumptions presupposed to have a perfectly competitive equilibrium as described here. If these assumptions are violated, competitive equilibrium is impossible or is not Pareto optimal, as will be discussed in the next chapter. What is more disappointing with the first half of the theorem is, however, the fact that Pareto optimality is not a sufficient condition for the desirability of the allocation, as is seen in Fig. 7.4. There may be a desirable allocation, which should, of course, be Pareto optimal, but not every Pareto optimal allocation is desirable. From the point of view of optimal resource allocation, therefore, what is more important is the possibility that any Pareto optimal allocation can be achieved through the perfect competition. This is the second half of the fundamental theorem of welfare economics.

7.7 Separating Hyperplane

Suppose a feasible allocation $(x_1, \dots, x_n, y_1, \dots, y_r)$ which satisfies (7.3) and (7.4) is Pareto optimal. To show that this allocation can be achieved through the competitive market mechanism, let us first consider some concepts on convex sets related to this allocation.

The set of all consumption vectors above the indifference curve passing the consumption vector x_i is called upper contour set and denoted as $\overline{U}_i(x_i) = \{x_i' \mid U_i(x_i') > U_i(x_i)\}$. In view of the nature of indifference curves discussed in Chap. 3, it is clear that this set is convex. Consider the direct sum (not union) of the upper counter sets of all x_i's, i.e., $\sum_i \overline{U}_i(x_i) = \overline{U}(x_1, \dots, x_n) = \left\{\sum_i x_i' \,\middle|\, U_i(x_i') > U_i(x_i) \text{ for all } i\right\}$. This is the set of all aggregate consumption vectors that can be distributed among n consumers so as to make them all better

Fig. 7.7

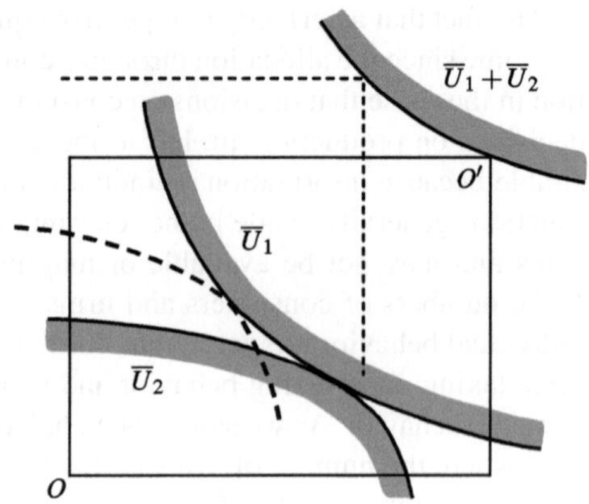

off than at the original allocation. It is a convex set, since it is the sum of convex sets. Figure 7.7 shows the construction of $\overline{U}_1 + \overline{U}_2$ in the case of $n = m = 2$. The box has a dimension of $(x_{11} + x_{21}) \times (x_{12} + x_{22})$ and x_1 and $\overline{U}_1$ are seen from O while x_2 and $\overline{U}_2$ are seen from O'. When $\overline{U}_1$ is slided along with the boundary of $\overline{U}_2$ with its boundary being kept tangent to that of $\overline{U}_2$, the locus of O' gives the boundary of $\overline{U}_1 + \overline{U}_2$.

The production possibility set of the k-th firm is denoted by $\overline{Y}_k = \{y'_k \mid f_k(y'_k) \leq 0\}$, where the production function is considered in inequality form (see Sect. 2.3). In other words, this set is the set of all the feasible input–output vectors which are technologically possible, including inefficient ones. As we discussed in Chap. 2, this set can be assumed convex. The aggregate production possibility set is defined as the direct sum of the production possibility set of individual firms, i.e., $\sum_k \overline{Y}_k = \overline{Y} = \left\{\sum_k y'_k \;\middle|\; f_k(y'_k) \leq 0 \text{ for all } k\right\}$. This is convex as the sum of convex sets. Consider the sum of aggregate production possibility set $\overline{Y}$ and a single point set $\overline{X} = (\overline{x}_1, \ldots, \overline{x}_m)$ of the initial stock vector, $\overline{Y} + \overline{X}$. This convex set is the set of technologically possible aggregate consumption vectors, which can be produced from the given initial stock and distributed to consumers.

We now have two disjoint convex sets, the aggregate upper counter set $\overline{U}(x_1, \ldots, x_n)$ and the aggregate supply possibility set $\overline{Y} + \overline{X}$. It is clear that two sets have no common points, since otherwise the allocation $(x_1, \ldots, x_n,\ y_1, \ldots, y_r)$ cannot be Pareto optimal. For two disjoint convex sets, we can find a hyperplane which separates them. If A and B are such m-dimensional sets, there exists a m-dimensional vector $p = (p_1, \ldots, p_m) \neq 0$ and $\sum_j p_j z_j \geq \sum_j p_j z'_j$ for any $z = (z_1, \ldots, z_m)$ in A and $z' = (z'_1, \ldots, z'_m)$ in B. Figure 7.8 shows the case of $m = 2$. Line $p_1 z_1 + p_2 z_2 = a$ separates the sets A and B. We can apply this separating hyperplane theorem to our sets $\overline{U}(x_1, \ldots, x_m)$ and $\overline{Y} + \overline{X}$.

Fig. 7.8

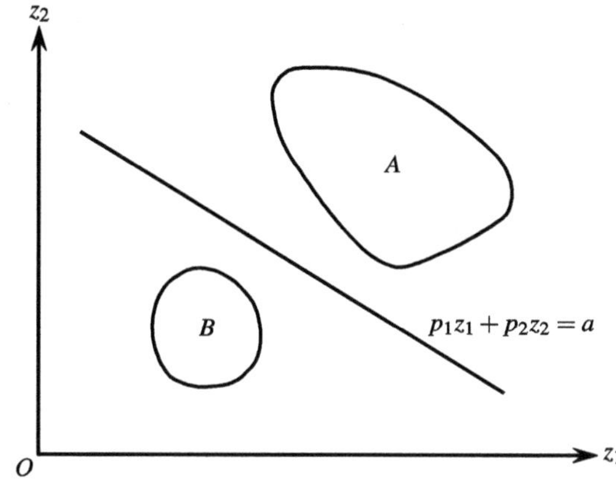

7.8 Fundamental Theorem (2)

To demonstrate that any Pareto optimal allocation $(x_1, \ldots, x_n,\ y_1, \ldots, y_r)$ can be achieved through competitive markets, let us apply the separating hyperplane theorem to $\overline{U}(x_1, \ldots, x_n)$ and $\overline{Y} + \overline{X}$ to have

$$p \sum_i x_i' \geq p \sum_k y_k' + p\overline{X} \tag{7.21}$$

for any x_i' in $\overline{U}_i(x_i)$, any y_k' in $\overline{Y}_k$, where $p = (p_1, \ldots, p_m) \neq 0$, $\overline{U}_i(x_i)$ is the upper contour set of x_i of the i-th individual, $\overline{Y}_k$ is the production possibility set of the k-th firm and $\overline{X}$ is the aggregate initial stock vector. Since x_i is on the boundary of the upper contour set $\overline{U}_i(x_i)$ and the utility function is continuous, (7.21) is also satisfied by x_i instead of x_i' in $\overline{U}_i(x_i)$. Since any Pareto optimal allocation $(x_1, \ldots, x_n,\ y_1, \ldots, y_r)$ satisfies the feasibility condition (7.4), we have

$$p \sum_i x_i = p \sum_k x_k + p\overline{X} \tag{7.22}$$

by multiplying p to both sides of (7.4). From (7.21) and (7.22), then,

$$\sum_j p_j \Big(\sum_i x_{ij}' - \sum_i x_{ij}\Big) + \sum_j p_j \Big(\sum_k y_{kj}' - \sum_k y_{kj}\Big) \geq 0 \tag{7.23}$$

for any x_i' in $\overline{U}_i(x_i)$ (including $x_i' = x_i$), and for any y_k' in $\overline{Y}_k$.

To show that $(p,\ x_1, \ldots, x_n,\ y_1, \ldots, y_r)$ is a competitive equilibrium, let us first note that $p \geq 0$. To see this, let us make the assumption of free disposal for a firm, say, for the first firm that $f_1(y_1') \leq 0$ for any $y_1' \leq y_1$. Then, substituting $x_{ij}' = x_{ij}$

(for all i, j), $y'_{kj} = y_{kj}$ (for all k, j except for $k = 1, j = j'$), and $y'_{1j'} = y_{1j'} - 1$, into (7.23), we have

$$p_{j'} \geq 0 \quad (j' = 1, \ldots, m). \tag{7.24}$$

We can, therefore, interpret that the p vector obtained from the separating hyperplane is a competitive price vector.

Against this price vector, it is easily see that y_k maximizes the profit $\sum_j p_j y_{kj}$ being subject to $f_k(y_k) \leq 0$. To see this, let us substitute x_{ij} for x'_{ij} for all i, j, and y_k for all y'_k for all k except for $k = k'$, in (7.23). Then,

$$\sum_j p_j y_{k'j} \geq \sum_j p_j y'_{k'j} \tag{7.25}$$

for any y'_k in $\overline{Y}_{k'}$, i.e., y'_k such that $f_{k'}(y'_{k'}) \leq 0$ for $k' = 1, \ldots, r$.

Finally, let us substitute y_{kj} for y'_{kj} for all k, j, and x_i for x'_i for all i except for $i = i'$, in (7.23). Then,

$$\sum_j p_j x'_{i'j} \geq \sum_j p_j x_{i'j} \tag{7.26}$$

for any $x'_{i'}$ in $\overline{U}_{i'}(x_{i'})$, i.e., $x'_{i'}$ such that $U_{i'}(x'_{i'}) \geq U_{i'}(x_{i'})$, for $i' = 1, \ldots, n$. This implies that

$$U_{i'}(x_{i'}) > U_{i'}(x''_{i'}) \tag{7.27}$$

for any $x''_{i'}$ which satisfies

$$\sum_j p_j x_{i'j} > \sum_j p_j x''_{i'j} \tag{7.28}$$

if we can assume that $\sum_j p_j x_{i'j} > 0$. Then from the continuity of the utility function,

$$U_{i'}(x_{i'}) \geq U_{i'}(x''_{i'}) \tag{7.29}$$

for any $x''_{i'}$ which satisfies

$$\sum_j p_j x_{i'j} \geq \sum_j p_j x''_{i'j} \tag{7.30}$$

for $i' = 1, \ldots, n$. In other words, x_i $(i = 1, \ldots, n)$ maximizes utility being subject to the budget condition (7.30), when the income distributed to the i-th consumer is $\sum_j p_j x_{ij}$.

Thus, the second half of the fundamental theorem of welfare economics insists that any Pareto optimal allocation can be achieved through perfect competition, if incomes are properly distributed among consumers. Unlike in the case of the first half of the theorem, convexity assumptions on utility and production functions are explicitly made so as to apply the theorem of separating hyperplane. In addition to these assumptions, furthermore, we have to assume that the income to be distributed to each consumer is strictly positive. Otherwise, the minimum expenditure (7.26) does not necessarily implies the maximum utility (7.29), as was seen in Sect. 4.5.

As we saw in Sect. 4.1, the theory of income distribution among consumers in a competitive economy explains that income accrues to a consumer from two sources, initial stocks of goods held by the consumer and the distribution of profit obtained in firms. The proper income distribution assumed in the second half of the fundamental theorem implies, therefore, some income redistribution policy through taxes and subsidies. In other words, unlike in the case of the first half, Pareto optimal allocation in the second half of the theorem cannot be a decentralized one. Income redistribution should be made through lump-sum taxes and subsidies so that identical marginal rates of substitution established by competition are not distorted by income redistribution. Unfortunately, however, there is a very good reason for the lack of information necessary to carry out such transfers. If consumers knew the basis on which lump-sum redistribution is to be arranged, they would have incentive to conceal or distort the information needed to implement such lump-sum transfers.

Problems

7.1. When the demand curve is downward sloping, the consumers' surplus is expressed by the area *DFA* in Fig. 7.2. How can the consumers' surplus be expressed in the case of Giffen paradox (Sect. 3.6)?

7.2. Reinterpret Fig. 7.2 for the case in which the good in question is a factor of production, which is supplied by consumers' households and demanded by firms. Specify the areas representing consumers' and producers' surpluses.

7.3. By introducing the possibility to import or export the good in the consumers' surplus analysis of Fig. 7.2, show that the free trade is better than the imposition of import or export tariff for a small country (constant foreign prices).

7.4. The utility possibility set, the shaded area in Fig. 7.4, is not a convex set in general. Show, however, it is convex if utility functions are all concave functions.

7.5. Demonstrate that the direct sum of two convex sets is a convex set.

7.6. Replace the feasibility condition (7.4) in Sect. 7.4 by $\sum_i x_{ij} \leq \overline{X}_j + \sum_k y_{kj}$ $(j = 1, \ldots, m)$. Discuss the case of a free good by assuming that the feasibility condition for the j-th good is satisfied with the strict inequality at a Pareto optimal allocation so that the corresponding competitive price is $p_j = 0$.

Literature

For further studies in general, see Malinvaud, op. cit., pp. 76–104, and Varian, op. cit., pp. 136–157.
For consumers' surplus analysis, in particular, see Hicks, op. cit., pp. 38–41, and Varian, op. cit., pp. 207–223. Rigorous proofs of the fundamental theorem of welfare economics are given in Arrow, op. cit. (see Chap. 3, Bibliography), Debreu, op. cit, pp. 90–97, and Arrow and Hahn, op. cit., pp. 90–97 (see Chap. 4, Bibliography). See P. Hammond, "Welfare Economics," G.R. Feiwel (ed.), *Issues in Contemporary Microeconomics and Welfare* (1985), for a critical discussion on the fundamental theorem from the point of view of recent developments in welfare economics.

Chapter 8
Market Failures

8.1 Laissez-Faire or Not

The so-called fundamental theorem of welfare economics is demonstrated in the preceding chapter. Apart from the problem of income distribution, the competitive market mechanism can generate an optimal social state in the sense that the resultant allocation of resources is Pareto optimal. Several conditions are, of course, assumed explicitly and implicitly to prove the theorem. If one regards these conditions approximately realistic, the best conceivable policy is that of laissez-faire, as far as the allocation of resources is concerned. Indeed, the fundamental theorem of welfare economics is the modern foundation of the historically celebrated doctrine of free trade.

There can be, however, an alternative interpretation of the fundamental theorem, if one regards the required assumptions for the theorem highly unrealistic and considers that cases in which these assumptions are violated are very important and cannot be assumed away as exceptional. The implication of the theorem is rather negative, if such strong assumptions are required to prove such a weak optimality as Pareto optimality. We cannot rely on the competitive markets even for a limited purpose of resource allocation, let alone for the purpose of income distribution. Government should actively interfere with the behavior of markets so as to achieve not only the optimal distribution of income but also the optimal allocation of resources by using such policy measures as tax and subsidy, public pricing, supply through public enterprises, direct control and prohibition of private productions, and production of public goods.

Assumptions required to demonstrate the fundamental theorem of welfare economics are (1) there exist sufficiently large number of markets so that all the conceivable goods can be traded in markets, (2) there exists no external effects in the sense that utility functions and production functions are functions of variables which can be controlled by the respective consumers or firms, (3) the feasible sets of firms' production are convex so that there is no possibility of increasing returns or diminishing costs, and (4) there are incentives for consumers and firms to behave

T. Negishi, *Elements of Neo-Walrasian Economics*, Advances in Japanese Business and Economics 5, DOI 10.1007/978-4-431-54535-4_8, © Springer Japan 2014

as if they are taking prices given. If these conditions are not assumed, there may be market failure in the sense that markets fail to generate Pareto optimal allocation of resources. In other words, either there may be no competitive equilibrium or competitive equilibria are not Pareto optimal.

The rest of this chapter will be devoted to discuss some of the well known examples of market failure. It will be seen that the reason for a particular case of market failure can be interpreted in different ways as to which assumption for the fundamental theorem is violated. This is because the assumptions given above are not mutually independent but rather interrelated. What makes the matter complicated is the possibility that the removal of the reason of a market failure generates the reason for another market failure. For example, the creation of a new market for a good, which did not exist before, may create monopoly that has no incentive to behave competitively.

If one considers market failures seriously, one has to give up laissez-faire and expects the government to interfere with markets so as to allocate resources optimally. The government is, however, not always *deux ex machina*, since there may not be incentives for the government to do so. Like markets, the government may also fail to allocate resources and distribute income optimally. In other words, there is a problem of how a modern society can make non-market decisions so that the result is optimal from some reasonable points of view. This is a part of the problem of the social choice, which will be discussed in the following chapter.

8.2 Diminishing Cost

The most simple case of the diminishing cost in which markets fail to allocate resources optimally may be that of the diminishing average cost of single product firms due to the existence of the fixed cost which does not vary with the level of output (see Sect. 2.7). To make the story simple, let us suppose that the variable unit cost is constant, so that the average cost curve is always downward sloping, converging to the horizontal marginal cost curve. No perfectly competitive equilibrium with positive output can exist in this case, since the equilibrium conditions require not only that the price of the product is equalized to the non-decreasing marginal cost but also that the average cost is not diminishing so that it is not lower than the marginal cost. While the former is the marginal condition of the maximum profit, the latter is the total condition which assures that the maximized profit is at least non-negative so that the firm is not bankrupt.

There may, of course, a perfectly competitive equilibrium with zero output of the product in question, if there is no demand at all at the price not lower than the constant marginal cost. Except for this trivial case, markets fail to allocate resources optimally, since the price cannot be equalized to the marginal cost at whatever possible equilibrium in the market of the product in question, whether it is a natural monopoly or not, so as to assure non-negative level of profit for the relevant firms.

Fig. 8.1

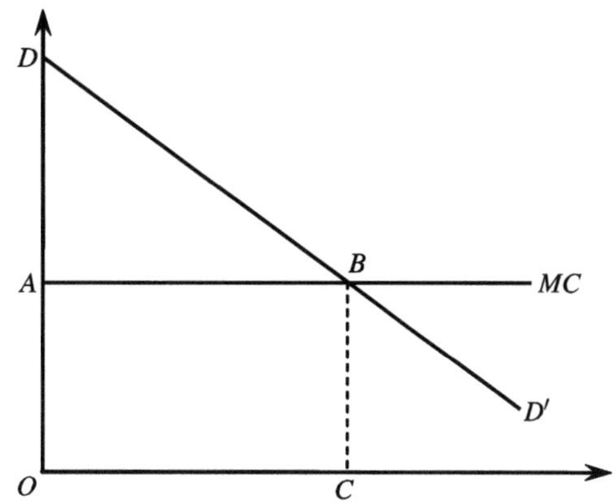

We can, conversely, easily imagine a Pareto optimal situation in which a positive level of output of the product is required. For a heuristic purpose, let us first consider by using consumers' surplus analysis. In Fig. 8.1 where the level of output is measured horizontally and the price and cost, vertically, *MC* signifies the constant marginal cost and the curve *DD′* is the demand curve for the product. As we saw in Sect. 7.3, the sum of consumers' surplus and producers' surplus is maximized at the level of output OC. Let us note, however, that the area $ABCO$ represents merely the variable cost for the level of output OC and the fixed cost should be added to this to obtain the total cost. If the price *OA* is paid for each unit of the product, then, the producers' surplus is negative by the amount of the fixed cost. Still, however, the sum of consumers' and producers' surpluses is positive, if the consumers' surplus *DBA* is larger than the fixed cost. This is the total condition for the optimality of the level of output OC in Fig. 8.1.

Using the general equilibrium model (Sect. 7.4), let us next suppose that an allocation $(x_1, \ldots, x_n,\ y_1, \ldots, y_r)$ is Pareto optimal. Without loss of generality, let us consider that the first s firms are identical single product firms with diminishing average cost due to the existence of the fixed cost. From the assumption of Pareto optimality, we can suppose that $y_1 \neq 0$, $y_k = 0$ for $k = 2, \ldots, s$. Pareto optimality requires that $\overline{U}(x_1, \ldots, x_n)$ which is the sum of n individual upper counter sets $\overline{U}(x_i)$ and $\overline{Y} + \overline{X}$, i.e., the sum of the production possibility set and the initial resource vector, have no common points. In particular, it is required for $y_1 \neq 0$ that $\overline{X} + \sum_{k \neq 1} y_k$ does not belong to $\overline{U}(x_1, \ldots, x_n)$. Since $\overline{Y} + \overline{X}$ is no longer convex, there is no separating hyperplane between them so that the second part of the fundamental theorem of welfare economics does not hold.

To see this, let us consider a simple two good economy. In Fig. 8.2, the first good is measured vertically and the second good, horizontally. Suppose there is only one firm which produces the second good from the input of the first. *OA* signifies the fixed set-up cost while the slope of *AB* shows the constant variable cost to produce the second good. $\overline{Y}$ is represented by the shaded area. *OAB* is shifted to

Fig. 8.2

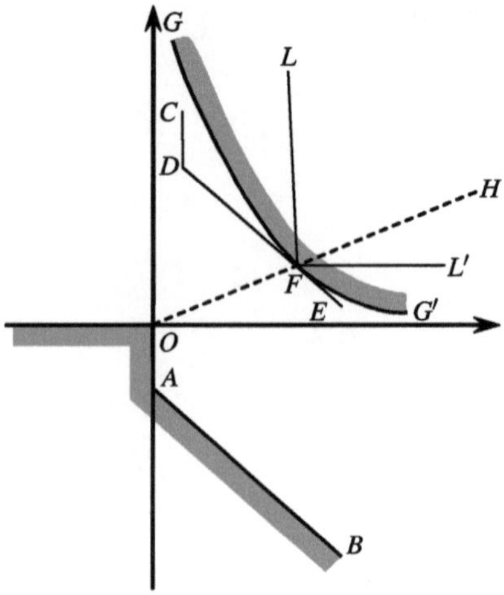

CDE since C is the initial resource point $\overline{X}$. The Pareto optimal allocation is F and the curve GG' is the boundary of $\overline{U}(x_1, \ldots, x_n)$ which is shown as the shaded area. The positive production of the second good is required, since C is not contained in $\overline{U}(x_1, \ldots, x_n)$. A sufficient condition for this is that two goods are complete complements for consumers (see Problem 3.11) so that GG' is transformed to LL' and the initial stock of the second good is relatively scarce so that C is located to the left of the dotted line *OH*.

As is seen in Fig. 8.2, the production possibility set $\overline{Y}$ is not convex and there is no separating hyperplane between $\overline{U}(x_1, \ldots, x_n)$ and $\overline{X} + \overline{Y}$. If there is no fixed cost and O and A (C and D) coincide, the line *DE* is a part of the separating hyperplane between $\overline{U}(x_1, \ldots, x_n)$ and $\overline{X} + \overline{Y}$, which is now convex. The Pareto optimal allocation can be achieved through competitive market where relative price of two goods is given by the slope of the line *DE* (*AB*). If there is fixed cost *OA* (*CD*), however, such a relative price gives rise to a negative profit for the firm. Since the total condition of the competitive equilibrium is not assured for the firm, the second good is not produced by the competitive firm, though the positive production of the good is required for the optimality.

8.3 Public Enterprises

Examples of industries with diminishing cost can be found particularly in the areas of public utilities, i.e., energy (electricity, gas, water), communication (telephone, postal services) and transportation (airlines, railroads, urban traffic, toll bridges). Many of them are examples of natural monopolies, since it is cheaper to produce goods by a monopoly than by many firms and it is easy to prevent the entry of new firms. To avoid the exploitation of the market by private enterprises in such industries, public enterprises are established or private enterprises are publicly regulated in many countries. In such cases, the products are publicly priced.

From the point of view of the fundamental theorem of welfare economics, the principle of the public pricing should be that of the marginal cost pricing. Since the average cost is diminishing and higher than the marginal cost, however, the marginal cost pricing implies that the total cost cannot be covered by the revenue from the sale of products. Marginal cost pricing firms with diminishing cost have, therefore, to be subsidized so that they are not bankrupt. Since the diminishing average cost is due to the existence of the fixed cost, whole or at least part of the fixed cost should be subsidized so that firms can cover the total cost of production. In other words, consumers of each unit of the product pay only the unit variable cost and does not pay the per unit fixed cost. Those who believe in the beneficiary-pay principle may object the marginal cost pricing principle and insist the self supporting accounting system that the unit price should be equalized to the average cost including per unit fixed cost.

To deal with this possible objection against the marginal cost pricing principle, let us consider the nature of the fixed or overhead cost which does not vary with the level of production. From the point of view of a consumer of the marginal unit of the production, what he should pay as a beneficiary seems to be the marginal cost, since the fixed cost is incurred independent of whether he consumes the marginal unit or not. If so, then, the cost for what is the fixed or overhead cost? We may argue that such cost is necessary to produce something like a public good (see Sect. 8.6) which is different from each unit of the product in question. Let us suppose that the utility of the i-th consumer is $U_i(q_i, x, M_i)$, where q_i is the quantity of the product in question he consumes, M_i is the quantity of money he holds and represents the consumption of all the other goods, and x is something which is created by the fixed or overhead cost. If such a cost is incurred, $x = 1$, otherwise $x = 0$. Since the supply of the product in question is possible if and only if such a cost is incurred, we may consider that $U_i(q_i, x, M_i) = U_i(q_i x, M_i)$.

The so-called consumers' surplus is

$$U_i(\overline{q}_i \times 1, \overline{M}_i - c\overline{q}_i) - U_i(0 \times 1, \overline{M}_i) \tag{8.1}$$

where c is the marginal cost price of the product, $\overline{q}_i$ is the quantity of the product consumed at the price c, and $\overline{M}_i$ is the initial income of the consumer. The benefit, on the other hand, which the consumer obtains from something like a public good created by the fixed or overhead cost is,

$$U_i(\overline{q}_i \times 1, \overline{M}_i - c\overline{q}_i) - U_i(0 \times 0, \overline{M}_i) \tag{8.2}$$

which is identical to the consumers' surplus. Since the consumption of the marginal unit does not yield consumers' surplus, which accrues to the consumption of intra-marginal units, then, the beneficiary-pay principle cannot insist to charge the cost to create the consumers' surplus to the consumer of the marginal unit. From the point of view of consumers, therefore, it is reasonable to pay the marginal cost price for each unit of the product, and to pay additionally for the consumers' surplus to finance subsidy to be given to firms to cover the fixed cost.

As a matter of fact, however, subsidies to public enterprises are often financed by taxes imposed on consumers who are currently not consuming the products of those enterprises. If so, such taxes cannot be justified as the prices for the consumers' surplus, unless the uncertainty is introduced into consideration. As we saw in Sect. 2.7, the fixed or overhead cost is the cost of factors of production, which are used by firms for a long period. As a result of such cost incurred, consumers are assured for opportunities to buy the product at the marginal cost whenever they wish so that they can enjoy the consumers' surplus. Consumers may need the product in the near future, even though he is currently not consuming it. According to the theory of expected utility (Sect. 3.11), risk averting consumers are willing to pay taxes to be assured for such opportunities. In other words, they wish to be insured for the possibility of need for the product in the future.

Public enterprises are expected to maximize welfare and not permitted to maximize their own profits. If the profit is not to be maximized, there is no incentive to minimize the cost to produce the given level of output. The price equalized to marginal cost has no welfare implication, if the marginal cost itself is not minimized. It is, of course, not so easy to raise the price of the product of public enterprise, since there are some countervailing powers like consumers' union and critical journalism. There are, then, some incentives to minimize cost and not to raise the price, whether it is equalized to the marginal cost or to the average cost. If the fixed cost is subsidized, however, there is not much incentive to minimize it. While consumers have strong incentive to lower the price, the government bureaus in charge of subsidies are likely to try to increase their budgets. If so, the self supporting accounting system (average cost pricing) might be better than the marginal cost pricing, even though the marginal conditions for Pareto optimum are not satisfied in the former.

8.4 Externality

There are two different kinds of externality. Pecuniary external economies (diseconomies) are, firstly, defined as the favorable (unfavorable) effect through markets of actions of a firm or those of a consumer on profits of other firms or on the budget of other consumers. Pecuniary externality itself is not a market failure. It rather shows how markets function well as a system to allocate resources. Market failures sometimes called pecuniary externality appear only when they are involved in such difficulties as economy of scale, lumpiness, etc. These problems are similar to that of diminishing cost, which was discussed in preceding sections. Secondly, technological external economies (diseconomies) are defined as the favorable (unfavorable) non-market, i.e., free (uncompensated) effects of actions of a firm (input and/or output of goods) or those of a consumer (consumption of goods) on production function of other firms or utility function of other consumers. An

Fig. 8.3

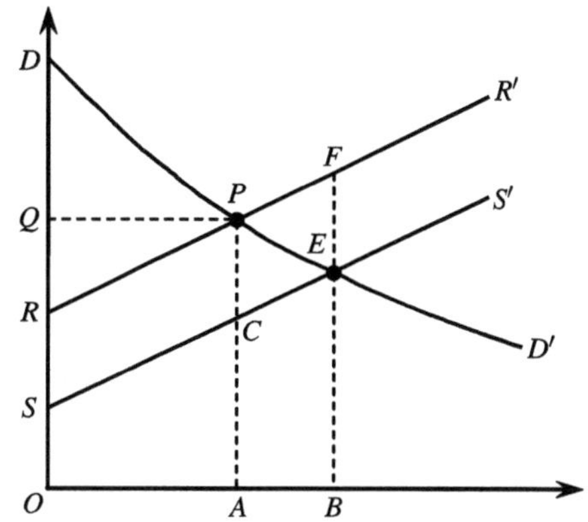

example of technological external diseconomies is the pollution like the emission of smoke. Competitive markets fail to generate Pareto optimal allocation of resources if these external economies and diseconomies are present, and some interference with market mechanism is necessary so that the modified market system can bring forth Pareto optimal allocation.

As an example, consider an industry, i.e., a group of firms which generates technological external diseconomies to other firms and consumers. Figure 8.3 shows the demand curve for the industry and the supply curve, i.e., the marginal cost curve of the industry. Prices and costs are measured vertically, and the quantity of the good the industry produces, horizontally. The problem is whether the competitive equilibrium E is optimal in the presence of the external diseconomies. The curve SS' is called the private marginal cost curve, since it is based only on the cost which firms in the industry actually pay. In the presence of technological external diseconomies, however, the private marginal cost is lower than the social marginal cost, which includes the cost incurred by other firms and consumers. If the external diseconomies can be shown as a function of the level of output of the industry, then, the social marginal cost curve of the industry is RR' in Fig. 8.3, where PC, AC and AP are, respectively, the marginal external effect, the private marginal cost and the social marginal cost. The intersection of the demand curve DD' and the social marginal cost curve RR' gives the optimal point P, where the difference of consumers' total valuation of the good $DPAO$ and the social cost of production $RPAO$ is maximized. Let us note that the external diseconomies do not vanish at the optimal point. PC and $RPCS$ are the optimal level of marginal and total external diseconomies. Since P and E do not coincide, there is a market failure and it is necessary to reduce the competitive output from OB to OA.

By using the general equilibrium model of Sect. 7.4, let us suppose that the output of the first good of the first firm has external diseconomies on the production function of the second firm. The production function of the second firm is now

$$f_2(y_{21}, \ldots, y_{2m}, y_{11}) = 0 \tag{8.3}$$

while that of the first firm remains unchanged as

$$f_1(y_{11}, \ldots, y_{1m}) = 0 \tag{8.4}$$

where y_{kj} denotes the k-th firm's output (if positive) or input (if negative) of the j-th good. Without loss of generality, we may assume that $f_{kj} = \dfrac{\partial f_k}{\partial y_{kj}} > 0$ and $f_{211} = \dfrac{\partial f_2}{\partial y_{11}} > 0$. In other words, for an increase in y_{11}, the second firm has to either reduce the output or increase the input of goods so as to keep (8.3) satisfied.

Consider an infinitesimally small change in the allocation such that $dy_{11} > 0$, $dy_{12} < 0$, $dy_{22} < 0$, $dx_{11} > 0$, $dx_{12} < 0$ and all other dx_{ij}'s and dy_{kj}'s are zero, which satisfies

$$f_{11}dy_{11} + f_{12}dy_{12} = 0, \tag{8.5}$$

$$f_{211}dy_{11} + f_{22}dy_{12} = 0, \tag{8.6}$$

$$dx_{11} = dy_{11}, \tag{8.7}$$

and

$$dx_{12} = dy_{12} + dy_{22} \tag{8.8}$$

where, of course, x_{ij} is the i-th consumer's consumption of the j-th good. At a Pareto optimal allocation, the utility of the first consumer $U_1(x_{11}, \ldots, x_{1m})$ cannot be changed by such a change in the allocation, so that

$$dU_1 = U_{11}dx_{11} + U_{12}dx_{12} = 0 \tag{8.9}$$

where $U_{ij} = \dfrac{\partial U_i}{\partial x_{ij}}$. From (8.5) to (8.9), a necessary condition for the Pareto optimality is

$$\frac{U_{11}}{U_{12}} = \frac{f_{11}}{f_{12}} + \frac{f_{211}}{f_{22}}. \tag{8.10}$$

Since at the competitive equilibrium,

$$\frac{U_{11}}{U_{12}} = \frac{f_{11}}{f_{12}} = \frac{p_1}{p_2} \tag{8.11}$$

where p_j is the competitive price of the j-th good, (8.10) cannot be satisfied and the competitive market mechanism fails to allocate resources optimally.

8.5 Correcting Externalities

In the presence of technological externalities some interference with markets is necessary so as to achieve Pareto optimal resource allocation. As policy measures for such a purpose, Pigou proposed taxes on and subsidies to the party which effects external economies and diseconomies on others. Of course, such a Pigouvian policy of taxes and subsidies is not the only conceivable remedy to externalities. Bargaining or trade among parties concerned is certainly another solution, which amounts to creating additional markets for artificially created commodities, i.e., the services due to the external economy effects and disservices or negative services (the negative amount of services) due to the external diseconomies. A classical example is the creation of the patent system, a new market for technological knowledge and information, the free use of which is a typical case of external economies. The aim of this section is to emphasize that taxes, subsidies and creation of new markets are equivalent, if the costs of such policy measures themselves are ignored, in the sense that Pareto optimal allocation is achieved and that the only difference among them is the difference in the resulting income distribution.

Let us start with Fig. 8.3, i.e., a case of external diseconomies generated by firms in an industry. A way to reduce the output from *OB* to *OA* is to impose a tax *PC* on each unit of the product, so that the supply curve of the industry is shifted from the private marginal cost curve *SS′* to the social marginal cost curve *RR′*. The same effect can be, however, expected by giving a subsidy *FE* for a unit reduction of the output from *OB*. The only difference is distributional, since the tax revenue *RPCS* can be returned to tax payers while the subsidy *FECP* has to be financed by an increase in the general tax. In view of (8.10) in the general equilibrium model of the preceding section,

$$\frac{p_1}{p_2} = \frac{f_{11}}{f_{12}} + \frac{f_{211}}{f_{22}} \tag{8.12}$$

has to be satisfied at a Pareto optimal competitive equilibrium. Since the first firm which generates external diseconomies to the second firm equates the marginal rate of substitution to the ratio of prices adjusted by tax or subsidy, the rate of externality correction tax or subsidy should be $\frac{p_2 f_{211}}{p_1 f_{22}}$, as is seen from

$$\frac{f_{11}}{f_{12}} = \frac{p_1 - p_2 \frac{f_{211}}{f_{22}}}{p_2}. \tag{8.13}$$

Fig. 8.4

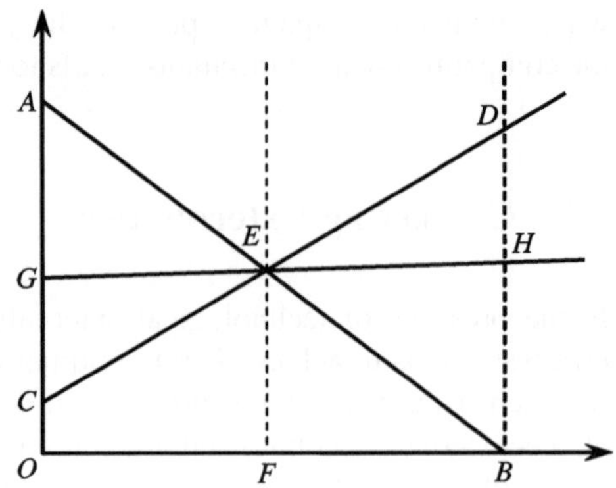

While Pigouvian taxes and subsidies are concerned only with the party which generate external effects, the creation of new market to solve externality naturally involves both the externality generating party and the externality receiving party, i.e., demanders and suppliers of the artificially created new goods. To show that the latter solution of externality is also identical to Pigouvian policies, let us consider Fig. 8.4 in which the level of output of the firm which generates external diseconomies is measured horizontally, and such monetary values as profit, price, cost, etc., vertically. The curve *AB* is the marginal profit curve of the first firm which generates external diseconomies while the curve *CD* is the marginal cost curve of the second firm which receives the external diseconomies. The profit of the first firm is maximized under laissez-faire at the level of output *OB*, but the socially optimal level of its output is *OF*. Pigouvian tax at the rate of *EF* on the output reduces the level of output from *OB* to *OF* and generates the tax revenue *GEFO*, while Pigouvian subsidy at the rate of *HB* on the reduction of output also reduces the level of output to *OF* and requires the total subsidy *EHBF*.

Suppose now that a new market is created in which the right of the first firm to generate external diseconomies is sold. If the first firm has no such right initially, it has to buy it in the market and the curve *AB* is its demand curve for such right. The curve *CD* is the second firm's supply curve of the right. The equilibrium price of the right of externality is determined by the intersection of demand and supply curves as *EF*. As in the case of Pigouvian tax, the first firm's level of output is *OF*, and the first firm pays *GEFO*, not as the tax, but as the price of the right to generate external diseconomies to the second firm. Unlike the case of Pigouvian tax, the second firm's profit is increased by *GEC*, i.e., the difference between the first firm's payments and the cost incurred to the second firm by the first firm's external diseconomies. If the first firm has already the right to generate external diseconomies initially, the second firm has to buy it back from the first so as to reduce the level of the first firm's output. From the origin *B*, the curve *DC* is the second firm's demand curve of the right and the curve *BA* is the first firm's supply curve. The equilibrium price is again *EF* and the level of output of the first firm is reduced to *OF*. As in the case of Pigouvian subsidy, the first firm receives *EHBF* which is, however, not the subsidy but the price of the right of external diseconomies sold to the second firm. Unlike the case of Pigouvian subsidy, the second firm has to pay what the first firm receives.

In the general equilibrium model considered in Sects. 7.4 and 8.4, let us add the $m+1$-th market where the right to generate external diseconomies as traded as the $m+1$-th good in the economy. The production function of the second firm (8.3) is simply rewritten as

$$f_2(y_{21},\ldots,y_{2m},y_{2,m+1})=0 \tag{8.14}$$

where $y_{2,m+1}>0$ is the supply of the right of external diseconomies. The condition for the equilibrium of the $m+1$-th market is

$$y_{1,m+1}+y_{2,m+1}=0 \tag{8.15}$$

where $y_{1,m+1}<0$ denote the demand for the right of external diseconomies, which is identical to $-y_{11}$. Since the first firm maximizes $\sum_{j\neq m+1} p_j y_{1j}-p_{m+1}y_{11}$, then, at the competitive equilibrium

$$\frac{f_{11}}{f_{12}}=\frac{p_1-p_{m+1}}{p_2} \tag{8.16}$$

while

$$\frac{f_{2,m+1}}{f_{22}}=\frac{p_{m+1}}{p_2} \tag{8.17}$$

from the profit maximization of the second firm. The condition for Pareto optimal allocation (8.12) is satisfied, therefore, at the competitive equilibrium, since f_{211} is by definition $f_{2,m+1}$.

While Pigouvian taxes and subsidies require the centralization of information on individual utility and production functions, the solution by the creation of new markets can enjoy the merits of decentralization. The latter solution has, however, difficulties of its own. As pointed out by Starrett, firstly, the feasible solution corresponding to the production function (8.14) may not be convex. In Fig. 8.5, the output of the second firm considered as a single product firm is measured vertically, and the amount of the externality right sold, horizontally, holding all inputs at fixed levels. The feasible set *OADC* is not convex. There is no competitive equilibrium, since the firm supplies an infinite amount of the right for any positive price, while it supplies no right for zero price. The difficulty remains, unless the feasible set can be restricted safely as *OAEB*, where *OB* is larger than *OB* in Fig. 8.4, i.e., the maximum level of the demand from the first firm. Secondly, there may be no incentive for the price taking behavior of firms participating in the newly created markets, unless the first and second firms discussed in the above are respectively the representative firms

Fig. 8.5

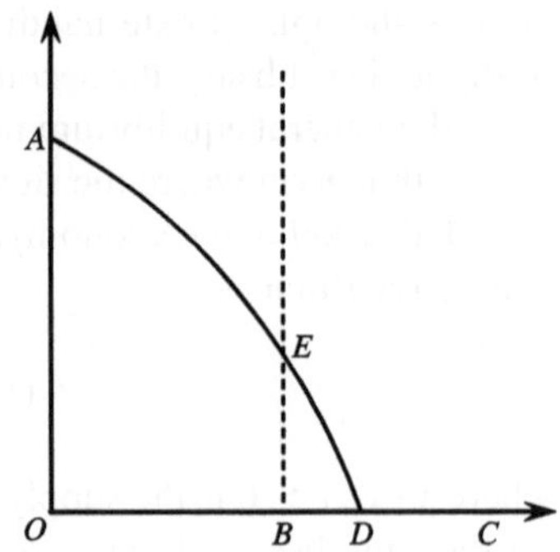

of many identical firms (see Sect. 4.3). If, for example, either the demand side or the supply side is monopolized, the equilibrium of the market is not optimal.

8.6 Public Goods

Another market failure, which is closely related to the externality, is the case of public goods. Consumers can jointly consume public goods and no one can be excluded from the consumption. In other words, each consumer can equally consume the total supply of a public good. In the case of a private good, each consumer consumes different units of the good and one is excluded from consuming a particular unit of the good, if the other already consumed it. Public goods do not have these properties. An example is the broadcasting service. It is a good produced from the input of certain factors of production. The amount of the service supplied to a given area is fixed, but all the people there have the same potential consumption. If one consumes the service, furthermore, it does not preclude the consumption of others.

In the case of a private good, the optimal level of output is determined by the intersection of demand and supply curve of the industry. This implies that the marginal cost of production is equalized to the marginal valuation of each consumer, i.e., the maximum amount of money he is willing to pay for the marginal unit, since the demand curve for the industry is the horizontal sum of individual demand curves, which show the marginal valuation of individual consumers. In the case of a public good, however, the sum of consumers' and producers' surpluses is maximized by the intersection of the social marginal cost curve and the social marginal valuation curve which is the vertical sum of individual demand (marginal valuation) curves. In other words, the sum of individual marginal valuations is equalized to the marginal cost of production at the optimal level of production. This can be easily seen in Fig. 8.6, where the output of a public good is measured horizontally, and costs and valuations, vertically. The curve MC is the marginal cost curve, the curve $ABCD$ is

Fig. 8.6

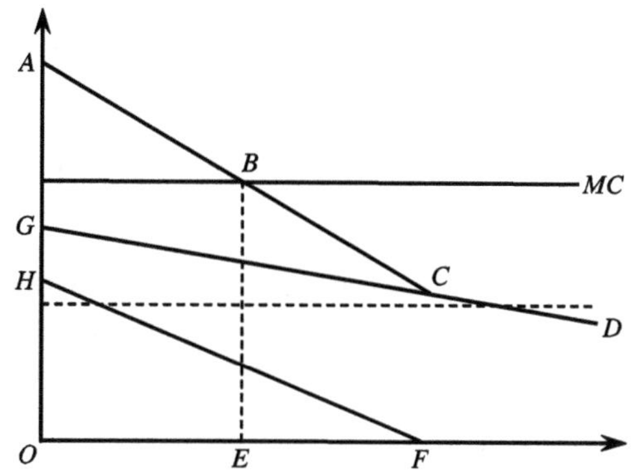

the social marginal valuation curve, vertically aggregated from individual marginal valuation curves *GD* and *HF*. The optimal level of output is *OE*.

In the general equilibrium model of allocation (Sect. 7.4), suppose the first good is a public good, the second good is the service of labor, and the public good is produced by the first firm. By definition, utility functions of consumers are now

$$U_i(x_1, x_{i2}, \ldots, x_{im}) \quad (i = 1, \ldots, n) \tag{8.18}$$

where x_1 denotes the total supply of the public good, which should be equalized to the output of the first firm y_{11}. To see the condition for Pareto optimality, consider an infinitesimal change of allocation from a Pareto optimal one such that

$$U_{i1}dx_1 + U_{i2}dx_{i2} = 0 \quad (i = 1, \ldots, n), \tag{8.19}$$

$$f_{11}dy_{11} + f_{12}dy_{12} = 0, \tag{8.20}$$

$$-dx_1 + dy_{11} = 0, \tag{8.21}$$

and

$$-\sum_i dx_{i2} + dy_{12} = 0 \tag{8.22}$$

where, of course, $U_{i1} = \dfrac{\partial U_i}{\partial x_1}$, $U_{ij} = \dfrac{\partial U_i}{\partial x_{ij}}$ $(j \neq 1)$, and $f_{1j} = \dfrac{\partial f_1}{\partial y_{1j}}$. Condition (8.19) is the one to keep Pareto optimality, while conditions (8.20)–(8.22) keep the feasibility of allocation satisfied, including the production function of the first firm and the demand and supply equality of two goods. By summing conditions in (8.19) and substituting from (8.22), (8.20) and (8.21) successively, we have the optimal condition for the supply of the public good,

$$\sum_i \frac{U_{i1}}{U_{i2}} = \frac{f_{11}}{f_{12}}. \tag{8.23}$$

In other words, the sum of the marginal rate of substitution between the public and the private goods is equal to the marginal rate of transformation (i.e., substitution in production) between them.

If public goods are defined as in (8.18), markets fail to supply them, since a consumer can enjoy them without paying the prices for them. As in the case of broadcasting services, such public goods have to be supplied either by governmental or public institutions, or as the by-products of other activities of private firms like advertisement. Ultimately, of course, the cost of production has to be paid by consumers, but not in proportion to the amount of individual consumption. Each consumer wishes, therefore, to consume the total supply, if the marginal valuation remains positive. Because of the special physical property of goods, i.e., non-rivalry in consumption, however, there is no congestion in the consumption of public goods.

Actually, there are not so many examples of such a pure public goods as defined in (8.18). What is more important is the case of the public supply of ordinary private goods. Since consumers are not charged in proportion to the amount of individual consumption, it is very likely that there appears the congestion in consumption and consumers have to be rationed by qualifications (ages, education, illness, etc.), queues or waiting lines, and lotteries. Instead of (8.18), then, utility functions of consumers are

$$U_i(a_i x_1, x_{i2}, \ldots, x_{im}) \quad (i = 1, \ldots, n) \tag{8.24}$$

where x_1 is the total supply of the first private good, which is to be supplied publicly, and a_i is the fixed ratio of the good to be given to the i-th consumer, so that $\sum_i a_i = 1$. Since a_i's are constants, the condition for Pareto optimality remains unchanged as (8.23), where $U_{i1} = \dfrac{\partial U_i}{\partial(a_i x_1)}$. It is a problem of the social choice to be discussed in next chapter whether a certain private good has to be supplied publicly as is defined by (8.24). Education, medical care, road service, etc. are some examples which have been supplied in different societies either privately through market or publicly like public goods.

8.7 Revelation of Preference

In the case of a private good supplied in a competitive market, a consumer has strong incentive to reveal his preference, i.e., the marginal valuations by demanding the quantity of the good he wishes to buy at the market price, since otherwise he cannot obtain the desirous amount of the good. In other words, consumers pay the price which is equal to their marginal valuations of the good. The optimal amount of the good is, then, supplied, since the marginal cost is equalized through the market price to such revealed marginal valuations of consumers. If a consumer also reveals his true preference and pays his price of a public good or a good publicly supplied, which is equalized to his marginal valuation, the governmental or public supplier can supply the optimal output by equating the marginal cost to the sum of the prices paid by consumers (see Fig. 8.6). In such a Lindahl solution, however, consumers have no incentive to reveal their true preference, since they all consume the equal or proportional amounts of the goods, irrespective of their marginal valuations and therefore of their shares of the cost. To save his share of the cost, every individually rational consumer tries to understate his marginal valuation. From the point of view of Pareto optimality, fortunately, it is not necessary, as is done in Lindahl solution, to equate individual marginal valuation to the individual share of the cost. What is necessary is only to equate the sum of individual marginal valuations to the marginal cost.

Even if the share of the cost is not related to individual marginal valuation, however, consumers may not necessarily have incentive to reveal their true preference. Suppose, in Fig. 8.6, the marginal cost *MC* is equally shared by two consumers. For a consumer whose marginal valuation curve is *HF*, the most desirous level of output is less than the social optimal level *OE*, since it is determined by the intersection of *HF* and the dotted horizontal line indicating the half of *MC*. He will understate his true marginal valuation so as to reduce the level of output determined by the intersection of *MC* and the sum of the individual marginal valuations. Similarly, the consumer whose marginal valuation curve is *GD* has also no incentive to reveal the true preference. Since the intersection of the dotted horizontal line and *GD* gives his most desirous level of output which is higher than *OE*, he will exaggerate his marginal valuation so as to increase the level of output determined by the intersection of *MC* and the sum of individual marginal valuations. The result of such strategic behavior cannot be easily expected, but it is likely that the resulted level of output is higher than the optimal one, in view of the fact that the extent of the understatement is bounded while that of the exaggeration is not.

It is possible, however, to induce consumers to reveal their true preference by a special tax imposed on them. Suppose the marginal cost and therefore the unit cost of a public good is constant like C in Fig. 8.7, where the level of output is measured horizontally and costs and valuations, vertically. The share of the i-th consumer in the marginal cost T_i is also constant such that $\sum_i T_i = C$. $C - T_i$ in Fig. 8.7 shows the cost consumers other than the i-th one have to bear for each unit of the good. The curve D indicates the sum of all the individual marginal valuations of consumers, while the curve $D - D_i$ is the sum of individual marginal valuations except the i-th consumer's marginal valuation D_i. The optimal level is *OQ* as determined by the intersection of D and C. If the preference of the i-th consumer D_i is not counted for the determination of the level of output, even though he shares the cost by T_i, the level of output would be *OA* as determined by the intersection of $D - D_i$ and $C - T_i$. In other words, the loss of consumers' surplus for the consumers other than the i-th

Fig. 8.7

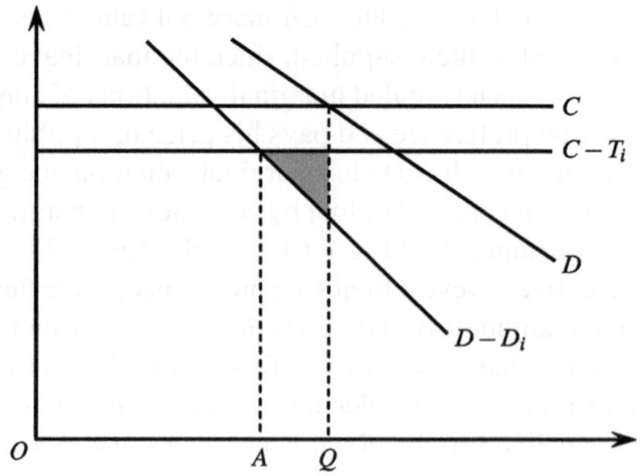

Fig. 8.8

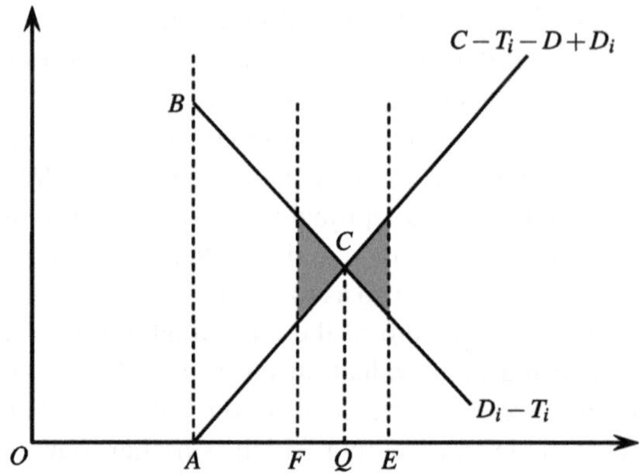

one caused by taking the i-th consumer's preference into consideration is the shaded triangle, which represents the incentive tax on the i-th consumer to induce him to reveal the true preference.

In Fig. 8.8, which is similar to Fig. 8.7, $D_i - T_i$ shows the net marginal valuation of the i-th consumer while $C - T_i - D + D_i$ indicates the loss incurred to other consumers caused by increases in output from the level OA. The shaded triangle in Fig. 8.7 is now represented by the area ACQ. The increase in the consumers' surplus of the i-th consumer is maximized as ABC at the level of output OQ, where $D_i - T_i$ and $C - T_i - D + D_i$ coincide, so that $D = C$. This is because he has to pay the incentive tax ACQ while his net valuation of the good is increased by $ABCQ$, if the level of output is increased from OA to OQ. There is nothing to be gained for the i-th consumer by understating his marginal valuation D_i so as to reduce the level of output to OF. The increase in consumers' surplus is smaller by the shaded triangle located to the left of C in Fig. 8.8 than at the level of output OQ. Similarly, if the output is increased to OE by the exaggeration of the marginal valuation D_i, the increase in the consumers' surplus is smaller by the shaded triangle located to the right of C. The honest revelation of his true marginal valuation schedule D_i is the optimal strategy of the i-th consumer.

8.8 Public Goods in Production

Public goods or private goods publicly supplied are used, not only by consumers as we considered in the preceding sections, but also by firms as intermediate goods in production. Some examples are technological information supplied by public research institutes, transformation service of roads in industrial areas, and activities to recreate environments disrupted by industrial activities. Analogously to (8.18) and (8.24) in Sect. 8.6 in the case of public goods or private goods publicly supplied for consumption, intermediate public goods and the public supply of intermediate private goods are respectively defined by production functions of user-firms as follows. If the first good is a public good, the production function of the k-th firm is

$$f_k(y_1, y_{k2}, \ldots, y_{km}, K_k) = 0 \tag{8.25}$$

where y_1 denote the total supply of the public intermediate good, y_{kj} $(j \neq 1)$ is the k-th firm's output (if positive) or input (if negative) of the j-th good, and K_k signifies the input of the fixed factors of production (see Sect. 2.4), or the capital stock of the k-th firm. Similarly, if the first good is a publicly supplied ordinary private intermediate good, the production function of the k-th firm is

$$f_k(a_k y_1, y_{k2}, \ldots, y_{km}, K_k) = 0 \tag{8.26}$$

where y_1 is the total supply of the first good and a_k is the fixed ratio of the good to be rationed to the k-th firm, so that $\sum_k a_k = 1$.

The optimal condition for the supply of public intermediate goods or publicly supplied intermediate goods is similar to the optimal condition for the supply of consumption public goods. The sum of the marginal productivity of a public intermediate good (publicly supplied intermediate good) for user-firms is equalized to the marginal cost of production of such a good. What is different from the case of the consumption is that the difference in the homogeneity property between (8.25) and (8.26) implies different effects on the allocation of capital in the long-run. An implicit function $f(x_1, \ldots, x_m) = 0$ is defined as homogeneous, if $f(hx_1, \ldots, hx_m) = 0$ for any $h > 0$. By differentiating f with respect to h at $h = 1$, we have Euler's theorem

$$\sum_j f_j x_j = 0 \tag{8.27}$$

where $f_j = \dfrac{\partial f}{\partial x_j}$ $(j = 1, \ldots, m)$.

The case of public intermediate goods (8.25) corresponds to the case which Meade called as the atmosphere creation, since the production function is homogeneous with respect to $y_{k2}, \dots, y_{km}$ and K_k. In other words, the condition (8.25) remains satisfied if $y_{k2}, \dots, y_{km}$ and K_k are proportionally changed and y_1 is kept unchanged. The case of the creation of atmosphere is exemplified by the free information on technology supplied by public research institutes. Another example is the free transportation service of roads, if they are so wide that there is no congestion and y_1 is measured by the length of roads. Since there is no congestion and no rivalry in the use of y_1, the firm's output can be increased proportionally if the input of non-public goods, including capital, are increased proportionally, with the level of y_1 being kept constant.

Capital is mobile in the long run and the rate of profit

$$r = \sum_{j \neq 1} \frac{p_j y_{kj}}{K_k} \tag{8.28}$$

is equalized among firms. In view of Euler's theorem

$$\sum_{j \neq 1} f_{kj} y_{kj} + f_{kK} K_k = 0 \tag{8.29}$$

where $f_{kK} = \dfrac{\partial f_k}{\partial K_k}$, and the equality of the marginal rates of substitution and relative prices in a competitive economy, (8.28) implies that

$$\frac{f_{kK}}{f_{kj}} = \frac{r}{p_j} \quad (j \neq 1). \tag{8.30}$$

In other words, in a competitive economy, the marginal rates of substitution between private goods including capital are equalized among firms in the long run, even if there exist some public intermediate goods. The profit as residue exactly corresponds to the marginal productivity of capital.

The case of public supply of ordinary intermediate goods (8.26) corresponds to the case which Meade called as the unpaid factors of production. For an example, we may consider the case of a road of the given length, the use of which is rationed among firms by a non-pecuniary method, say, by limiting the number of licensed cars, so as to avoid congestion and the width of which is measured by y_1. Alternatively, we may suppose that y_1 is an activity to recreate environments disrupted by industrial activities, with the level of disruption legally permitted to each firm properly arranged so as to keep the resulted level of total environments at the given desired level. Since the use of y_1 is limitational, the outputs cannot be increased proportionally when inputs are increased proportionally, unless the amount of y_1 is also increased proportionally. In other words, the production function in (8.26) is homogeneous not with respect to $y_{k2}, \dots, y_{km}$ and K_k, but with respect to $y_1, y_{k2}, \ldots, y_{km}$ and K_k. This is no wonder since the role played by $a_k y_1$ in the production is not different from those played by ordinary factors of production.

In view of Euler's theorem,

$$f_{k1} a_k y_1 + \sum_{j \neq 1} f_{kj} y_{kj} + f_{kK} K_k = 0 \tag{8.31}$$

where $f_{k1} = \dfrac{\partial f_k}{\partial (a_k y_1)}$, and the rate of profit defined in (8.28), then, instead of (8.30), we have

$$\frac{f_{kK} + \dfrac{f_{k1} a_k y_1}{K_k}}{f_{kj}} = \frac{r}{p_j} \quad (j \neq 1). \tag{8.32}$$

If some intermediate goods are supplied publicly, the marginal rates of substitution between capital and other private goods $\dfrac{f_{kK}}{f_{kj}}$ are not equalized among firms in the long run competitive equilibrium. The reason is that contributions to the production made by intermediate goods publicly supplied is imputed to the private capital used by firms, the rate of profit as residue defined in (8.28) exceeds the marginal productivity of capital, and that the equalization of the rate of profit among firms does not imply in general the equalization of the marginal productivity of capital. Public supply of private intermediate goods generates the distortion of the long run allocation of capital.

Problems

8.1. Criticize the following statement. "Public pricing like marginal cost pricing is the pricing of the products of public enterprises."

8.2. The self supporting accounting system of public enterprises does not satisfy the marginal conditions of Pareto optimality. Consider, however, the second best problem of a joint-output firm subject to the balanced budget (zero profit) condition. Maximize the sum of consumers' and producers' surplus, assuming the inverse demand functions (marginal valuation functions) are independent among different products of the firm.

8.3. Read J.M. Buchanan and Wm. Craig Stubblebine, "Externality" (A.E.A. *Readings in Welfare Economics* (1969)), and critically discuss their criticism of the Pigouvian tax and subsidy.

8.4. H.R. Bowen suggested the determination of the supply of a public good by voting. Suppose, as in Fig. 8.6, that the constant marginal cost is shared equally among consumers and that each consumer votes for the quantity which maximizes his consumers' surplus. If the average of quantities voted is to be supplied, what condition is necessary on individual marginal valuation curves for the supply so determined to be optimal?

8.5. By using the general equilibrium model, derive the optimal condition for the supply of public goods in production.

8.6. Discuss the efficacy of incentive tax in the case in which the quantity *OA* is larger than the quantity *OQ* in Figs. 8.7 and 8.8.

Literature

For further studies in general, see Malinvaud, op. cit., pp. 200–229, and Varian, op. cit., pp. 197–207. Also useful is A.E.A. *Readings in Welfare Economics* (1969).
See Chaps. 7 and 8 of D. Bös, *Public Enterprise Economics* (1986), for advanced discussions on the marginal cost pricing and Ramsey pricing (see Problem 8.2) of the products of public enterprises. The problem of revealing preferences on public goods is discussed in Chap. 4 of D.C. Mueller, *Public Choice* (1979).
For the literature on the externality and public goods in production, see respectively Negishi, op. cit. (1972), Chap. 4 and Negishi, op. cit. (1979), Chap. 14.

Chapter 9
Optimal Income Distribution

9.1 Voting Paradox

In the previous chapter, it was shown that there are many cases in which competitive markets fail to allocate resources optimally. Even if we disregard the existence of such difficulties, however, what competitive markets can do is only to achieve a Pareto optimal allocation, which may not be the optimal organization of an economy, since Pareto optimality is, though necessary, by no means sufficient for it. To choose the optimal organization of the economy from many Pareto optimal allocations is the problem of the optimal distribution of incomes, in view of the second half of the fundamental theorem of welfare economics, which insists that any Pareto optimal allocation can be achieved through perfect competition if incomes are properly distributed among consumers (Sect. 7.8). Since different individuals have different opinions on how should incomes be distributed, and the market mechanism cannot be relied on to solve it, the problem of optimal income distribution is a social choice which has to be made politically through voting in a democratic society.

The method of majority decision fails, however, sometimes to satisfy the condition of rationality. The famous example of the paradox of voting is as follows. Consider a society, which consists of three individuals, facing the problem of social choice among three alternatives A, B and C. Table 9.1 shows how three individuals I, II and III, rank three alternatives A, B and C, i.e., I prefers A to B and B to C, II prefers B to C and C to A, and III prefers C to A and A to B. By the method of majority decision, A can defeat B by two votes (I and III) to one (II), and B can defeat C by two votes (I and II) to one (III). If the social ranking has to satisfy transitivity as the condition of rationality, then, A should defeat C in a vote too. But, in fact, C defeats A by two votes (II and III) to one (I). Thus, the method of majority decisions leads to inconsistencies.

This inconsistency of the majority decision can be avoided by the use of the so-called rank order method of voting. A certain number of marks are given to each alternative according to each individual's ranking, and the total number of marks

T. Negishi, *Elements of Neo-Walrasian Economics*, Advances in Japanese Business and Economics 5, DOI 10.1007/978-4-431-54535-4_9, © Springer Japan 2014

Table 9.1

Individuals	Alternatives A	B	C
I	1	2	3
II	3	1	2
III	2	3	1

Table 9.2

Individuals	Alternatives A	B	C
I	1	2	3
II	2	1	3
III	1	2	3

received by each alternative is added up so as to decide the social ranking. In the three alternative case of Table 9.1, let 1 be assigned for being first, 2 for being second, and 3 for being third. The alternative with the smallest score is to win. Then, A, B and C, each receives six marks, so that the outcome is not an inconsistency but a tie. This method has, however, a different difficulty. Suppose Table 9.1 is changed to Table 9.2. Every one's ranking of A vis-a-vis B remains unchanged, but individuals II and III change their minds about an irrelevant alternative for the comparison of A and B, i.e., C and decide that it is worse than both A and B. In Table 9.1, the outcome is a tie between A and B, each receiving six marks. In Table 9.2, however, A with the score of four defeats B with the score of five. While every one's ordering of A and B remains unchanged, the social choice between A and B is not the same.

Both the method of majority decision and the rank order method transfer individual orderings into the social ordering. In general, a rule which transforms a set of n individual orderings, R_i $(i = 1, \ldots, n)$ into the social ordering R is called Arrowian Social Welfare Function. Like individual orderings, of course, the social ordering must satisfy the conditions of rationality, i.e., reflexibility, transitivity and completeness (see Sect. 3.5). It is desirable to impose certain conditions of reasonableness on such social welfare function.

The first condition is that the social welfare function must work for every logically possible configuration of individual orderings. This is called the condition of unrestricted domain (condition U), since the domain of the social welfare function is the set of individual orderings. We have just seen that the method of majority decision does not satisfy condition U, since it fails to transform the particular configuration of individual orderings given in Table 9.1 into the social orderings which by definition must satisfy transitivity.

While the rank order method can satisfy condition U, its outcome is not independent of rankings of irrelevant alternatives, as we saw in the case of change from Table 9.1 to Table 9.2. Secondly, therefore, we wish to avoid this difficulty by imposing the condition of independence of irrelevant alternatives (condition I) that social choice over a set of alternatives must depend on individual orderings only over those alternatives and not on rankings of alternatives that are not involved in this choice. The method of majority decision satisfies, of course, this condition I.

Thirdly, the social welfare function must satisfy the Pareto principle that the society must prefer A to B if every individual prefers A to B (condition P). Condition P is satisfied by both the method of majority decision and the rank order method. This condition is very reasonable, particularly from our point of view, since Pareto optimality is a necessary condition of the optimal organization of an economy and the problem of optimal income distribution is considered to be a problem of social choice over Pareto optimal allocations.

Among three conditions on the social welfare function, U, I and P, the method of majority decision violates condition U while the rank order method does not satisfy condition I. Is there any social welfare function which satisfies all of three conditions? If there is such a social welfare function, unfortunately, it can be shown that there must be an individual who is called a dictator in the sense that the society must prefer A to B, whenever he prefers A to B. In other words, if we impose the condition of non dictatorship (condition D) on the social welfare function, we have Arrow's general impossibility theorem that there is no social welfare function which satisfies conditions U, I, P and D.

9.2 Arrow's Theorem (1)

To sketch the proof of Arrow's general impossibility theorem for social welfare function, let us consider a society in which there are at least two individuals (so that condition D is relevant) and assume that there are at least three alternative social states like different income distributions (so that transitivity does matter). Let an individual ordering xR_iy denote that the social state x is at least as good as the social state y for the individual i, and xP_iy denote xR_iy but not yR_ix, i.e., x is better than y for i. For any set of individual orderings $R_1, \ldots, R_n$ in an n individual society, a social welfare function specifies the social ordering R such that xRy denotes x is at least as good as y for the society and xPy denotes xRy but not yRx. Both individual and social orderings satisfy reflexibility, transitivity and completeness.

Let us define that a set of individuals V is decisive for x against y if xPy when xP_iy for every i in V. Note that being decisive x against y is different from being decisive y against x. We shall first show that if there is some individual J who is decisive for any ordered pair of alternatives, then a social welfare function satisfying conditions U, I and P implies that J is a dictator. Then, Arrow's theorem will be proved by showing that given conditions U, I and P, there must be an individual who is decisive over some ordered pair of alternatives.

Suppose that individual J is decisive for some x against some y and let z be another alternative. To show first that J is a dictator over any three alternatives containing x and y, we have to show that he is also decisive for x against z, z against y, y against z, y against x, and z against x. After showing this, we shall show that J is decisive for all possible ordered pairs of alternatives u and v.

To see that J is decisive for x against z, let i refer to all individuals other than J and assume that $xP_J y$, $yP_J z$ and that $yP_i x$, $yP_i z$. It is condition U that makes such assumptions possible. Since J is decisive for x against y and $xP_J y$, we have xPy. From condition P, furthermore, yPz, since $yP_J z$ and $yP_i z$. But xPy and yPz implies xPz from the transitivity of R. From condition I, however, the assumption that $yP_i z$ and $yP_i x$ has no effect on the social choice between x and z, since it is the assumption on an irrelevant alternative y. Hence, xPz must be the consequence of $xP_J z$ alone and is independent of our assumption on P_i. In other words, J is decisive for x against z.

Similarly, J can be shown to be decisive for z against y. Assume that $zP_J x$, $xP_J y$ while $zP_i x$, $yP_i x$. By condition P, we have zPx. Since J is decisive for x against y and $xP_J y$, furthermore, we have xPy. By transitivity, then, zPy. The assumption $zP_i x$ and $yP_i x$ has, however, no effect on zPy from condition I. Hence, J is decisive for z against y, since zPy when $zP_J y$.

Being decisive for y against z can be seen as follows. We have already shown that an individual who is decisive for x against y is decisive for z against y. Interchanging y and z, we can similarly show that an individual who is decisive for x against z is decisive for y against z. Since J was shown to be decisive for x against z, however, he is also decisive for y against z.

The individual J is also decisive for y against x. We have shown that an individual who is decisive for x against y is decisive for x against z. Putting x in place of z, z in place of y, and y in place of x, then, we can similarly show that an individual who is decisive for y against z is decisive for y against x. Since J was shown to be decisive for y against z, however, he is decisive for y against x.

Finally, J is decisive for z against x. We have shown that an individual who is decisive for x against y is decisive for z against y. By interchanging x and y, then, we can show that an individual who is decisive for y against x is decisive for z against x. Since J was shown to be decisive for y against x, however, he is decisive for z against x.

Thus, J who is decisive for x against y is a dictator over any set of three alternatives containing x and y, since he is decisive for every ordered pair of alternatives (six in all) from the set of three alternatives x, y and z, given conditions U, I and P. To show that J is a dictator over any set of alternatives, however, we have to show that he is decisive for all possible ordered pairs of alternatives. Consider any two alternatives u and v. If one of u and v is the same as one of x and y, say, u and x are the same, take the triple consisting of x $(= u)$, y and v. Since J is decisive for x against y, i.e., decisive for u against y, it follows that he is also decisive for u against v and for v against u. Suppose, finally, that both u and v are different from x and y. First, take the triple consisting x, y and u. J is, of course, decisive for x against u. Then, take the triple consisting of x, u and v. Since J is decisive for x against u, it follows that he is also decisive for u against v and decisive for v against u.

9.3 Arrow's Theorem (2)

In the previous section, it was shown that an individual who is decisive for any ordered pair of alternatives is a dictator, given conditions U, I and P. Now, we are ready to prove Arrow's theorem that there is no social welfare function which satisfies conditions U, I, P and D. This will be done by showing that given conditions U, I and P, there must be an individual who is decisive for some ordered pair of alternatives. To show it, we make the contrary supposition that there is no such individual and show that it leads to an inconsistency. Then, Arrow's theorem will follow, since such an individual is a dictator.

For any pair of alternatives, there is at least one decisive set V of individuals, since the set of all individuals is decisive for any pair of alternatives (condition P). Compare all the sets of individuals that are decisive for some pair of alternatives, and from them choose the smallest one. Call this set W and assume that it is decisive for x against y. If this W contains only one individual, then he is a dictator and there is no need to proceed further. If, however, W contains two or more individuals, divide W into two parts, i.e., W_1 containing only a single individual, and W_2 containing the rest of W.

From condition U, we can assume any logically possible combination of individual orderings. Let us assume, then, that for all i in W_1, $xP_i y$, $yP_i z$ and that for all j in W_2, $zP_j x$, $xP_j y$. Since W is decisive for x against y and every individual in W prefers x to y, we have xPy. As for y and z, W_2 members prefer z to y, so that if zPy, then W_2 is a decisive set. But W is the smallest decisive set and W_2 is smaller than W by an individual who belongs to W_1. Therefore, it is not true that zPy. It is defined that zRy and not yRz implies zPy. The negation of zPy implies, then, yRz. But xPy and yRz implies xPz. Since the only individual in W_1 prefers x to z, however, he is decisive for x against z. Hence there is a contradiction in our original supposition that there is no individual who is decisive for some ordered pair of alternatives.

If there is such an individual, however, he must be a dictator, as was shown in Sect. 9.2. Given conditions U, I, P and D, therefore, there is no social welfare function, which is Arrow's theorem. In general, in other words, the social ordering cannot be generated rationally and democratically from individual orderings.

Arrowian social welfare function is defined as a function which aggregates individual orderings into a social ordering. Traditionally in welfare economics, however, a social welfare function has been defined as a function which gives the level of social welfare W as a function of individual utilities U_i $(i = 1, \ldots, n)$ in an n individual economy. We may call such a function an individualistic Bergsonian welfare function. Figure 9.1 is a reproduction of utility frontier AB in Fig. 7.4 (Sect. 7.4) where U_1 and U_2 denotes respectively the utilities of the first and second

Fig. 9.1

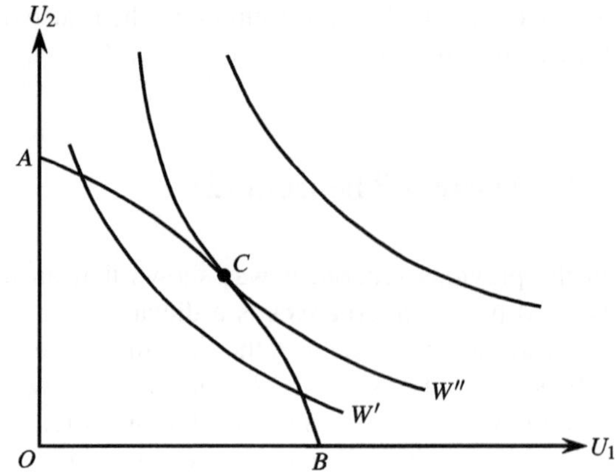

individuals in a two individuals economy. Curves W', W'', etc. are indifference curves of $W(U_1, U_2)$, a Bergsonian welfare function. They are drawn under the assumptions that the function W is Paretian, i.e., increasing with respect to U_i $(i = 1, 2)$, and that the function W is a strictly quasi-concave function (see Sect. 3.3). The social welfare W is maximized at the point C in Fig. 9.1. In other words, a Bergsonian social welfare function is used to find the point of the optimal income distribution from Pareto optimal utility combinations AB.

The lesson from Arrow's theorem is that such a Bergsonian social welfare function as a social ordering R cannot be obtained rationally and democratically from individual orderings R_i $(i = 1, \ldots, n)$. In other words, it is a dictator J's ordering. Since different individuals have different views on how incomes should be distributed, we should rather consider the Bergsonian welfare function W_i of the i-th individual, $i = 1, \ldots, n$, as his individual ordering R_i over social states, which express his value judgements on income distribution. It is true that W_i cannot be the Bergsonian social welfare function, unless the i-th individual is a dictator. Unlike the case of individual's utility function which express his taste, however, individual's ordering of social states like income distribution which express his ethical value judgement can be changed through education, persuasion, and propaganda. If there is any hope to change individual rankings of social states toward the unanimity, then, it is not entirely useless to review some reasonable Bergsonian social welfare functions as possible candidates of the social welfare function which may be supported by individuals almost unanimously.

9.4 Pareto Optimal Redistribution

Let us start with the problem of the so called Pareto optimal redistribution, which makes clear some implications of Bergsonian social welfare functions. As was shown in Chap. 4 (Problem 4.1), Pareto optimal allocation achieved by ideal competitive markets implies the maximization of $\sum_i a_i U_i$, where U_i denotes the utility of the i-th individual and a_i's are any arbitrary given positive numbers. Since a_i's can be changed by the redistribution of income among individuals, competitive markets fail to determine the optimal distribution of income. This indeterminacy does not necessarily arise from the assumption of egoistic individual in the sense that his utility depends only on his income and is independent of others' income. To see this, let us assume that an individual's utility is a function not only of his own income but also of others' income, by taking into consideration such facts as charity and envy among individuals.

Consider a two individual economy where

$$U_A = U_A(Y_A, Y_B) \tag{9.1}$$

and

$$U_B = U_B(Y_A, Y_B) \tag{9.2}$$

are, respectively, the utility of individual A and B, and Y_A and Y_B are, respectively, the income given to individual A and B. We assume, of course, that $\frac{\partial U_A}{\partial Y_A}$ and $\frac{\partial U_B}{\partial Y_B}$ are positive, while $\frac{\partial U_A}{\partial Y_B}$ and $\frac{\partial U_B}{\partial Y_A}$ can generally be anything, if they are positive they show the positive marginal utility of charity, and negative, the existence of envy among individuals.

Suppose that in a competitive allocation $Y_A = \overline{Y}_A$ and $Y_B = \overline{Y}_B$ and, without loss of generality, that $\overline{Y}_A > \overline{Y}_B$. Unlike in the case of no interdependent preference, there is still a possibility of increasing both of U_A and U_B through income redistribution, if $\frac{\partial U_A}{\partial Y_B} > 0$ and $\frac{\partial U_B}{\partial Y_B} > \frac{\partial U_B}{\partial Y_A}$. In Fig. 9.2, Y_A is measured vertically, and Y_B is measured horizontally. The slope of the line *OE* is $+1$, and that of the line *AB*, -1. Starting from the point C of original income $\overline{Y}_A$ and $\overline{Y}_B$, and transferring income from the rich A to the poor B, we proceed along *CE* from C down to E. If the curve *FDG* is an indifference curve of individual A, obtained from (9.1), then, point D is the point of Pareto optimal redistribution of income, since a further redistribution from individual A to individual B decreases the utility of A. This point of Pareto redistribution remains unchanged even if the point of original income C is shifted to any point located on the line *AB* between A and D.

Is this point of Pareto optimal redistribution, then, also the point of optimal distribution of income? Definitely not. The location of point D is, though not locally, but globally, not independent of the location of the point C of the original income distribution. To see this, let us interchange the roles of two individuals A and B and assume that $\overline{Y}_B > \overline{Y}_A$. In Fig. 9.2, points C and D are now located

Fig. 9.2

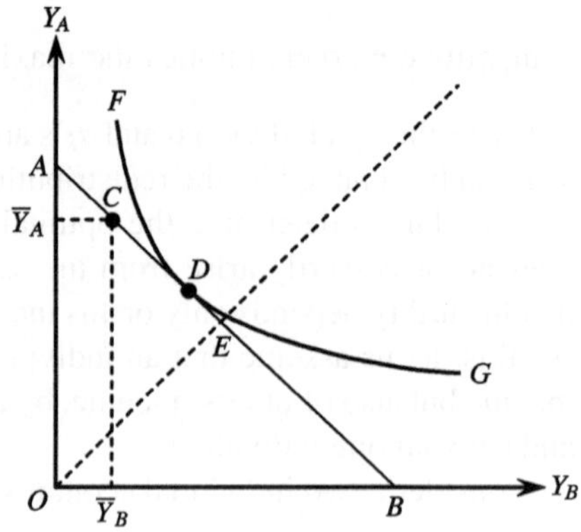

on the line AB between E and B, unless the function $U_B(Y_A, Y_B)$ in (9.2) is not much different from the function $U_A(Y_B, Y_A)$, i.e., the function U_A in (9.1) with Y_A and Y_B interchanged. Of course, D remains unchanged, if $U_A(Y_A, Y_B)$ in (9.1) and $U_B(Y_A, Y_B)$ in (9.2) are identical functions, so that the curve *FDG* is also an indifference curve of *UB* in Fig. 9.2.

In other words, utility functions of interdependent preference, U_A and U_B in (9.1) and (9.2), are Bergsonian social welfare functions of individuals A and B. Unless different individuals have same social welfare function so that there exists a consensus on the optimal distribution, it is generally impossible to find the point of optimal redistribution, which is independent of the point of original income distribution in Fig. 9.2.

9.5 Utilitarianism (1)

The oldest and still most well-known example of Bergsonian social welfare function is that of utilitarianism. It insists "the greatest happiness of the greatest number" and "everybody to count for one, no body for more than one." From the point of view of utilitarianism, Bergsonian social welfare function of an n individuals society

$$W = W(U_1, \ldots, U_n) \tag{9.3}$$

where U_i denotes the utility of the i-th individual, is an additive separable function so that

$$W = U_1 + U_2 + \cdots + U_n. \tag{9.4}$$

The social welfare function (9.4) has been called the Cambridge social welfare function, since Pigou used it to insist the equal distribution of national income, by assuming that different individuals have rather similar utility functions and that the marginal utility of income is diminishing. It may be interesting, however, to know that Edgeworth in Oxford also used (9.4) to insist unequal distribution of income, by emphasizing that different individuals have different utility functions.

It can be shown that (9.3) is reduced to (9.4) if utilities are ordinal,

$$\frac{\partial W}{\partial U_i} > 0 \quad (i = 1, \ldots, n) \tag{9.5}$$

and

$$\frac{W_r}{W_s} = W_{rs}(U_r, U_s) \quad (r, s = 1, \ldots, n) \tag{9.6}$$

where $W_r = \dfrac{\partial W}{\partial U_r}$ $(r = 1, \ldots, n)$. In other words, Bergsonian social welfare function is utilitarian, if it is Paretian so that (9.5) is satisfied and if the marginal rate of substitution of U_r and U_s in W is independent of U_t for $t \neq r, s$. The latter condition implies that the social order of two different social states can be judged from utilities of individuals who are not indifferent between two states, irrespective of the utilities of individuals who are indifferent between them. It is a natural extension of the former condition that the social welfare increases if utilities of some individuals increase while those of no individuals decrease.

To show that (9.5) and (9.6) implies (9.4), let us first show that (9.6) implies that there is a set of functions $w_1(U_1), \ldots, w_n(U_n)$ such that

$$\frac{W_r}{W_s} = \frac{w_r(U_r)}{w_s(U_s)} \quad (r, s = 1, \ldots, n). \tag{9.7}$$

Since from (9.6)

$$\frac{W_r}{W_s} = \frac{\dfrac{W_r}{W_t}}{\dfrac{W_s}{W_t}} = \frac{W_{rt}(U_r, U_t)}{W_{st}(U_s, U_t)} \tag{9.8}$$

for all $r, s, t = 1, \ldots, n$, we have

$$\log\left(\frac{W_r}{W_s}\right) = \log W_{rt}(U_r, U_t) - \log W_{st}(U_s, U_t) \tag{9.9}$$

and

$$\frac{\partial^2 \log\left(\dfrac{W_r}{W_s}\right)}{\partial U_r \partial U_s} = 0 \tag{9.10}$$

so that

$$\log\left(\frac{W_r}{W_s}\right) = A_r(U_r) + A_s(U_s) + C \tag{9.11}$$

where C is some constant and therefore

$$\frac{W_r}{W_s} = A_r(U_r)A_s(U_s). \tag{9.12}$$

By defining that $w_r(U_r) = A_r(U_r)$ and $w_s(U_s) = \dfrac{1}{A_s(U_s)}$, then, we can eliminate U_t in (9.8) and have

$$\frac{W_r}{W_s} = \frac{w_r(U_r)}{w_s(U_s)}. \tag{9.13}$$

In other words, there is a set of functions $w_i(U_i)$ ($i = 1, \ldots, n$, but $i \neq t$), which satisfy (9.7).

Similarly, by eliminating U_s ($s \neq t$), from

$$\frac{W_r}{W_t} = \frac{W_{rs}(U_r, U_s)}{W_{ts}(U_t, U_s)} \tag{9.14}$$

we can show that there is a set of functions $v_j(U_j)$ ($j = 1, \ldots, n$, but $j \neq s$), which satisfy

$$\frac{W_r}{W_t} = \frac{v_r(U_r)}{v_t(U_t)}. \tag{9.15}$$

Let us define that

$$w_t = \frac{v_t(U_t)w_1(U_1)}{v_1(U_1)} \tag{9.16}$$

by assuming, without loss of generality, that $t \neq 1, 2$. Since from (9.7) and (9.15)

$$\frac{v_t w_1}{v_1} = \frac{W_t w_1}{W_1} = \frac{W_t w_2}{W_2} = \frac{v_t w_2}{v_2} \tag{9.17}$$

we have also

$$w_t = \frac{v_t(U_t)w_2(U_2)}{v_2(U_2)}. \tag{9.18}$$

It follows that w_t is a function of U_t alone, since it is independent of U_2 in the right hand side of (9.16) and independent of U_1 in the right hand side of (9.18). Moreover, $\frac{w_t}{w_1} = \frac{v_t}{v_1} = \frac{W_t}{W_1}$. Therefore, we can conclude that there is a set of functions $w_1(U_1), \ldots, w_n(U_n)$ which satisfy (9.7).

Secondly, from (9.7), we can show that there exist functions $F_1, \ldots, F_n$ and G such that

$$W = G(F_1(U_1) + F_2(U_2) + \cdots + F_n(U_n)). \tag{9.19}$$

Consider a function H such that for each r, $\frac{\partial H}{\partial U_r} = w_r(U_r)$ $(r = 1, \ldots, n)$. Then,

$$dH = \sum_r w_r(U_r) dU_r. \tag{9.20}$$

Therefore, we can define F_r by

$$H = \int \sum_r w_r(U_r)\, dU_r = \sum_r F_r(U_r). \tag{9.21}$$

Since by definition,

$$dW = \sum_r W_r dU_r, \tag{9.22}$$

the partial derivatives of functions H and W are always proportional. It follows, therefore, that $dH = 0$ if and only if $dW = 0$, and that any two sets of $U_1, \ldots, U_n$ yield equal W if and only if they yield equal H. Hence W is a function of H, and from (9.21)

$$W = G(H) = G(F_1(U_1) + \cdots + F_n(U_n)). \tag{9.23}$$

In view of (9.5), $G'F_i > 0$ for all i. Since we can make $G' > 0$ and $F_i' > 0$ for all i, without loss of generality, now we can arrive at the utilitarian welfare function (9.4) by redefining ordinal indicators of welfare and utilities with $G^{(-1)}W, F_1(U_1), \ldots, F_n(U_n)$, where $G^{(-1)}$ is the inverse function of G.

9.6 Utilitarianism (2)

To argue for the equal distribution of income, however, it is necessary to assume that the marginal utility of income is diminishing, which implies that social welfare and individual utilities cannot be ordinal. As was discussed in Sect. 3.11, utility can be considered as cardinal, if we assume that the behavior of people facing risks can be described by the maximization of the expected utility. Then, the utility function is unique up to the increasing linear transformation. Let us suppose that both social welfare and individual utilities are cardinal in this sense. In this case, we can show that the Bergsonian social welfare function (9.3) can be reduced to an additive function (9.4), without making such an assumption as (9.6). Let W be chosen so that $W = 0$ if for all the n individuals $U_i = 0$ $(i = 1, \ldots, n)$, where W and U_i denote, respectively, the social welfare and the utility of the i-th individual. We can make W a single valued function by assuming that if every individual is indifferent between two social states, then the society is also indifferent between them.

To show that W can be written as an additive function (9.3) of U_i's, we first show that W is a homogeneous function of the first order of U_i's. In other words, if $U_i = u_i$ $(i = 1, \ldots, n)$, and $W = w$, then $W = kw$ when $U_i = ku_i$ $(i = 1, \ldots, n)$.

Consider first the case where $0 \leq k \leq 1$. Suppose that $U_i = 0$ for all the individual and therefore $W = 0$ in the social state A while $U_i = s_i$ $(i = 1, \ldots, n)$, and $W = v$ in the social state P. Consider a social state Q which is a combination of A with the probability $(1 - p)$ and P with the probability p. Welfare and utilities in Q can be obtained as the expected welfare and expected utilities from welfare and utilities in A and P, i.e., $W = pv, U_i = ps_i$ $(i = 1, \ldots, n)$. If we write $k = p$, and compare welfare and utilities in P and Q, we can show that W is homogeneous of order one with respect to U_i's for the case where $0 \leq k \leq 1$, since being the probability p cannot be larger than 1 or smaller than 0.

Next let us consider the case $k < 0$. Suppose the social state R is such that the social state A is equivalent to the combination of the social state R with probability p and the social state P with probability $(1 - p)$. The social welfare and individual utilities in R should be such that

$$W = \left(1 - \frac{1}{p}\right)v, \quad U_i = \left(1 - \frac{1}{p}\right)s_i \quad (i = 1, \ldots, n)$$

since the welfare and utilities in A are weighted average of those in R and P, with weights being p and $(1 - p)$. If we write $k = 1 - \dfrac{1}{p}$ and compare welfare and utilities in R and those in P, we can show that W is homogeneous of order one with respect to U_i's for the case of $k < 0$, since we can make k equal to any negative number by a suitable choice of the probability p.

Finally, for the case where $k > 1$, consider the social state S such that the social state P is equivalent to the combination of the social state S with the probability p and the social state A with the probability $(1 - p)$. The welfare and utilities in such a state as S should be that

$$W = \frac{1}{p}v, \quad U_i = \frac{1}{p}s_i \quad (i = 1, \ldots, n)$$

since welfare and utilities in P are the expected values of those in S and those in A. If we write $k = \frac{1}{p}$, then, we can make k equal to any number larger than one by appropriate choice of p. From the comparison of utilities and welfare in P and S, we can show the homogeneity of the first order of W with respect to U_i's for the case of $k > 1$.

Now we are ready to show that the social welfare function can be written as an additive function (9.4) of utilities. Let a_i $(i = 1, \ldots, n)$ be the value of W when $U_i = 1$, and $U_j = 0$ for all $j \neq i$. Let furthermore S_i be a social state in which $U_i = u_i$ and $U_j = 0$ for all $j \neq i$. From the homogeneity of W, then, $W = a_i u_i$ in the social state S_i. Consider a social state T which is a combination of $S_1, \ldots, S_n$, each with probability $\frac{1}{n}$. The social welfare and individual utilities in this state T are

$$W = \frac{1}{n} \sum_i a_i u_i, \quad U_i = \frac{u_i}{n} \quad (i = 1, \ldots, n).$$

Then, in view of the homogeneity of order one of W, the social welfare function can be written as

$$W = \sum_i a_i U_i. \tag{9.24}$$

Since $U_1, \ldots, U_n$ are unique only up to the increasing linear transformation, we can make (9.24) reduced to (9.4) by redefining U_i $(i = 1, \ldots, n)$ with $a_i U_i$.

9.7 Social Contract

An alternative Bergsonian social welfare function is proposed by J. Rawls from the point of view of the theory of the social contract, the traditional rival of utilitarianism. Rawls criticises the social welfare function (9.4) of utilitarianism that it subordinates individuals to the common good, or to the end of attaining the greatest net balance of satisfaction, since it allows the case where the greater gains of some, even if they are better off, may offset the losses of others less fortunate. The social welfare function suggested is, then,

$$W = W(U_1, \ldots, U_n) = \min_i (U_1, \ldots, U_n) \tag{9.25}$$

which implies that the level of the welfare of a society is indicated by the level of utility of individuals who are most unfortunate. Figure 9.3 shows indifference curves of the social welfare for the case of social welfare function (9.4) and (9.25). The utility of the first individual, U_1, is measured horizontally, and that of the second,

Fig. 9.3

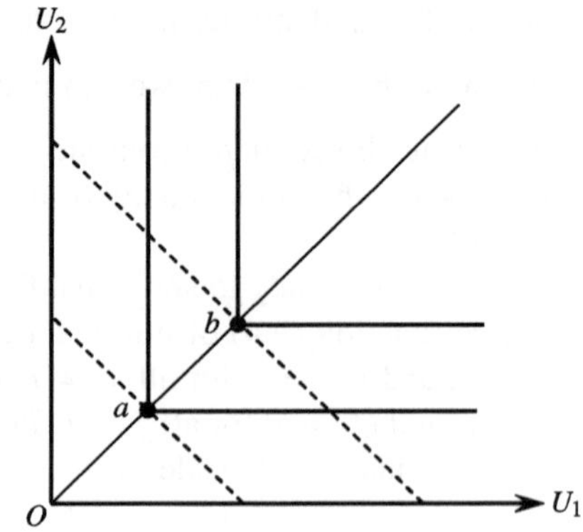

U_2, vertically. While indifference curves of (9.4) are straight dotted lines, those of (9.25) are L shaped with kinks at points of equal utilities like a and b.

The social welfare function can be explained from the point of view of the theory of social contract as the maximin behavior criterion of a rational individual facing uncertainty. Suppose the social contract on the distribution of income is made among individuals in an initial or original situation, the significant feature of which is that no one knows his position in the society, nor even his place in the distribution of natural talents and abilities. Given the circumstances of this initial or original position, it is rational for an individual to behave as if he were designing a society in which his enemy is to assign him his place. Thus it is rational to be conservative, to assume that he would be the worst-off and to behave in accordance with the maximin principle so as to maximize the utility of the worst off. Though every individual is trying to maximize his own utility, they arrive at an agreement in the sense that the utility of the poorest should be maximized.

Of course, one might argue that the maximin criterion is too risk-averse or too conservative as the behavior criterion of individuals facing uncertainty. Suppose, without losing the generality, individuals can be ordered according to the level of utility to be enjoyed in the society to come so that $U_1 > U_2 \cdots > U_n$. With the complete ignorance on the place to be assigned to him in the society, a rational individual at the social contract may assume equal chance to all the places from the first down to the n-th in this ranking of utility. Then, an additive social welfare function

$$W = W(U_1, \ldots, U_n) = \frac{1}{n} \sum_i U_i \tag{9.26}$$

is obtained as the expected utility of a risk-neutral individual so that the utilitarian social welfare function (9.4) can also be explained from the theory of social contract.

If so, it may be interesting to compare the resulting distributions suggested by the two different welfare functions (9.4) and (9.25). The inequalities in the distribution are justified, of course, if and only if the value of such social welfare functions can

Fig. 9.4

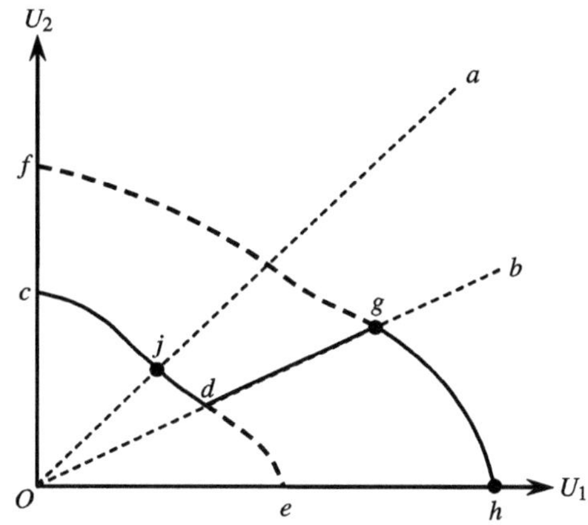

be made larger by unequal distributions. Conversely, which social welfare function requires larger inequality to maximize the social welfare? To see this, consider a two individuals economy and suppose, in Fig. 9.4, that the first individual whose utility U_1 is measured horizontally represents talented individuals, while the second individual whose utility U_2 is measured vertically represents ordinary untalented individuals. Let us assume that the special ability of the first individual cannot be mobilized unless there exists an incentive that his utility is higher relative to that of the second individual.

In Fig. 9.4, line *Oa* indicates equal distribution of utilities while line *Ob* shows the minimum required utility difference. Utility frontier, i.e., the boundary of the set of utilities possible under resources and technological constraints, is curve cjde when there is no incentive for the first individual. If there is a sufficient incentives for him, on the other hand, utility frontier is shifted into curve *fgh*. Since the minimum required incentive is indicated by line *Ob*, utility combinations between f and g are actually impossible. Realizable utility frontier is, therefore, considered to be *cjdgh*, having a rising porting *dg*.

If we superimpose Fig. 9.3 on Fig. 9.4, we can see that the social welfare function (9.25) is maximized at point g, where higher utility of the first individual is justified on the ground that it makes the lower utility of the second individual higher than it is otherwise, for example, at the point j of the equal distribution. On the other hand, the social welfare function (9.26) which can be reduced to (9.4) is maximized at a point which lies between g and h on the utility frontier. In other words, utilitarianism recommends greater inequality. As Rawls argued, this is because it allows to offset the loss of the poor by the greater gains of the rich. While the point g can be admitted ex post even by the less fortunate second individual, points to the right of the point g induces ex post resentment to unjust treatment. If the poor insist the points located to the left of the point g, however, Rawls considers that it is based not on resentment but on envy which is one of Kant's "vices of hating mankind."

Fig. 9.5

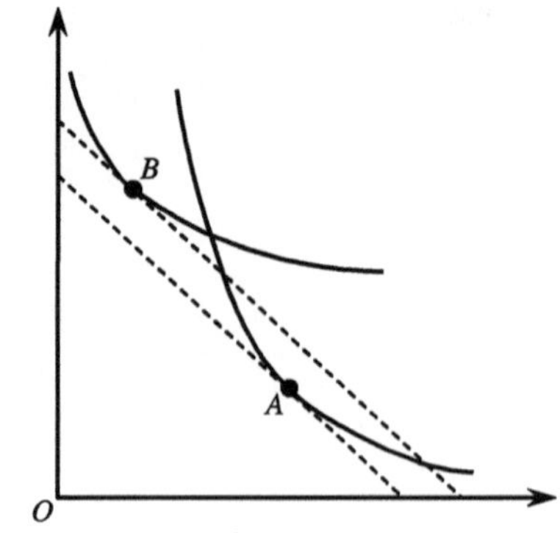

9.8 No Envy Criterion

In spite of Rawls, however, let us consider a criterion of the optimal distribution that no individual feels envy of other individuals in the distribution. If x_i denotes the consumption vector of the i-th individual and $U_i(x_i)$ denotes his utility function, $i = 1, \ldots, n$, no envy criterion is that

$$U_i(x_i) \geq U_i(x_j) \quad (i, j = 1, \ldots, n). \tag{9.27}$$

In other words, no individual feels envy of other individuals, since the utility of consumption vectors of others are not higher than the utility of his own consumption vector, if they are evaluated by his own utility function. Let us call a distribution fair if the condition (9.27) is satisfied at a Pareto optimal allocation.

Suppose a Pareto optimal allocation is achieved by the perfect competition. It is easily seen that the equal distribution of income is a fair distribution. Since all the individuals face an identical budget constraint, it is impossible that the optimal consumption vector chosen by an individual has less utility for him than consumption vectors chosen by ocher individuals. The converse is, however, not necessarily true. A fair distribution does not necessarily imply the equal distribution of income, when goods arc cvaluated by Pareto optimal (perfectly competitive) prices.

Consider an example shown in Fig. 9.5. The first good is measured horizontally, and the second good, vertically. Points A and B indicate, respectively, the consumption vectors distributed to individuals A and B. Curves passing points A and B are, respectively, indifference curves of individuals A and B. Marginal rates of substitution of A and B at A and B are identical, since Pareto optimality is assumed. Since individual A prefers point A to point B, and individual B prefers point B to point A, A does not feel envy at B and B does not feel envy at A, so that the distribution is fair. If goods are evaluated by Pareto optimal prices given by the common marginal rate of substitution at A and B, however, the income of B is larger than the income of A.

We can have this kind of examples quite often, if two individuals have different utility functions. In the case of Fig. 9.5, individual B has larger income, because relatively he evaluate the second good higher so that he is given in a fair distribution relatively large quantity of the second good while the price of the second good is relatively higher. When individuals have similar utility functions, on the other hand, no-envy criterion (9.27) implies that their incomes are not much different each other. If the number of individuals is very large, furthermore, each individual can find some individuals who have utility functions very similar to his own so that their incomes are not much different from his income in a fair distribution. Can we conjecture, then, that a fair distribution is an equal distribution in a large economy?

To prove this conjecture, let us consider that each point in a closed interval [0, 1] represents an individual. Let $x(t)$ denote the commodity vector to be given to an individual $t \in [0, 1]$ and let the utility of the individual t be denoted by

$$U_t(x(t)) = U(t, x). \tag{9.28}$$

By denoting $U_{t_0}(x(t))$ with $V_{t_0}(t)$, we can express the condition that an individual t_0 does not feel envy at others as

$$V_{t_0}(t_0) \geq V_{t_0}(t) \quad \text{(for all } t \in [0, 1]). \tag{9.29}$$

In other words, $V_{t_0}(t)$ should be maximized at $t = t_0$.

Suppose that $x(t)$ is differentiable. If t_0 is an interior point of [0, 1], the condition for the maximization of $V_{t_0}(t)$ at $t = t_0$ is

$$\begin{aligned}\frac{dV_{t_0}(t)}{dt} &= \frac{d[U_{t_0}(x(t))]}{dt} \\ &= \sum_i \frac{\partial U_{t_0}(x(t))}{\partial x_i}\frac{dx_i(t)}{dt} \\ &= 0\end{aligned} \tag{9.30}$$

where $x(t) = [x_1(t), \ldots, x_m(t)]$ and x_i denotes the quantity of the i-th commodity in x. In a Pareto optimal allocation,

$$\frac{\partial U_{t_0}(x(t))}{\partial x_i} = \lambda_{t_0} p_i \tag{9.31}$$

where p_i denotes the optimal price of the i-th commodity and λ_t denotes the positive marginal utility of income. In view of (9.31), then, (9.30) implies

$$\lambda_{t_0} \sum_i p_i \frac{dx_i(t)}{dt} = 0. \tag{9.32}$$

Therefore, in a fair distribution, we have

$$\sum_i p_i \frac{dx_i(t)}{dt} = 0. \tag{9.33}$$

Let us now define the income of t as

$$y(t) = \sum_i p_i x_i(t). \tag{9.34}$$

The equal distribution of income means that $y(t)$ is constant with respect to t, i.e.,

$$\frac{dy(t)}{dt} = \sum_i p_i \frac{dx_i(t)}{dt} = 0. \tag{9.35}$$

From the comparison of (9.33) and (9.35), then, it is clear that a fair distribution is an equal distribution if $x(t)$ is differentiable in a large economy.

Problems

9.1. Show graphically that the utilitarian social welfare function is maximized by the equal distribution of a given total income between two individuals, if individuals have identical utility functions and the marginal utility of income is diminishing. From the point of view of utilitarianism, can you defend the equal distribution, even if different individuals have different utility functions but you are completely ignorant of which individual has higher or lower marginal utility of income at such a distribution?

9.2. Discuss the following criticism of Arrow against the arguments in Sect. 9.6. The theory of the expected utility "is a very useful matter from the point of view of developing the descriptive economic theory of behavior in the presence of random events, but it has nothing to do with welfare consideration, particularly if we are interested primarily in making a social choice among alternative policies in which no random elements enter. To say otherwise would be to assert that the distribution of the social income is to be governed by the tastes of individuals for gambling."

9.3. Discuss the following criticism of Arrow against the arguments in Sect. 9.6. "Even if, for some reason, we should admit the measurability of utility for an individual, there still remains the question of aggregating the individual utilities. At best, it is contended that, for an individual, his utility function is uniquely determined up to a linear transformation; we must still choose one out of the infinite family of indicators, to represent the individual, and the value of the aggregate (say a sum) are dependent on how the choice is made for each individual."

9.4. If different individuals have different utility functions, does the maximization of social welfare function (9.25) in Sect. 9.7 require the equal distribution of the given total income?

9.5. Unless all individuals have a common identical utility function, the social welfare function (9.26) in Sect. 9.7 should read as

$$W = \frac{1}{n} \sum_{i} U(X_i, Y_i)$$

where U is the utility function of a particular individual who maximizes his expected utility, X_i is the income given to the i-th individual, and Y_i is the aggregate of subjective features of the i-th individual, $i = 1, \ldots, n$. Explain the difference between this welfare function and the welfare functions discussed in Sects. 9.5 and 9.6.

Literature

For further studies in general, see Malinvaud, op. cit., pp. 86–99, and Varian, op. cit., pp. 225–228.
The explanation of Arrow's theorem in Sects. 9.2 and 9.3 is based on K.J. Arrow, *Social Choice and Individual Values* (1951, 1963), and A.K. Sen, *Collective Choice and Social Welfare* (1970). Section 9.4 is a critical review of H.M. Hochman and J.D. Rodgers, "Pareto optimal redistribution," *American Economic Review* (1969). E.S. Phelps (ed.), *Economic Justice* (1973) contains articles of M. Fleming, J.C. Harsanyi, P.K. Pattanaik, J. Rawls and E.S. Phelps, on which arguments in Sects. 9.5, 9.6 and 9.7 are based. For Sect. 9.6, see particularly the article of Harsanyi. See also H.A. John Green, *Aggregation in Economic Analysis* (1964), pp. 17–20 for Sect. 9.5. No envy criterion and fair allocation are discussed in H.R. Varian, "Equity, Envy and Efficiency," *Journal of Economic Theory* (1974), and H.R. Varian, "Two Problems in the Theory of Fairness," *Journal of Public Economics* (1976).

Chapter 10
Microeconomic Foundations of Macroeconomics

10.1 Macroeconomics

Economic theory can be divided into microeconomics and macroeconomics. The neoclassical theory of microeconomics has been much influenced by the theory of classical mechanics in physics. In the latter theory, a system which consists of a number of particles can be fully described by specifying mass, position, and velocity of each single particle. Similarly, microeconomic theory tries, as we saw in preceding chapters, to describe the behavior of an economy by specifying the behavior of each single consumer and the input–output activity of each single firm. There is, however, an alternative approach in physics. Consider the behavior of the gas contained in a balloon. The gas consists of different molecules and the behavior of these molecules like the collisions among them obeys the laws of classical mechanics. If we know the position, velocity and mass of each of these molecules, therefore, we can describe, at least in principle, the behavior of the gas. From the more practical point of view, however, it is much more important to measure the balloon's volume, its pressure, its temperature, etc., to describe the behavior of the gas. For example, it can be described by the universal gas equation, $pV = NRT$, where p denotes pressure, V volume, N the number of mols, R the universal gas constant, and T the absolute temperature.

Similarly, macroeconomic theory tries to describe the behavior of an economy in terms of the aggregate level of output, the aggregate demand, the level of total employment, the general price level, etc., without describing the behavior of each single consumer and the activity of each single firm. The historically most celebrated equation of macroeconomics, which looks like the universal gas equation, is the equation of exchange in the quantity theory of money, $MV = PT$, or the Cambridge equation, $M = kPT$, where M is the stock of money, V is its velocity of circulation, P is the general price level, T is the physical volume of transactions or the level of aggregate output, and k is a constant which is called Marshallian k. Traditionally, the main problem of the macroeconomics was to explain the change in the general price level P caused by changes in the supply of money, while the

T. Negishi, *Elements of Neo-Walrasian Economics*, Advances in Japanese Business and Economics 5, DOI 10.1007/978-4-431-54535-4_10, © Springer Japan 2014

aggregate level of output T is considered to be at the level of full employment, which is unchanged, at least, in the short-run, i.e., under the given technology and the given labor population. After the so-called Keynesian revolution, however, macroeconomic theories are also concerned seriously with the short-run variations in the aggregate level of output. This is true, not only for Keynesian theories which consider that the demand and supply are not necessarily equalized in some important markets, but also for classical theories which assume that the demand and supply are equalized in all markets.

As was in microeconomics, it is also convenient in macroeconomics to describe the economy in a state of equilibrium which repeats itself through time, at least in the short-run. As was suggested by A. Marshall, however, it is not necessary for this purpose to consider that all the consumers and the firms in the economy are simultaneously in equilibrium. It is possible for an aggregate economy to be in equilibrium, even though most of consumers and firms are in disequilibrium and changing their plans of demand and supply. What is required is that the adjustments made by individual consumers and firms are mutually cancelled out so that the average consumer and the average firm are in equilibrium. In other words, the condition for an equilibrium of an aggregate economy is the equilibrium of the representative consumer and that of the representative firm, which jointly make a small replica or a miniature of the whole aggregate economy. To the extent that the behavior of an aggregate economy can be explained by the behavior of the representative consumer and the representative firm, macroeconomics is based on foundations of microeconomics. Although the macroeconomics itself is beyond our scope, it may not be unreasonable to devote the final chapter of a text book of microeconomics to the consideration of microeconomic foundations of macroeconomics.

10.2 Time and Money

Microeconomic theories developed in the preceding chapters are static or timeless ones of a real economy, where the role of money is not taken into the consideration. To consider the behavior of the representative consumer and of the representative firm, which serve as microeconomic foundations of macroeconomics, however, we have to extend our models of consumers and of firms into dynamic or multi-period ones and introduce the money which serves as the unit of account (the numeraire), the medium of exchange, and the store of value through time. This section is, therefore, devoted to an informal sketch of multi-period models of consumers and firms in a monetary economy. Both consumers and firms have to make their plans of demand and supply not only for the current period but also for the all future periods in their time horizons (possibly for infinite periods). Let us assume the perfect competition so that consumers and firms are price takers. While the current prices are given to them as market prices, consumers and firms have to expect prices which might prevail in future periods on the basis of current prices. In view of macroeconomic theories which are interested only in the level of aggregate output and that of total employment, let us assume that there is a single produced good which can be either consumed or used as capital in production and that labor is the only primary factor of production.

Consider first the multi-period model of a firm. Production functions are given not only for the current period but also for all the future periods and define the maximum possible net output in each period as a function of labor input and capital available in the period. While the available capital in the current period is given as a result of investments in the past periods, the capital in each future period is a variable which can be changed by investments in the previous periods. If the capital available in the t-th period is denoted by K_t and the investment made in the s-th period by I_s,

$$K_t = K_0 + \sum_{s=0}^{t-1} I_s. \tag{10.1}$$

The profit to be distributed in the k-th period is defined as

$$\pi_t = p_t Y_t - w_t L_t - p_t I_t \tag{10.2}$$

where p_t is the price of the product, Y_t is the maximum possible net output which keeps the level of capital unchanged, w_t is the rate of wage, and L_t is labor input, all in the t-th period. The firm maximizes

$$\sum_t \pi_t' \tag{10.3}$$

where π_t' is the discounted present value of the profit to be distributed in the t-th period, i.e.,

$$\pi_t' = \frac{\pi_t}{(1+i_0)(1+i_1)\cdots(1+i_{t-1})}, \quad \pi_0' = \pi_0 \tag{10.4}$$

and i_t is the rate of interest prevailing in the t-th period. This is because π_t and π_{t-1} are of equal significance to the firm if $\pi_t = \pi_{t-1}(1 + i_{t-1})$. Even though the discounted present value of total profits (10.3) is positive, however, the profit to be distributed in the current period π_0 may be negative, if the investment in the current period is fairly large. In such a case, the firm has to finance the investment, at least partly, by issuing bonds which promise to pay certain amount of money in the next period. The price of a bond issued in period t, which promises to pay a units of money in period $t + 1$, is $\dfrac{a}{1+i_t}$. For simplicity, we assume that firms do not hold money.

At the end of Chap. 5, it is argued that the introduction of money is necessary in the non-tâtonnement model of market adjustments. If equilibrium has been achieved on completion of the preliminary process of tâtonnement, exchange of goods can, in principle, be achieved by barter without using money. It is highly inconvenient, however, since not only direct barter but also indirect barter, i.e., repeated barter, is necessary to achieve the required allocation. For example, someone who wishes to obtain good A by supplying good B may first have to exchange good B for good C and then exchange good C for good A. This is very inconvenient if good C is perishable. It will be very convenient, even in the world of tâtonnement, if everyone agrees to use money as a medium of exchange, i.e., as a special good that is specialized to play the role of good C. For the sake of simplicity, let us suppose that only the household of individual consumers demand such a convenient balance and that such a demand for money is uniquely related to the value of consumers' goods and bonds to be purchased by households. Of course, money as such has no direct utility, though people demand money for the sake of convenience in transactions.

In the multi-period model of a consumer, it is assumed that the life-time utility function is maximized being subject to the life-time budget constraint. In our simplified model, the utility depends, directly, only on the amount of the consumption of the single produced good and that of the leisure (labor not supplied) in each period. The lifetime budget constraint can be decomposed into budget constraints for single periods, the first two of which are as follows.

$$p_0C_0 + \frac{a}{1+i_0}B_0^d + m_0 + w_0l_0 = w_0\overline{L} + d_0 + m_{(-1)}, \tag{10.5}$$

$$p_1C_1 + \frac{a}{1+i_1}B_1^d + m_1 + w_1l_1 = w_1\overline{L} + d_1 + w_0 + aB_0^d \tag{10.6}$$

where C_t, B_t^d, m_t, l_t, $\overline{L}$, d_t are, respectively, the demand for the consumption good, the demand for the bond issued by the firms, the demand for money, the demand for the leisure, the total available time for leisure and labor supply, the profit distributed from firms, and $t = 0$ is the current period.

If we assume that no bond was issued in the last period ($t = -1$) and that current investments are fully financed by issuing bonds, the sum of profits distributed to all the consumers in the current period equals to the sum of $(p_0Y_0 - w_0L_0)$ of all the firms. Let us assume that the demand for money is uniquely related to the value of the consumers' demand for the good and the bond, so that

$$m_0 = k(i_0)\Big(p_0C_0 + \frac{a}{1+i_0}B_0^d\Big) \tag{10.7}$$

where k is the micro version of the Marshallian k. Although the money is introduced as a medium of exchange, it can also serve as a store of value as we saw in (10.5) and (10.6). If the rate of interest is raised and the bond becomes more attractive as a store of value, the consumer sacrifices the convenience in transactions for the higher yields of the bond and reduces the demand for money, so that k is a decreasing function of the rate of interest in (10.7).

10.3 Classical Macroeconomics

Let us consider an aggregate macro economy, composed by four markets, i.e., markets for the aggregate products, labor, money and bonds. The classical macroeconomic theory presupposes that the general price level, the rate of wage and the rate of interest are all flexible and that all the markets are cleared, i.e., the demand and supply are equalized in every market.

In view of the model of a firm sketched in Sect. 10.2, the aggregate level of output Y, the aggregate level of labor input L and the aggregate level of investment I can generally be assumed to be functions of the general price level p, the rate of wage w and the rate of interest i in the current period, since future p, w and i are expected as functions of current p, w and i. It can also easily be seen that Y and L are actually independent of i. If the expectations are static, furthermore, Y, L and I are homogeneous of degree zero in p and w. Since the current investments are assumed to be financed by issuing bonds, the aggregate supply of bonds B^s in the current period is

$$B^s = \frac{\frac{pI}{a}}{1+i} \tag{10.8}$$

so that it is homogeneous of degree one in p and w.

Similarly, from the model of a consumer sketched in Sect. 10.2, the aggregate level of consumption C, the aggregate demand for money M^d, the aggregate supply of labor L^s and the aggregate demand for bonds B^d are functions of p, w, i and the supply of money $\overline{M}$ which is given exogeneously. If expectations are static and the current distribution of profit is assumed to be equal to $pY - wL$, as was done in Sect. 10.2, C and L^s are functions of p, w, i, $\overline{M}$ and pY, homogeneous of degree zero in p, w and $\overline{M}$, and M^d and B^d are functions of p, w, i, $\overline{M}$ and pY, homogeneous of degree one in p, w and $\overline{M}$, since $L = L^s$ in equilibrium.

Equilibrium conditions are,

$$C\left(\frac{w}{p}, Y\left(\frac{w}{p}\right), \frac{\overline{M}}{p}, i\right) + I\left(\frac{w}{p}, i\right) = Y\left(\frac{w}{p}\right) \tag{10.9}$$

for the good market,

$$L\left(\frac{w}{p}\right) = L^s\left(\frac{w}{p}, Y\left(\frac{w}{p}\right), \frac{\overline{M}}{p}, i\right) \tag{10.10}$$

for the labor market,

$$B^d\left(p, w, pY\left(\frac{w}{p}\right), \overline{M}, i\right) = B^s(p, w, i) \tag{10.11}$$

for the bond market,

$$M^d\left(p, w, pY\left(\frac{w}{p}\right), \overline{M}, i\right) = \overline{M} \tag{10.12}$$

for the money market. Three unknowns p, w and i are determined by any three conditions among (10.9)–(10.12), since not all four conditions are independent from Walras' law. This equilibrium of markets in the current period is the so-called Hicksian temporary equilibrium in the sense that it may not repeat itself through future periods, because the future level of capital accumulation, for example, may be different from the current one.

In the classical macro model (10.9)–(10.12), money is neutral, since proportional changes in $\overline{M}$, p and w keep the equilibrium conditions unviolated, which can easily be seen from the homogeneity of degree one of B^d, B^s and M^d with respect to p, w and $\overline{M}$. In other words, changes in the supply of money have no real effects on the economy and merely induce proportional changes in the general price level and the rate of wage. Sometimes, small effects are boldly disregarded in macroeconomics. If there is no real balance effect on consumption so that C is independent of $\frac{\overline{M}}{p}$ in (10.9) and L^s is assumed to be a function of $\frac{w}{p}$ only in (10.10), the system is dichotomized in the sense that real variables are determined by real equations and monetary equation(s) can determine only the absolute level of price. The real wage is determined in (10.10), and then the rate of interest is determined by the equality of saving and investment

$$I\left(\frac{w}{p}, i\right) = S\left(\frac{w}{p}, Y\left(\frac{w}{p}\right), i\right) \tag{10.13}$$

which is derived from (10.9) by the definition of the saving $S = Y - C$.

10.4 Classical Unemployment

Since the labor market is cleared in (10.10), there exists no involuntary unemployment in classical macroeconomics. Voluntary and frictional unemployments, however, do exist even in classical equilibrium theory, and the changes in aggregate level of employment can be explained if we leave the world of static expectation.

Friedman, for example, describes the following effects of an increase in the supply of money. Because prices of products typically respond to an unanticipated rise in nominal demand faster than the prices of factors of production, real wages received go down—though real wages anticipated by employees go up since at first they are likely to evaluate the wages offered at the unchanged price level. This simultaneous fall *ex post* in real wages to employers and rise *ex ante* in real wages to employees is what increases both demand and supply of labor and enables employment to increase. But soon employees begin to consider rising prices and demand higher nominal wages. To keep the supply of labor larger than the equilibrium supply, real wages now have to be higher than the equilibrium ones. Any rise in real wages, however, decreases the demand for labor and tends to return employment to its former equilibrium level. Temporary increase in employment comes not from inflation *per se*i, but from unanticipated inflation.

Similarly, we can consider the effects of a decrease in the supply of money as follows. Because prices of products respond to an unanticipated decrease in nominal demand faster than prices of factors of production, as the supply of labor is temporarily decreased by the reduction in wages to below the anticipated normal level, real wages received go up—though real wages anticipated by employees go down since at first they tend to evaluate the wages offered at the unchanged price level. This simultaneous rise *ex post* in real wages to employers and fall *ex ante* in real wages to employees reduces both demand and supply of labor and enables voluntary unemployment to increase. However, employees soon realize that prices have fallen and accept lower nominal wages. To keep the level of voluntary unemployment higher than the equilibrium rate, real wages must now be lower than the equilibrium ones. Any fall in real wages, however, increases the demand for labor and tends to return voluntary unemployment to the equilibrium level. A temporary decrease in employment comes not from deflation *per se* but from unanticipated deflation.

Another example of the classical equilibrium theory of unemployment is the so-called job-search unemployment theory. This theory is based on two fundamental postulates. Firstly there is a search cost differential in an unorganized labor market in the sense that more and better information on alternative wage offers can be obtained more easily and quickly if the searcher is not currently employed and is devoted to the search activity. Secondly, a supplier of labor service will not change his reservation wage instantly but will initially continue searching for jobs with higher wages when actual wage offers fall short of the reservation wage.

Suppose that suppliers of labor formulate subjective estimates of the distribution of money wage rate offers over either space or time. These estimates are inelastic with respect to the mean of the distribution of actual wage rate offers, W. Let W^* represent the mean of the inter-household distribution of the mean of household's estimated distribution of money wage offers. Similarly, let P^* represent the mean of the inter-household distribution of the mean of household's estimated distribution of the price of the consumers' goods, estimates being inelastic with respect to the mean of the distribution of actual prices of the consumers' goods, P. An aggregate employment-acceptance function may be specified as $L^s\left(\frac{W^*}{P^*}, \frac{W}{W^*}\right)$, where the employment accepted in the short run is an increasing function of $\frac{W^*}{P^*}$ and an increasing function of $\frac{W}{W^*}$, reflecting the short-run speculative behavior of individual suppliers to accept (reject) an actual wage offer that is higher (lower) than the mean of his estimated distribution of wage offers. Similarly, an aggregate consumption demand function would be $C\left(\frac{W^*}{P^*}, \frac{P}{P^*}\right)$, which is an increasing function of $\frac{W^*}{P^*}$ and a diminishing function of $\frac{P}{P^*}$.

Now (10.9) and (10.10) are replaced by

$$C\left(\frac{W^*}{P^*}, \frac{P}{P^*}\right) + A = Y\left(\frac{W}{P}\right) \tag{10.14}$$

and

$$L\left(\frac{W}{P}\right) = L^s\left(\frac{W^*}{P^*}, \frac{W}{W^*}\right) \tag{10.15}$$

where A represents the autonomous demand. From (10.14) and (10.15) it is easily seen that an exogeneous change in aggregate demand for current output induces changes in the same direction in P and W, and also a change in the same direction of the amount of employment accepted.

10.5 Keynesian Macroeconomics

The Keynesian macroeconomic system is consist of two equations, *IS* and *LM* equations. The *IS* equation

$$I(i) = S(Y, i) \tag{10.16}$$

represents Keynes's theory of investment multiplier and requires that the aggregate level of output Y should be determined so as to equate the Saving it generates with the given Investment, when the rate of interest i is given. The *LM* equation, on the other hand, represents Keynes's liquidity preference theory of interest that the rate of interest is determined so as to equate people's demand for Liquidity with the supply of Money. In our terminology, therefore, it may be formulated as

$$M^d(Y, i) = \overline{M} \tag{10.17}$$

where, of course, $\overline{M}$ denotes the given supply of money. Unlike the case of (10.12), however, Keynesian theory emphasizes the role of the speculative demand for money that money is demanded by people who consider the current level of the rate of interest (prices of long-term bonds) too low (high). In other words, the equilibrium of demand and supply in the bond market is reflected in (10.17). Demand and supply in the labor market are, however, not equalized and there exists involuntary unemployment

$$F^{-1}(Y) < L^s\left(\frac{w}{p}\right) \tag{10.18}$$

when Y and i are determined by (10.16) and (10.17), where F^{-1} is the inverse function of the production function $Y = F(L)$ in the current period.

If we compare Keynesian system (10.16) and (10.17) with the classical system (10.9)–(10.12), the most striking deference is that there is no role for p and w in (10.16) and (10.17) so that Y is determined not by $\frac{w}{p}$ but directly by the effective demand $C + I$, since (10.16) can be rewritten as

$$Y = C(Y, i) + I(i). \tag{10.19}$$

From the point of view of macroeconomics itself or that of the monetary economics, of course, there are many important problems in the financial markets which exist behind (10.17). From the point of view of the microeconomic foundations of macroeconomics, however, we have to concentrate on the questions like why the role of prices (and wages) is limited, how the aggregate level of output is determined by the effective demand, and why involuntary unemployment continues to exist. To consider such questions which are real rather than monetary, we shall simplify the monetary aspect of our model in the below.

Suppose the representative firm's Walrasian demand for labor and supply of the products are decreasing functions of $\frac{w}{p}$, when it takes w and p given in the markets, but it does not make investment and distribute the current profit to consumers, so that no bond is issued. Let us denote the aggregate Walrasian demand for labor as $L_1 = L\left(\frac{w}{p}\right)$ and the aggregate Walrasian supply of the product as $Y_1 = Y\left(\frac{w}{p}\right)$.

Suppose the current utility of the representative consumer is

$$U = a_1 \log C_0 + a_2 \log m_0 + a_3 \log l_0 \tag{10.20}$$

where a_i's are positive constants, and his current period budget constraint is

$$pC_0 + m_0 + wl_0 = m_{(-1)} + w\overline{L} + d_0 \tag{10.21}$$

where $C_0, m_0, m_{(-1)}, l_0, \overline{L}$ and d_0 are as explained in the case of (10.5) in the above. Consumers do not demand for bonds. This is because there is no supply and the rate of interest is 0, so that demand and supply are trivially equated in the bond market. The representative consumer's Walrasian demand for the product C_0 and supply of labor $\overline{L} - l_0$ are obtained by the maximization of (10.20), subject to (10.21). We can denote the aggregate Walrasian demand for the product as $Y_2 = \dfrac{a_1}{a_2}\dfrac{\overline{M}}{p}$ and the aggregate Walrasian supply of labor as $L_3 = n\overline{L} - \dfrac{a_3}{a_2}\dfrac{\overline{M}}{w}$, where n is the number of consumers, if consumers are assumed to expect that $pY_2 - wL_3$ is the profit distributed from firms.

Combinations of real wages and real balance, i.e., $\dfrac{w}{p}$ and $\dfrac{\overline{M}}{p}$ are grouped as follows according to the sign of Walrasian excess demand in the product and labor markets,

I $\quad Y_2 - Y_1 > 0, \quad L_1 - L_3 < 0,$
II $\quad Y_2 - Y_1 < 0, \quad L_1 - L_3 < 0,$
III $\quad Y_2 - Y_1 > 0, \quad L_1 - L_3 > 0,$
IV $\quad Y_2 - Y_1 < 0, \quad L_1 - L_3 > 0.$

This is represented in a $\left(\dfrac{\overline{M}}{p}, \dfrac{w}{p}\right)$ diagram, Fig. 10.1, where the downward sloping curve Y_1Y_2 is the equilibrium locus of the product market, and the upward sloping curve L_1L_3 is the equilibrium locus of the labor market. In area I in Fig. 10.1, Walrasian excess demand exists in the product market and Walrasian excess supply in the labor market, which may be called stagflation. In area II (III), Walrasian excess supply (demand) prevails both in the product market and the labor market, i.e., deflation (inflation). Finally, in area IV we have Walrasian excess demand in the labor market and excess supply in the product market.

If the law of demand and supply works as in the classical macroeconomics wages are bid up in areas III and IV and bid down in areas I and II. Similarly, prices are bid up in areas I and III, while they are bid down in areas II and IV. Only at the point of intersection of the curves Y_1Y_2 and L_1L_3, i.e., point A, is Walrasian general equilibrium established and there are no changes in either p or w. In the Keynesian macroeconomics, however, the law of demand and supply does not work and it is assumed that p and w are not changed even if the markets are in disequilibrium. In view of the existence of unemployment (10.18), the Keynesian macroeconomics seems to be concerned with areas I and II in Fig. 10.1. We have to note, however, that the classification of areas in Fig. 10.1 is based on Walrasian excess demands, which are obtained from the assumption that consumers and firms behave as if they can demand and supply whatever amounts they wish at the given prices and wages. It is

Fig. 10.1

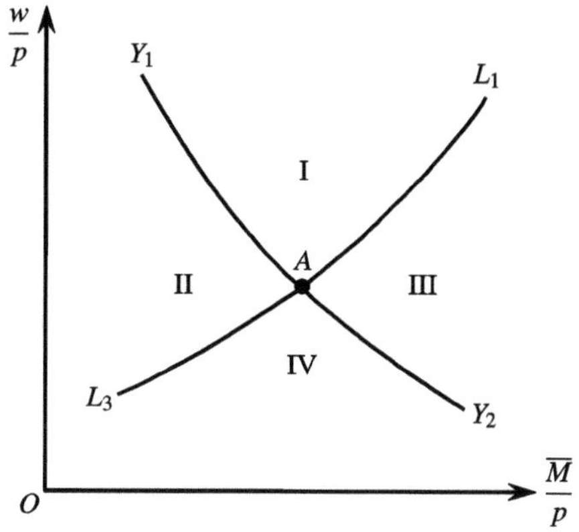

clear that such a Walrasian assumption can be justified only when the markets are cleared smoothly by the working of the law of demand and supply. To discuss the Keynesian macroeconomics, therefore, we have to modify the area classification in Fig. 10.1, in view of Keynesian assumption of the limited role of the law of demand and supply.

10.6 Quantity Constraints and Dual Decisions

Let us consider that consumers and firms take quantity constraints into their consideration when markets are in disequilibrium which cannot be expected to be cleared soon. If there is Walrasian excess demand in a market, they consider that the quantity they can purchase is given by the supply in the market and make dual decisions on their plans of demand and supply in the other markets. Similarly, they consider that the quantity they can sell is given by the demand in the market and modify their plans of demand and supply in the other markets, when they found Walrasian excess supply in a market. This is called the short-side principle, since only the consumers and firms on the short side (i.e., suppliers if there is excess demand, demanders if there is excess supply) can realize their Walrasian demand or supply.

In area I of Fig. 10.1, firms are not constrained and the effective and Walrasian demands and supplies of firms are identical, since Y_1 and L_1 are realized according to the short-side principle. Consumers are, on the other hand, constrained and have to make dual decisions on demand in the product market and on supply in the labor market, subject to the quantity constraints perceived in the other markets. The aggregate effective demand for the product Yde is obtained using the budget constraint

$$pC_0 + m_0 = m_{(-1)} + \frac{wL_1}{n} + d_0 \qquad (10.22)$$

instead of (10.21), since the representative consumer is now on the long-side of the labor market and cannot sell more labor than $\frac{L_1}{n}$. From the maximization of utility (10.20), subject to (10.22), we have $Y^{de} = \frac{a_1}{a_1 + a_2}\left(\frac{\overline{M}}{p} + Y_1\right)$, by considering that consumers expect the distribution of profit as $pY_1 - wL_1$. The excess effective demand in the product market is then

$$Y^{de} - Y_1 = \frac{a_2}{a_1 + a_2}(Y_2 - Y_1) \tag{10.23}$$

since we defined as $Y_2 = \frac{a_1}{a_2}\frac{\overline{M}}{p}$. Similarly, the aggregate effective supply of labor L^{se} is obtained using

$$m_0 + w(l_0 - \overline{L}) = m_{(-1)} + d_0 - pC_0 \tag{10.24}$$

since the representative consumer is on the long-side of the product market. The maximization of (10.20), subject to (10.24), gives the excess effective demand in the labor market as

$$L_1 - L^{se} = \frac{a_2}{a_2 + a_3}(L_1 - L_3) \tag{10.25}$$

since the aggregate profit is $pY_1 - wL_1$ and $L_3 = n\overline{L} - \frac{a_3}{a_2}\frac{\overline{M}}{w}$. The sign of the effective excess demand is, therefore, the same as the sign of Walrasian excess demand in area I.

In area II, Walrasian supplies Y_1 and L_3 are not realized in both markets and it is expected that effective demand will not be greater than Walrasian demand, with the sign of effective excess demand again unchanged by dual decisions. Since firms are not constrained in the labor market, Y_1 remains as the effective supply in the product market. Since the representative consumer is constrained in the labor market, however, the aggregate effective demand for the product Y^{de} is again obtained using the budget constraint

$$pC_0 + m_0 = m_{(-1)} + \frac{wL}{n} + d_0 \tag{10.26}$$

where L is the realized aggregate employment. As a result of maximizing (10.20), this gives $Y^{de} = \frac{a_1}{a_1 + a_2}\left(\frac{\overline{M}}{p} + Y\right)$, in view of the fact that the aggregate profit is $pY - wL$, where Y is the realized purchase of the product. Since consumers are on the short-side of the product market, we should have $Y = Y^{de}$. The excess effective demand for the product is

$$Y^{de} - Y_1 = Y_2 - Y_1 < 0 \tag{10.27}$$

in view of the definition of Y_2. In the labor market, on the other hand, the effective supply L^{se} coincides with Walrasian supply L_3, if we consider the effect of the difference between the realized profit and the expected one as negligible. Effective demand in the labor market is, however, different from Walrasian demand since firms are on the long-side of the product market. Firms have to base their plan of demand for labor L^{de} on realized sales in the product market, i.e., Y_2. The excess effective demand for labor is

$$L^{de} - L_3 = F^{-1}(Y_2) - L_3 \tag{10.28}$$

which is less than $L_1 - L_3 < 0$. As expected, excess effective supply dominates both the labor and the product markets in area II.

In area III, Walrasian demands Y_2 and L_1 are not realized in both markets and therefore effective supply is not expected to be greater than Walrasian supply, with the sign of effective excess demand unchanged by dual decisions. Since firms are on the short-side of the product market, the effective demand for labor is the same as the Walrasian demand L_1. Consumers have, however, to make dual decisions on the supply of labor since they are constrained in the product market. The effective supply of labor L^{se} is again obtained by maximizing (10.20), subject to

$$m_0 + wl_0 = m_{(-1)} + d_0 + w\overline{L} - \frac{pY}{n} \tag{10.29}$$

where Y is the realized aggregate purchase of the product. This gives $L^{se} = n\overline{L} - \frac{a_3}{a_2}\frac{\overline{M}}{w} = L_3$, since consumers who are on the short-side of the labor market expect that the aggregate profit is $pY - wL^{se}$. Therefore, the excess effective demand in the labor market is

$$L_1 - L^{se} = L_1 - L_3. \tag{10.30}$$

In the product market, on the other hand, the effective demand coincides with the Walrasian demand Y_2 since consumers are not constrained in the labor market and there are no dual decisions to be considered, if we ignore the effect of the difference between the expected and realized profits. The effective supply in the product market Y^{se} is, however, different from the Walrasian since firms are on the long-side of the labor market and have to make dual decisions on the supply of the product. Firms must base their plan of supply on the realized purchase of labor which is L_3. The excess effective demand in the product market is then

Fig. 10.2

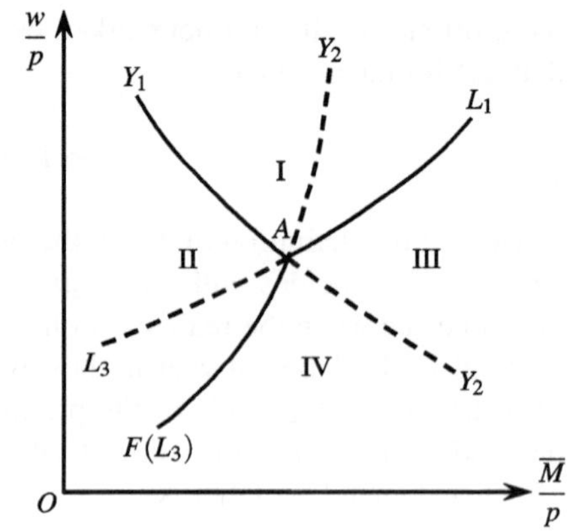

$$Y_2 - Y^{se} = Y_2 - F(L_3) \tag{10.31}$$

which is larger than $Y_2 - Y_1$. As expected, excess effective demand exists in both the labor and product markets in area III.

Finally, in the case of area IV, consumers are not constrained and make no dual decisions with the result that effective demand in the product market and effective supply in the labor market are the same as the Walrasian ones, i.e., Y_2 and L_3. Firms are, on the other hand, constrained in both markets and dual decisions have to be made on demand in the labor market and on supply in the product market. Effective demand in the labor market is $F^{-1}(Y_2)$, since supply from firms in the product is constrained at Y_2, and effective supply in the product market is $F(L_3)$, since the demand from firms in the labor marker is constrained at L_3. Therefore, after making dual decisions, excess demand can be anything in both markets, depending on the relative magnitude of Y_2 and $F(L_3)$. Figure 10.2 is obtained from Fig. 10.1 by adding the $Y_2F(L_3)$ curve which shows the combination of $\frac{w}{p}$ and $\frac{\overline{M}}{p}$ satisfying the condition that $Y_2 = F(L_3)$. Any point to the left of this curve satisfies the inequality $Y_2 < F(L_3)$ and any point to the right satisfies $Y_2 > F(L_3)$. In the subarea of area IV in Fig. 10.1 which is located on the left of $Y_2F(L_3)$ in Fig. 10.2, excess supply exists in both the labor and product markets. Since consumers are now constrained in the labor market and firms are constrained in the product market, we have (10.27) and (10.28) again as the result of further dual decisions. In Fig. 10.2, therefore, area II is enlarged to include this subarea where effective excess demand is negative in both the labor market ($F^{-1}(Y_2) < L_3$) and the product market ($Y_2 < Y_1$). Similarly, in the subarea of area IV located to the right of $Y_2F(L_3)$ curve, excess demand dominates both markets. Dual decisions repeated by consumers constrained in the product market and firms constrained in the labor market imply (10.30) and (10.31) again, where effective demand is positive in both the product market ($Y_2 > F(L_3)$) and the labor market ($L_1 > L_3$). Therefore, area III is enlarged to include this subarea in Fig. 10.2.

The Keynesian macroeconomics is to be concerned with the enlarged area II in Fig. 10.2, since firms are constrained in the product market so that the level of output is determined by the effective demand (10.19), and consumers are constrained in the labor market so that there exists involuntary unemployment (10.18).

10.7 Fixprice Method

Keynesian macroeconomic model is that of fixprice method in the sense of Hicks. Prices and wages are not governed by the law of supply and demand, and not reduced in the face of excess supplies in the product and labor markets. An important task of microeconomic foundations of Keynesian macroeconomics is to explain why excess supplies are not cleared by adjustments in prices and wages. As for the product market, we have already an explanation given in Sect. 6.8, i.e., the theory of kinked demand curves which are due to the asymmetric behavior of consumers. The representative firm facing the demand constraint in the product market perceives a kinked demand curve which is kinked at the point of the current price and the level of effective demand (Fig. 6.6). Although the marginal cost is lower than the current price, it is impossible to sell more at such a price. There exists an effective excess supply (10.27). Nor is it profitable, however, to sell more by reducing the price. The price is, therefore, not reduced in the face of excess supply.

As for the labor market, perhaps one of the most interesting explanation of unchanged wage is the theory of implicit contracts between employers and employees. An implicit contract is said to exist when an employer or employee, by behaving consistently in a particular manner, can induce another employer or employee to act to a large degree as if the former were legally constrained to act in that manner. It has often be suggested that the difference between employers and employees with respect to risk aversion can explain why transactions in the labor market typically involve implicit long-term contracts, particularly those with unchanged wage rates. If employees are averse to risk, they would prefer to be employed at lower expected wages with a small variance than at higher expected wages with a larger variance. If employers are risk neutral they would be willing to accommodate the employees in their interests of obtaining cheaper labor. If employers are faced with demand constraints in their product markets, furthermore, we can show that implicit contracts can be with a variable level of employment. In other words, the full employment is not assured and unchanged rate of wage and unemployment can coexist.

Suppose there are only two possible states of nature with different levels of the effective demand for the product. The state 1 occurs with probability $a > 0$ and the state 2, with probability $1 - a > 0$. If the state i occurs, the general price level is q_i and the representative firm expects a price $\overline{p}_i$ for its product, which it cannot exceed, and possible sales $\overline{z}_i$ at this price, $i = 1, 2$. The relation between the level of output z_i and the price p_i which enables this output to be sold, i.e., the perceived demand function, is $p_i = p_i(z_i)$ which satisfies $p_i = \overline{p}_i$ for $z \leq \overline{z}_i$ and $p_i < \overline{p}_i$ for $z_i > \overline{z}_i$,

$i = 1, 2$. In other words, it has a kink at $(\overline{p}_i, \overline{z}_i)$. The short-run production function of the representative firm is $f(k)$, where k is the number of employees employed.

The length of working hours for a unit period is assumed to be institutionally constant, L, for the representative employee. The utility v of the representative employee is a function of his real wage income and leisure; and without loss of generality this can be given by $u\left(\frac{w}{q}\right) = v\left(\frac{wL}{q}, \overline{L} - L\right)$, $v(0, \overline{L} - L) = 0$, $v(0, \overline{L}) = K \neq 0$, where w, q and $\overline{L}$ are, respectively, the level of wages, the general price level and the length of the unit period. The function u represents the utility of being employed and K the utility of being unemployed.

The representative firm offers a contract (w_i, k_i) which denotes that it will pay wage w_i and employ k_i persons in state i. This contract is constrained by the fact that it must give the risk averting employee just as much expected utility u_0 as he could get in the Walrasian labor market,

$$a\left(\frac{k_1}{N}\right)u\left(\frac{w_1}{q_1}\right) + aK\frac{N - k_1}{N} + (1-a)\frac{k_2}{N}u\left(\frac{w_2}{q_2}\right) + (1-a)K\frac{N - k_2}{N} \geq u_0 \quad (10.32)$$

where N is the total number of employees divided by the number of firms, and the choice of those employed is assumed to be made at random so that $a\frac{N - k_1}{N}$ denotes the probability of being unemployed in state 1 and the like.

Being risk-neutral, the representative firm maximizes real expected profit

$$a\frac{p_1 z_1 - w_1 k_1}{q_1} + (1 - a)\frac{p_2 z_2 - w_2 k_2}{q_2} \quad (10.33)$$

with respect to z_i, w_i and k_i, subject to (10.32), and

$$k_i \leq N \quad (i = 1, 2), \quad (10.34)$$

$$f(k_i) \geq z_i \quad (i = 1, 2). \quad (10.35)$$

Let us suppose that the expectations are realized so that the value of z_i in the solution to this constrained maximization must be identical to $\overline{z}_i$ and therefore $p_i = \overline{p}_i$ $(i = 1, 2)$. Since the firm tries to make the real wage $\frac{w_i}{q_i}$ as low as possible, the condition (10.32) must be satisfied with the equality at the constrained maximum. The marginal rate of substitution between $\frac{w_1}{q_1}$ and $\frac{w_2}{q_2}$ in (10.32) must be equalized with that in (10.33) at the constrained maximum, so that $u'\left(\frac{w_1}{q_1}\right) = u'\left(\frac{w_2}{q_2}\right)$. In other words, the optimal contract has to keep the real wage unchanged. To see

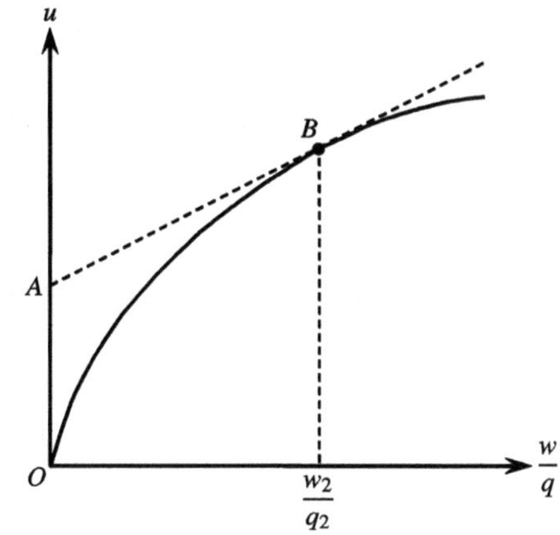

Fig. 10.3

whether the full-employment is assured in the optimal contract, let us suppose that $k_2 = N$ and reduce the value of k_2 slightly. To keep the condition (10.32) with equality, w_2 should be increased. Since the marginal rate of substitution between k_2 and w_2 in (10.32) is $\frac{q_2[u(w_2/q_2) - K]}{k_2} u'\left(\frac{w_2}{q_2}\right)$ and that in (10.33) is $\frac{w_2}{k_2}$, the optimal contract does not assure the full employment $k_2 = N$, if

$$u\left(\frac{w_2}{q_2}\right) - K < u'\left(\frac{w_2}{q_2}\right)\frac{w_2}{q_2}. \tag{10.36}$$

In Fig. 10.3, this condition implies that K is larger than *OA*.

Problems

10.1. In a multi-period model of a firm in Sect. 10.2, show that the optimal output Y_0 and labor input L_0 in the current period is independent of the rate of interest.

10.2. Write down the single life-time budget constraint in a multi-period model of a consumer in Sect. 10.2.

10.3. Derive Walras' law and show that not all the equations (10.9)–(10.12) are independent.

10.4. Show that P and W change in the same direction as A does in (10.14) and (10.15).

10.5. In Sect. 10.5, derive Y_2 and L_3 as functions of p, w and M, and explain why Y_1Y_2 curve is downward sloping and L_1L_3 curve is upward sloping in Fig. 10.1.

10.6. In Sect. 10.6, derive Y^{de} in (10.23), L^{se} in (10.25), Y^{de} in (10.27) and L^{se} in (10.30) as functions of p, w and M.

10.7. Explain why $Y_2F(L_3)$ curve in Fig. 10.2 is upward sloping.

10.8. Interpret the situation of the enlarged area III in Fig. 10.2 as that of a planned economy.

10.9. Why can we assume that employers are risk-neutral and employees are risk-averting in the theory of implicit contracts (Sect. 10.7).

10.10. Show that the optimal contract assures the full employment in Sect. 10.7, if the product market is Walrasian with flexible prices to clear the markets.

Literature

For the relation between economics and physics, see P. Mirowski, "Physics and the Marginalist Revolution," *Cambridge Journal of Economics* (1984), and M. Faber, H. Niemes and G. Stephan, *Entropy, Environment and Resources* (1987), pp. 77–103.
The classical and Keynesian models in macroeconomics are rigorously developed in T.J. Sargent, *Macroeconomic Theory* (1979), pp. 6–73. For microeconomic foundations of classical macroeconomics, see M. Friedman, "The Role of Monetary policy," *American Economic Review* (1968), H.I. Grossman, "Aggregate Demand, Job Search and Employment," *Journal of Political Economy* (1973), and E.S. Phelps et al., *Microeconomic Foundations of Employment and Inflation Theory* (1970). General references for micro-foundations of Keynesian macroeconomics are, for example, J.P. Benassy, *Macroeconomics, An Introduction to the Non-Walrasian Approach* (1986), E. Malinvaud, *The Theory of Unemployment Reconsidered*, 2nd ed. (1985), and Negishi (1979), op. cit. For implicit contract theory, see C. Azariadis, "Implicit Contracts and Underemployment Equilibria," *Journal of Political Economy* (1975). The implication of the fixprice method is explained in J.R. Hicks, *Capital and Growth* (1965), pp. 76–78. See also J.M. Grandmont (ed.), *Temporary Equilibrium, Selected Readings* (1988), for Hicksian temporary equilibrium and fixprice method.

About the Author

Takashi Negishi
A member of the Japan Academy, professor emeritus of University of Tokyo, former president of the Econometric Society and former president of the Japanese Society for History of Economic Thought. Major publications include *General Equilibrium Theory and International Trade* (1972), *History of Economic Theory* (1989), and *Collected Essays of Takashi Negishi*, three volumes (1994 and 2000).

Professor Negishi taught and conducted research at Stanford University, the University of Tokyo, the University of New South Wales, the University of Minnesota, and the London School of Economics.

His major contributions range from general equilibrium theory and welfare economics (existence, optimality, and stability), theory of monopolistic competitions (kinked demand curves), and micro foundations of Keynesian macroeconomics, to the history of economics. For the details of these contributions, see the *International Journal of Economic Theory*, volume 4, number 2, June 2008: A Special Issue on Social Welfare, Market Equilibrium and Stability in Honor of Professor Takashi Negishi.

T. Negishi, *Elements of Neo-Walrasian Economics*, Advances in Japanese Business and Economics 5, DOI 10.1007/978-4-431-54535-4, © Springer Japan 2014

Name Index

T. Negishi, *Elements of Neo-Walrasian Economics*, Advances in Japanese Business and Economics 5, DOI 10.1007/978-4-431-54535-4, © Springer Japan 2014

Subject Index

T. Negishi, *Elements of Neo-Walrasian Economics*, Advances in Japanese Business and Economics 5, DOI 10.1007/978-4-431-54535-4, © Springer Japan 2014

MIX
Papier aus verantwortungsvollen Quellen
Paper from responsible sources
FSC® C105338

If you have any concerns about our products,
you can contact us on
ProductSafety@springernature.com

In case Publisher is established outside the EU,
the EU authorized representative is:
Springer Nature Customer Service Center GmbH
Europaplatz 3, 69115 Heidelberg, Germany

Printed by Libri Plureos GmbH
in Hamburg, Germany